THERAPY OR COERCION

R. D. Hinshelwood

THERAPY OR COERCION

Does Psychoanalysis Differ from Brainwashing?

R. D. Hinshelwood

London
KARNAC BOOKS

First published in 1997 by
H. Karnac (Books) Ltd.
58 Gloucester Road
London SW7 4QY

British Library Cataloguing in Publication Data

Hinshelwood, R. D.
Therapy or coercion : does psychoanalysis differ from brainwashing?
1. Psychoanalysis 2. Medical ethics
I. Title
150.1'95

ISBN 1 85575 143 7

Edited, designed, and produced by Communication Crafts

Printed in Great Britain by BPC Wheatons Ltd, Exeter

10 9 8 7 6 5 4 3 2 1

For all the deeper, more personal kinds
of support and encouragement
that go beyond the merely intellectual,
to Anna

CONTENTS

PART TWO
THE PROBLEMS OF AUTONOMY

PART THREE
THE ETHICS OF INFLUENCING

PART FOUR
PERSONS AND SOCIETY

PREFACE

This book has been a long time developing. Perhaps it goes back to the 1960s, when the age of permissiveness was upon us, and I found myself both strongly identifying with those aspirations and, at the same time, as a young psychiatric doctor, helping nurses to struggle physically to get reluctant patients into the ECT room. That kind of conflict, between freedom and force, went rather deep, and it has taken a long time to come to terms with it—to come to terms with bridging the contradictions, which has implications for the practice of psychoanalysis and beyond.

My own career in psychiatry starting then involved a revulsion against traditional psychiatry, its methods, and its large institutions, which seemed to reduce the patient to a passive manipulated object—a kind of veterinary psychiatry. And the situation has not improved since then. R. D. Laing and Erving Goffman were enlightening critics who strengthened the doubts I had and helped in my thinking about my revulsion. I felt strongly aligned with alternatives—the therapeutic community, anti-psychiatry, and psychoanalysis. In the 1960s the strengthening of the individual's demands for freedom and autonomy, both inside the mental hospitals and in society at large, seemed an almost absolute principle. Internal autonomy, the freedom within one's own world of impulses and objects, appeared to be the psychoanalytic equivalent of the cultural climate, which held up the autonomous individual in society as the ideal. The limitations on personal autonomy seemed to be there in order to be removed—internal limitations by psychoanalysis, external ones by social and political change. To write this account of my intellectual and professional travels through this landscape has been difficult because I have been uncomfortably forced to the view that autonomy is not an absolute principle, even in psychoanalysis—perhaps especially not in psychoanalysis. The question arises: "Why is this so?" And then: "How do we judge our footing in this landscape, which has suddenly grown dangerously boggy and treacherous?"

I was struck by the message that one arrives at when one puts together, on the one hand, the experimental work on group pressures to conform, conducted by social psychologists such as Solomon Asch or S. Milgram, with, on the other hand, the aims in group therapy to use group pressure therapeutically to free people up in some way. In therapeutic groups, social pressure is exerted on the members to have more realistic views of themselves; but the problem lies in tracing what that reality within the group culture at the time is. I originally presented these ideas, in an early form, at the Ninth Anglo-Dutch Workshop on Therapeutic Communities at Windsor in 1986.

This original paper was met with a reaction that went roughly like this: "What is this all about? Surely we do, indeed, press our patients to modify their views—it is for their good. The general benevolence of the staff and of the groups has to be taken for granted. It is alarmist, and self-deprecating, to call our work into doubt in this way."[1] Eventually, despite this reaction, the paper was published, in a slightly modified form (Hinshelwood, 1990); and I remained unconvinced that we could be so absolutely sure

[1] Most articulate and helpful in expressing this paternalist argument was Geoff Pullen, and I am grateful to him for making this project into a much bigger, though more painful, struggle to survey this vast problem.

that the pressure we put on our patients is easily and comfortably distinguishable from that of all sorts of other influences. I was left still with my original hunch that we do, in fact, need—and I had the confidence we must be able to find—a criterion for distinguishing benevolent from malevolent influencing. Since then, I have presented, to a number of different audiences, various versions of these ideas, concerned more with individual psychoanalysis than with groups. In the course of time the ideas have become progressively modified. I have been particularly helped by Bill Fulford, whose endless patience, both with my writing habits and with the obscurities of psychoanalysis, has been extraordinarily important in keeping me encouraged and in improving the clarity of my discussion. Much of the basis of my argument appeared in his journal, *Philosophy, Psychiatry and Psychology* (Hinshelwood, 1995, 1997).

The present volume is an attempt to make a contribution to the understanding of the professional ethics of psychoanalysis. But as psychoanalysis has such important things to say about the nature of mind and about the relations of individuals to their social (and therefore ethical) context, the implications of a psychoanalytic ethics range freely from narrow professional ethics to the wider horizons of philosophy, society, and history. It is these wider horizons that have proved the greatest obstacles to the writing of this book, since it is a daunting prospect for a psychoanalyst to enter the turbulent waters of other people's contemporary discourse on such wide-ranging subjects and to survive with a creditable idea still intact. If my argument does, in fact, survive, then this is not because of my competence across such a range, but because of the value of the argument itself. I can only hope that my amateur efforts outside my own profession, and the glaring mistakes I may have overlooked, will not detract too much from an interest in the core question, and that the argument will be sufficiently engaging for others with a more thorough specialist knowledge that they will be prompted to work over those specialist areas more competently.

I am aware that most readers of technical books of this kind will dip into parts of it rather than passing from the beginning to the end of the whole argument, as in the case of a novel. The plot of the argument is probably as complex as that of most novels, and

I have tried to lay it out in as straightforward a way as possible. Nevertheless, strands lead in and out, and many ramifications drift away into various other disciplines. I have tried to keep an orderly manner. However, the book brings together many psychoanalytic issues with philosophical questions, and the chance of, in fact, keeping an orderly house in cross-currents like these is very difficult. It has been extremely difficult in the writing, and I think will probably prove so in the reading of it, as the encounters between ideas from different continents of thought are in danger of sparking off wildly imaginative consequences.

For this I have a regret and make apology, and wish the reader well in trying to follow a route in this interdisciplinary maze; and I assure the reader of my understanding if the frustration of following the lead of my argument proves too irking, and he throws the book aside.

A further regret is the problem of personal pronouns, so deeply involved in generating and sustaining a belief in one's personal identity. If my traditional and insolent use of "he", when some generic pronoun would be better, gives offence, I am truly sorry and regret that the generic pronoun has not yet been invented—or circulated.

I am deeply grateful to many people for help, encouragement, and persistent questioning, including: Stephen Braude, Mike Brearley, Irma Brenman-Pick, Marie Bridge, Prophecy and Walter Coles, Gail Grayson, Karl Figlio, Bill Fulford, Sebastian Gardner, Zaida Hall, Jeremy Holmes, Jim Hopkins, Michael Langenbach, Bradley Lewis, Richard Lindley, Chris Mace, Jane Milton, Red O'Shaughnessy, Geoff Pullen, Robert Royston, Cesare Sacerdoti, Joe Sandler, Janet and Sean Sayers, Graham Sleight, Patricia Sohl, Martin Stanton, Paul Sturdee, Bob Young. I am deeply indebted to the meticulous help that Klara King has given me in correcting the manuscript and preparing it for publication.

THERAPY OR COERCION

Introduction

Freud was pessimistic, if not cynical, about the real benefits of ethical injunctions and moral values, which have to struggle against instinctual desires for basic bodily satisfactions or their socially contorted derivatives:

> The commandment, "Love thy neighbour as thyself", is the strongest defence against human aggressiveness and an excellent example of the unpsychological proceedings of the cultural super-ego. The commandment is impossible to fulfill; and such an enormous inflation of love can only lower its value, not get rid of the difficulty. . . . "Natural", ethics, as it is called, has nothing to offer here except the narcissistic satisfaction of being able to think oneself better than others. [Freud, 1930a, p. 143]

Freud makes the depressing assumption that human aggression is inherent and that only the effects of civilization can ameliorate it. Such aggression is relentless, blind, and lacking in circumspection. It is met by an internalized "society", in the form of the superego, which has just the same qualities of relentlessness, blindness, and absence of circumspection.

Such a raw clash between the primitive and the sophisticated is not quite the position taken by Melanie Klein and her followers. Instead, she found internal reactions to such blind aggression, in children who struggled against these destructive and self-destructive states long before the superego could be observed. She regarded this, in effect, as a proto-morality. For Klein, whatever the specific ethical and moral values of a culture, the infant is born into it with a potentiality to develop a moral sense of good and bad. Morality does not, however, spring to life in mature form, from the moment of birth. The infant must, and does, struggle for it. In the first instance, an object that feeds it and is good to it by satisfying its needs and demands is loved and valued. This value is a very primitive affair, being one-dimensional and unsullied by any characteristics of hesitancy or rejection on the part of the object. It is not *good*, it is *wholly good*. The baby enjoys, as Wollheim (1984) calls it, "archaic bliss", a momentary state that we have all perceived in the faces of infants, after feeding, say, and lying gazing into the feeding mother's equally happy face.

In contrast, the infant, when pressed by bodily demands—such as unsatisfied hunger—experiences itself in the hands of an object that is totally evil and threatening it with suffering and death. This object, Klein supposed, was primordially experienced as bad. Bliss and evil are, for the infant, the primary signals of the value of objects in its world. Objects are loved and hated in accord with this binary experience. The infant, born into a world of unreality, has immediately to begin to grow out of it. It is from these "semi-biological" states that there emerges, in various normal or distorted ways, the capacity to perceive good and bad in the real and social world and to receive the world's demands to accept standards to correlate with those primary experiences. Development onwards, from an indulged infant towards an ethical being, proceeds, according to Klein, under the pressure of reality. In particular, the child must discover that its objects are not perfectly good or wholly evil. The capacity to learn adequately about the real world is intimately connected with the entry into it as a moral being.

> If these assumptions could be shown to be correct, then I would see no reason for holding truth to be any more objective than value, or value any less objective than truth. . . .

> Truth and value—in principle, one no less decidable than the other—would then together be part of the fabric of thought. [Cavell, 1992, p. 83]

The conjoining of knowledge of the world with its evaluation is important; it suggests, unexpectedly, that science and value go hand in hand.

Conducting a psychoanalysis upon a person's unconscious is, therefore, to enter a sensitive moral fabric.[1] We are surgeons using a scalpel to incise into the fine tissues of an ethical psyche. With Freud's (1923b) concept of the superego, psychopathology could be reduced to moral complications in the nature of man in general and in the particular lives of those who fall victim to those complexities. To a major extent, psychoanalysis became the analysis of a person's moral being—focused so often by Freud around "unconscious guilt".

To a major extent, too, there was some neglect of the ethical cutting edge of psychoanalysis itself. Freud especially was intent on the technical advance of knowledge rather than the ethics of psychoanalysis. Whilst psychoanalysis was simply the relief of symptoms through interpreting dream symbols, the ethical implications were minimally different from those of the rest of medicine. However, at the point where psychoanalysis became the analysis of character, it changed from a mere medical technique to a moral practice—that is, a practice upon a moral being. This development, arising in the 1920s and 1930s, has to an extent failed to keep pace with its own development and to keep its own psychoanalytic eye on the ethics of its practice.

Because of its roots as a medical technology, psychoanalysis has been alien to philosophical occupations. Freud, in considering Putnam's attempt to relate psychoanalysis to philosophy, was in doubt as to "which of the countless philosophical systems should be accepted". Instead, he advised:

[1] Though I refer simply to psychoanalysis, I think there may be no real divergence from my argument for any psychoanalytic psychotherapy based on a more rigorous frame of psychoanalytic thinking. However, where suggestions and other forms of influence come into the work, perhaps especially with psychotherapy on a much less frequent basis, other considerations may have to apply, some of which may be found in Chapter 13.

> It seemed more prudent to wait, and to discover whether a particular attitude towards life might be forced upon us with all the weight of necessity by analytical investigation itself. [Freud, 1921a, p. 270]

Philosophers, too, have taken rather less note than they might of psychoanalytic discoveries:

> . . . on the whole, philosophers, so far as they took notice of psycho-analysis at all, condemned its basic concepts as muddled and self-contradictory. And analysts silently responded by dismissing philosophy. [Money-Kyrle, 1958, p. 102]

The upshot is that despite the increasing sensitivity of the psychoanalytic "instrument", the parallel ethical (and philosophical) journey has barely started. In this country, philosophers originally became aware of psychoanalysis during the First World War. Bertrand Russell (1921) gave some thought to it when writing on the philosophy of mind; and when in later life he turned for a moment to writing fiction, he contrived a psychoanalyst's nightmare analysing Shakespeare's characters in a story published in the magazine, *The Courier*, in 1954. One of Russell's brightest students at Cambridge, Karin Costelloe-Stephens, eventually trained as a psychoanalyst. W. H. R. Rivers's book on *Dreams and the Unconscious* (1920) was noted by the Aristotelian Society, who in 1922 mounted a joint conference on it with the British Psychological Society, though Rivers unfortunately died just before the conference took place. However, philosophical interest was reserved, and the relevance (or not) of psychoanalysis for understanding the nature of mind was not taken up until the time of the Second World War. Wittgenstein (1942) and Sartre (1943) again expressed reservations. But from then on there began a steadily increasing exploration of the possible implications arising from psychoanalytic discoveries (Feuer, 1955; Hanley & Lazerowitz, 1970; Home, 1966; Hook, 1959; Kaplan, 1958; Matte-Blanco, 1975; Wisdom, 1953; Wollheim, 1974).[2] Dilman (1984), Wollheim (1984), and Lear (1990)

[2] On the whole, I concentrate on the Anglo-American tradition of philosophy. On the Continent, Habermas (1968), Ricoeur (1970), and many others, leading to Lacan and Derrida, have given Freud a very different and more exhaustive treatment than in the case of British philosophy.

are recent exponents, and the collections of Wollheim and Hopkins (1982) and Clark and Wright (1988) are important; Farrell (1981) and Grünbaum (1984) made more deeply critical contributions to the debates. Recently, an interest has developed in split minds (Parfit, 1984), and some (Gardner, 1993; Pears, 1982; Sturdee, 1995) have searched psychoanalysis for a contribution to this problem.

Many of the philosophical works debate the status and validity of psychoanalysis, its observations, and its theories. But there are other possible interactions between philosophy and psychoanalysis. Our observations and discoveries are potentially revelatory for the nature of mind. And psychoanalysis needs moral philosophy. In researching for this book, I have concluded that issues in the nature of mind and professional ethics cannot be separated. In short, for some 80 years psychoanalysis has so elaborated its theory of mind that its ethics cannot remain relevant without keeping pace. The mechanics of libido theory and the simple conflict between the human animal and civilization to which it gave rise have been surpassed long ago.

Today psychoanalysis is about the nature of the person. And eight decades later we have not only the many philosophies, but also all the psychoanalytical schools to take account of. The core set of concepts that we can turn to as a "lowest common denominator" amongst psychoanalysts is remarkably limited—perhaps only "the unconscious" and "transference". The implication of this to the "truth" of psychoanalysis demands (and receives) wide discussion. Hamilton's research demonstrated that differences in schools of psychoanalysis orbit within a domain of three (plus one) sets of questions (Hamilton, 1996). These questions concern (a) the concept of psychic reality and psychic truth; (2) the concept of analytic neutrality (rule of abstinence); (3) interpretation as either a hypothesis to investigate or a conclusion in the form of directive statements; and (4) related theoretically to the other three, the clinical applicability of the concept of the death instinct.

I address in this book a further divergence—a choice between repression and splitting. Psychoanalysts have not addressed this difference adequately. It bears on philosophical issues concerning the nature of irrationality and a "second mind", and psychoanalysts have not bequeathed to philosophers a clear outline of the issue—in part because psychoanalysts have not been sufficiently philosophers.

How the empirical findings concerning a divided mind relate to philosophical issues and then back again to the ethics of psychoanalysis emerges in this book. Nevertheless, the divided-mind issue has a central role, and most schools of psychoanalysis will make passing but inadequate reference to it. In addition to the Kleinian school, others challenge the philosophical concept of the discrete, coherent, and indivisible notion of the "self"—though couched in different terms. The shaky self-system described by self-psychologists would seem to be a case in point. In the 1920s and 1930s, it was ego-psychology that originally provoked the question: "How does character form and evolve?" In fact, ego-psychologists made observations that have recently been shown to be remarkably similar to the primitive processes I shall examine. I think particularly of "identification with the aggressor" (Anna Freud, 1936) and "role-responsiveness" (Sandler, 1976). This means that ego-psychologists have been tilling in the same backyard as Kleinians.

Winnicott's (1960) formulation of the "false" and "true" selves is a related idea, connected to an experienced "continuity of being". Winnicott worked out these ideas directly in contact with the Kleinian work on schizoid experiences in the 1950s. Fairbairn and Guntrip, in turn, were also addressing schizoid phenomena partly in interaction with Klein. Each strand of British object-relations psychoanalysis developed its own terminology (and matrix of theory) about "self" and identity. The differences in theory have less to do with the unreliability of their observations and more with personal rivalries that seem perversely inherent in the world of analysed psychoanalysts. Parallel to this and quite independent was Helene Deutsch's (1942) concept of the "as if" personality, which closely resembled Winnicott's "false self" idea.

In other words, there is an area of theorizing in each of the main psychoanalytic schools that derives from similar observations about the incoherence of the self. Well—Chris Mace (1997), who has commented on my argument, might still argue—it is arbitrary to take the terminology from only one of them. Even if, to avoid confusion, one system for thinking about these observations has to be consistently applied, I am not sure that it is arbitrary to take the Kleinian one. It might be argued that the Kleinian interest in psychosis, during the period between 1950 and 1970, entailed a developing understanding of disorders of identity to a degree that outreaches (or, more accurately, plumbs to greater depths than) others. The steadily widening interest in the concept of projective identification (which incorporates both splitting and projection) attests to the fact that there is a need by psychoanalysts from other schools to mine the work of Klein and Kleinians to understand the processes of identity that run deeper than common sense. Mace (1997) implies that it is arbitrary even to choose one of the object-relations schools of psychoanalysis (Kleinian, Fairbairn, or Winnicott) at all. He seems to oppose a "priority on object-relationships", but when we address the principles of right or wrong between people, as ethics does, a formulation in terms of object-relations would seem to be exactly what we do need to prioritize. It is true perhaps that Jung's theories of archetypes are, as Mace says, excluded from my array, and this demonstrates the radical difference between the direction taken by Jung and the character analysis that occupied psychoanalysts once Jung had left the Freudian movement. Jung's views on social formations derive, as I understand it, from a connectivity of the unconscious within cultural continuities. But it does seem to me that Jung's concept of individuation—in effect, the integration of highlighted and shadowy sides of the self (Samuels, 1985)—comes close to examining splits and incoherence in the self, and an integration of them, as the prime marker of psychic health. It would appear, therefore, to relate closely to this common strand.

Kleinian psychoanalysis deals most directly with the issue of the divided mind through its elaboration of the mechanisms of, and phantasies about, identification. It is true that I am examining the implications of that school of psychoanalysis with which I am most familiar. Perhaps, therefore, I need to content myself with speaking only to Kleinians. Nevertheless, Kleinian ideas are pertinent to the renewed philosophical interest in dissociated minds (Hilgard, 1977). Much time has elapsed since Freud encountered the idea of "dissociation" when he studied the French research on hypnosis by Charcot, Bernheim, and Janet. At that time, the divided person was at the basis of "empirical philosophy". Psychiatry and philosophy then informed each other—for example, Hughlings Jackson, the most eminent of nineteenth-century neurologists, wrote influentially on the mind–brain problem (Dewhurst, 1982; Jackson, 1931), which provoked philosophical interest in the nature and dissociation of mind. Study of mediums—Leonie by Janet (1892) and Sally Beauchamp in America by Morton Prince (1906)—showed that these mediums could exist in several states of mind and would now be diagnosed as multiple personality disorders. Each state of mind seemed to be completely disconnected from the other as the person assumed one identity after the other without recollection of their "alters". Freud employed this concept of dissociation in his theory of repression; he discovered that there were connections between different states of mind, but the connections were unconsciousness. Bleuler (1911) used the idea of dissociation in his eventual description of schizophrenia. Freud (1940e [1938]) eventually returned to the picture of the fragmented mind, as did Glover (1930, 1943), Fairbairn (1944), Winnicott (1945), and Klein (1946).

Psychoanalysis provides a method of revealing "findings". Its extension beyond the consulting room of the psychoanalyst may be justified by a continuity of the therapeutic method into other domains. For instance, similar phenomena can be observed and tested through interpretation in group therapy. The relevance of the psychoanalytic method in large groups and in the multigroup system of the therapeutic community suggests that the extension of it to everyday life is valid. Its validity within these therapeutic settings can be empirically assessed with the interpretative method, the evidence of validity being the patient's response. However, beyond these settings (of groups up to a maximum of, say, 100), we no longer have that method of validation. We have, instead, to rely on a more hermeneutic method—explanations based on psychoanalytic discoveries seem to create meaning and to make sense.

The Western world gives priority to the essential self, but this is not the case in other cultures. We are shocked by the low priority given to the individual in other contemporary cultures, where, apparently, "human life is cheap". For the Western world, it is expensive, and this expensiveness marks a discontinuity from our medieval heritage and from other countries.

The sources of benevolence, of meaning and purpose, have been drawn within the individual. This change in the public perception of the individual is correlated with a number of other cultural changes:

1. new religious attitudes after the Middle Ages;
2. the reformation of the Catholic Church recovering from its multiple moral hypocrisies;
3. the Enlightenment attitude towards rational thought;
4. a new view of nature, including:
5. a new attitude towards human nature;
6. the employment of rational thought in an instrumental way;
7. the development of applied science, technology, and industry;
8. the social changes and institutions accompanying the industrial development;
9. the development of monetary and financial accounting systems that could track very complex trading and banking arrangements.

Which of these is primary and which are dependent variables has for a long time been open for continuous debate. Whether it was changes in our experiences of ourselves (1–5) that produced the material changes in the way we do things (6–9) or vice versa, profound psychological, philosophical, and attitudinal changes have created a specific Western moral climate. This revolves around the way the individual and identity has come to be seen. In a striking sense, psychoanalysis has become a theory of personal identity. Particularly British psychoanalysis has grown deeply absorbed in a study of the phenomenon of projective identification,[3] which points exactly to the importance of the sense of identity.

[3] The term was first used in an addition to Melanie Klein's 1946 paper when it was republished in 1952. However, I have refrained from using the term "projective identification" as it has achieved a peculiar confusion of meaning through overuse and diverse distortions. In its original sense, it referred to the primitive mechanisms I describe—the loss of the part of the ego, or self, with the compulsive phantasy that the part now belongs to someone else's mind.

Together with the soaring value given to the individual comes an increasing anxiety about the misuse of people. Lifton (1961) and Seaborn-Jones (1968) both concern themselves with systematic brainwashing in China after the revolution. Gareth Seaborn-Jones (1968) has taken a starting point that is remarkably similar to my own: treatment or torture. However, his is a more technical account of practice than is satisfying to me. He contrasts "logical validity" with ethics and traces this through a comparison of psychotherapy with the techniques of thought-reform in China in the 1960s. Impressed by the similarity of the ingredients of psychotherapeutic treatment and torture—group pressure, incentives, and personal development through transference and suggestibility—he concludes:

> The powerful combination of transference, incentives and group interaction (TIG) could be used without danger of oppression only if it were applied by people who were impartial and independent of the administration. [Seaborn-Jones, 1968, p. 292]

The problem is to determine the independence and impartiality of those administering the treatment. Seaborn-Jones, however, does not show how we might evaluate the activity of treater or torturer in order to distinguish between them rigorously and in detail, and it is precisely this gap that we intend to examine.

There is no doubt that, in therapy, abuse of persons does exist and that people have been exploited in quite immoral and financial ways, apparently with their full cooperation (Foster, 1971; Jehu, 1994). The bond that grows between victim and torturer or terrorist (the Stockholm syndrome—Kuleshnyk, 1984) is quite counter-intuitive and requires explanation. Is there a connection between it and the powerful union between patient and analyst, which can result in unethical liaison? Explaining this phenomenon entails a full examination of the ethics of influencing another human being, of the philosophy of identity and its incoherence.

* * *

This book is in four parts. To know whether psychoanalysis differs from brainwashing, our first port of call is the professional ethics of medicine and psychiatry. However, there are problems in the standard model of medical ethics when adopting the model of the mind that is implicit in psychoanalysis. Moreover, I have become aware that in philosophy there has been a parallel trend in questioning certain aspects of the nature of mind—particularly its unity—from which medical ethics derived certain basic assumptions. Thus a philosophical attention to psychoanalysis could approach those flawed assumptions.

The first five chapters recount these issues and problems. Chapters 6 and 7 then present the psychoanalytic evidence that appears to me to be crucial. A knowledge of primitive psychological mechanisms leads to a conception of the person, and his mind, as capable of division and incoherence—a finding that seriously hampers the use of the key concepts of autonomy and rationality in medical ethics and at the same time provides the fundamentals for rethinking those concepts.

Part Two discusses autonomy and rationality in the light of primitive psychological mechanisms. A new and more fundamental concept emerges. This notion of integration lends itself, I claim, to being employed as an ethical principle that supports—or, rather, underlies—both autonomy and rationality. Closely associated with integration—now an ethical idea—is a psychological function of reflection, particularly self-reflection.

This sets the direction for Part Three to return to and review professional ethics and eventually to pass a verdict on the ethical status of psychoanalysis. In that process certain points require discussion concerning the nature of human sciences and the moral practices to which they give rise—and their contrast with the natural sciences and technology.

Finally, Part Four returns to more general considerations. I first address the conception of personal identity viewed, as it were, under the psychoanalytic microscope. Then, in the final two chapters, I extend the vista to wider, more general ethical issues. The principle of integration is turned upon questions of ethical action in society at large and, indeed, on the question of what would be the criteria for evaluating a particular society itself in ethical terms.

PART ONE

THE UNITY OF THE PERSON

CHAPTER ONE

Freedom or force

The way people interact is socially controlled by laws and customs. On the whole, these are established on an intuitive basis, but moral philosophy attempts to ground these laws and customs within a rigorous conceptual framework. One set of characteristics that applies to relations between people concerns the degree to which they allow each other to be individuals. Conversely, there is suspicion of relations in which one party attempts to control or impose its will on the other. This dimension of freedom and force has gained a higher priority as Western culture has developed a special emphasis on the individual, especially since the Enlightenment.

Clear frameworks for guiding conduct are especially necessary in professional relationships. These are particular social relationships in which a contract (usually involving money, another central pivot of Western culture) is established for rendering services. However, such are the complexities of these social arrangements that it has become increasingly difficult to distinguish good from bad practice. When the practice involves changing people—that is, changing them in themselves, as persons—there is particular suspicion. For the purposes of this book (which is by a psychoanalyst) the question has been phrased in the following form:

- How do we know that psychoanalysis is different from brainwashing?

However, the question is much more widely applicable—to the psychotherapies and therapy and, indeed, to psychiatry, medicine, and professional ethics in general.

Moral philosophy

In his search for principles that might address ethical questions in general (Raphael, 1981), Kant formulated his central moral principle in the form of an injunction:

> Act in such a way that you always treat humanity, whether in your own person or in the person of any other, never simply as a means, but always at the same time as an end.

This formula aims to apply to all actions and is, therefore, an absolute principle. Another similarly absolute principle was that of Jeremy Bentham and the Utilitarians:

> The action is right that produces the overall greatest amount of pleasure.

There are considerable problems in defending either of these approaches. Typically, the problem with Kant's principle is the instance of lying to a murderer. If a murderer asks you where his intended victim has gone and you know, should you tell him? On intuitive grounds, the morally best judgement is to lie to him, but this contradicts Kant's basic moral principle—by lying to him, you fail to treat him as an end in himself, to respect his autonomy and reason and so on. You treat him instrumentally as a means to an end of preventing a murder. Similarly, the test case for Utilitarianism is that of the gladiatorial contest. It would be morally right to put on contests in which gladiators hacked each other to pieces, if it provided enough pleasure for enough spectators to outweigh the disaster inflicted upon the gladiators. Again the principle seems to lead to a justification of something that, intuitively seems quite immoral. These arguments are not in any way comprehensive (Scheffler, 1988) but merely illustrative of the difficulties of finding and defending a single basic principle that can underlie all moral decisions.

To get out of the problems of searching for an absolute moral principle, another philosophical approach posits that there is no single absolute principle. Thus two or more principles have to be weighed against each other in any situation. Intuitive judgements are emphasized in practice. Various principles, such as honesty, benevolence, liberty, and so forth, have been proposed and argued over. Often these multiple principles are arranged in such a way that one principle takes precedence over another—for instance, one might argue: "Always be honest, but when honesty conflicts with the principle of benevolence (when, for instance, an honest remark would hurt someone), then observe the principle of benevolence." In that special circumstance, benevolence takes precedence over honesty. These kinds of *non-absolutist* views tend to be adopted in professional ethics.

John Stuart Mill (1859) attempted a solution on this basis by bringing together the Kantian and Utilitarian positions. He included in the Utilitarian injunction the need to respect liberty, not just pleasure. Freedom has become an important "good", but it takes its place at the head of a non-absolute set of ethical principles. Freedom—or its modern equivalent, autonomy (Lindley, 1986)—is central to current professional ethics. With the recent revelations of abuse within the setting of ordinary therapies, and even of the more sophisticated psychotherapies, and the increasingly litigious attitude towards professions in general, there have been many attempts to address the establishing of an ethical approach to psychotherapy—for instance, by London (1964), Lakin (1988), Austin, Moline, and Williams (1990), and Barker and Baldwin (1991). In contrast, more classical treatments (Szasz, 1965; the 1959–1960 seminars of Lacan, 1986) take a more metaphysical and less legalistic stance.

The significance of psychoanalysis for moral issues has attracted interest mostly amongst psychoanalysts. Freud introduced the concept of the superego as the moral principle in human beings (Freud, 1923b), with the implication that, prior to the development of the superego at around 3–5 years, children are amoral beings. Interestingly, he had already encountered apparently amoral adults—criminals who were, he understood, not fixated at a pre-moral stage but, instead, in thrall to an unusually strong unconscious morality (unconscious guilt) that was so severe that it actually crippled a moral sense altogether (Freud, 1916d). In contrast, Klein regarded the human being as born into a moral universe of conflicting and competing objects which, from the beginning, it evaluates as good or bad (Klein, 1932); amoral behaviour and criminality are, then, forms of acting out an internal state of persecution (1934). Money-Kyrle (1944, 1952) employed Klein's theory of the depressive position as a system of ethics. This psychoanalysis of morality in human beings has been a dominant trend for a long time: (e.g. Brierley, 1947; Feuer, 1955; Flugel, 1945; Hartmann, 1960). Following the major wars, there have been many attempts to enlist a psychoanalytic view, specifically regarding the destructive sadism of human beings, to explain war—Glover (1933), Strachey (1957), and Fornari (1966), among others.

This debate concerns the alternative roots of morality in human beings: either an inherent morality (not yet with specific morals) or purely socialization. There has been relatively less interest in the development of actual ethical principles concerning psychoanalysis. However, psychoanalysis and psychotherapy seem to create their own value system, which may be offered to, taught to, or imposed upon patients (Reid, 1955; Seaborn-Jones, 1968; Szasz, 1965). Recently, Holmes and Lindley (1989) have discussed what they call the "values" of psychotherapy. In this they delineate the values implicit in the work of psychotherapists, which they subtly expect their patients to converge towards. As a result, there is a potential concern about the morality of psychoanalysis (Lifton, 1976). In the aftermath of the Vietnam war, a symposium organized as a joint meeting of the American Psycho-Analytical Association and the American Association for the Advancement of Science (Ekstein, 1976; Erikson, 1976; Lifton, 1976; Michels, 1976; Serota, 1976; Wallerstein, 1976) addressed issues of the conduct of the professional in a war.

Because the notions of psychoanalysis are now inserted deep within Western culture—in terms of the concept of the individuality of the person, of the working of hidden motives for which the individual cannot be consciously responsible, and of the consequent emphasis on issues of personal freedom and autonomy—the values according to which the activities of psychoanalysts and psychotherapists are judged to be ethical derive in part from a psychoanalytic framework of thinking. Thus the emphasis on those principles that underlie the ethics of psychoanalysis is in part determined by psychoanalytic ideas and practice.

We discuss this circularity in the course of this book. But from the start we must note that the ethical conduct of professionals, including psychoanalysts, is publicly regulated by professional bodies that generally adopt standard medical ethics as their paradigm. The shortcomings of this model are addressed first. In the process, we will see that much of the impact of psychoanalysis on social and professional values derives from theories that developed at the beginning of psychoanalysis itself. Contemporary psychoanalysis has moved on and is itself a new vantage point for a critique of these values.

CHAPTER TWO

Medical ethics

At times in our work we sense that we must proceed *in spite of* the patient, and that this does not bring us—doctor, nurse, or psychoanalyst—into the category of torturer or brainwasher. Intuitively, we would agree that there are some conditions in which it is beneficial to go against the patient; but how can this be decided? To examine these situations carefully, we will turn to the paradigm of medical ethics, and then to the question of whether medical ethics can, in fact, apply to psychoanalytic work.

A priority of values

The resolution of ethical problems revolves around knowing when to apply which ethical principle. In medicine the principles governing treatment are non-absolutist, are clearly arranged, even though the discriminating criterion may be difficult to measure at times.

Roughly speaking, standard medical ethics is based on the following principles (Gillon, 1986):

1. *Autonomy:* Medical practice concerns doing good for the patient. It is the patient's right to expect this from his doctor. The doctor should respect the patient as the final arbiter of the choice of treatment. The patient has a right to receive good medical advice and to be put, by his doctor, in a position to be able to choose the best line of treatment. The patient has *autonomy*. He must be allowed to assert his right of *informed consent*.

   The principle of autonomy is clearly open to transgression by doctors who do not properly inform patients or who bring undue influence on them for various unprincipled reasons—such as financial considerations, sexual exploitation, and so on. However, most doctors, being of reasonably good character, do respect the patient's autonomous rights over his own body and his own decisions about health and about offers of treatment—an "informed consent"—and they will avoid clear exploitation and severe violation of the patient's autonomy.

2. *Paternalism:* The situation, however, is not always so simple. Not all patients are capable of making good decisions. "Autonomy" takes precedence *unless exceptional situations occur*. When a patient cannot contribute to the decision, the doctor has to override the patient's right to autonomy. Dyer (1988), for instance, stresses the fact that suffering may not be relieved for patients by too slavish a regard for autonomy. This is particularly common in psychiatry. The psychiatrist must, at times, adopt a position of knowing best what is good for the patient. This is an attitude of *paternalism*.

3. *Rationality:* The principles of autonomy of the patient and paternalism towards him would conflict unless they are managed by ordering the principles according to strict criteria. Thus the patient must always be given his autonomy, *unless* the patient is not capable of making good decisions about himself and his treatment; then the doctor is entitled to "know best" for the

patient and make paternalistic decisions on the patient's behalf about the treatment.

The tricky point is to know when exactly the doctor should relinquish his respect for the patient's autonomy and take it into his own hands to decide what is best—to become paternalistic. That is to say: how does the doctor decide that the patient cannot make good decisions? The issue turns on one criterion—the patient's degree of *rationality* (Gillon, 1986). If he is sufficiently rational, he should be allowed to make his own decisions (autonomy); but if he is irrational, in some relevant way and to a particular degree, then the doctor must decide for him (paternalism). This is straightforward enough, but it does depend on the doctor making an assessment of the rationality of the patient and of the degree of rationality that is sufficient in any specific case.[1] These exceptional instances occur particularly in psychiatry, when the patient is considered not to be of sound mind.

4. *Psychiatric paternalism:* Influencing people's minds for their own good is the activity of psychiatrists. This is a particular issue when patients are under compulsory orders for detention or treatment (Bloch & Chodoff, 1981; Dyer, 1988; Edwards, 1982), and the psychiatrist's responsibility may require him to go directly against the patient's deeply held convictions or fears. A severely paranoid patient may believe that his nurses are conspiring against his life; a severely depressed patient may be just too ill to be able to make a decision about having ECT. The psychiatrist has to take over the decision-making function of the patient; though some would dispute this (Laing, 1959; Szasz, 1961).
5. *Psychoanalytic consent:* We will examine in much greater detail the exact conditions that operate in a psychoanalysis; here we can recognize that psychoanalytic patients do not always cooperate with treatment. In fact, we know that something else

[1] Culver and Gert (1982), we shall see, have attempted to simplify this measurement by showing that it is easier to assess the degree of irrationality rather than that of rationality.

> happens: resistance, symptoms, the transference, acting-out, and so on. One important factor is the—often unconscious—intention to thwart or circumvent the "work" of the psychoanalyst.[2] One instance of this can be seen in Freud's case of Dora (Freud, 1905e [1901]), whose consent turned out to hinge on being able to use Freud to enact a successful revenge. At least, she seemed to have consented to treatment on the basis that this would be a part of her treatment. In addition, her leaving treatment as a form of acting-out suggested that her consent had been given on the basis that she was the one who knew which course of action was best for her difficulties, and she did not heed Freud's instruction at the time that she "should not take any important decisions affecting [her] life during the time of [her] treatment" (Freud, 1914g, p. 153).

The changes we expect in a patient's personality, and, indeed, in his unconscious, are, therefore, often very remote from the process that he wants, and to which he believes, unconsciously, he is submitting himself (and engaging the analyst to provide him with). Simply, the patient, unconsciously, comes in search of a mother-figure, say, despite meeting a professional advisor. With this inevitable conflict between what the patient, in some sense, consents to and what the psychoanalyst consents to, we are confronted with an unexpectedly complex ethical situation. It is comparable to the case of the doctor in a casualty department who wishes to give a blood transfusion to a road-traffic accident victim but finds that the patient is a Jehovah's witness and has a conscientious objection to transfusions. If there are, indeed, similar ethical problems, then, on the face of it, standard medical ethics would appear to be a good model for how to proceed with this conflict between psychoanalyst and patient. And in practice psychoanalytic ethics has until now taken medical ethics as just such a suitable model.

---

[2] The idea of unconscious intentions implied by transference and acting-out may make philosophers nervous (Hampshire, 1963); but the example of post-hypnotic suggestion (Erikson, 1939), as well as wish-fulfilments concealed in dreams from normal psychology (Dilman, 1988), adds empirical observation to psychoanalytic work that unconscious forms of intention do in fact exist.

However, we need a detailed examination of how the conditions in medical ethics—in cases where the patient does not cooperate with treatment—might correspond to the psychoanalyst proceeding despite the patient's resistance. Chapter 3 therefore presents an assessment of standard medical ethics as a basis for an ethics of psychoanalysis.

CHAPTER THREE

Rationality and irrationality

The key to what is permitted in medical practice is the degree of rationality (or irrationality) of the patient. This notion is philosophically and psychoanalytically complex. Psychoanalysis addresses irrationality itself—it cannot just respond ethically *to* it.

The place of reason in this is important. As an instrumental function of human beings, reason is regarded in the contemporary world as the underlying factor in the development of science and in the enormous explosion in the Western standard of living. Rationality and its role in enquiry and decision-making is, therefore, a fundamental principle of great value upon which our culture depends.

Reason also plays an important role in the way a person leads his life. It is a bedrock of the capacity for autonomous action, which has to be based upon rational decisions. In terms of the conditions of psychic reality itself, reason—as we shall see later—may form a bridge of thinking that can join up again the divisions in a mind. In this, its internal effects, it could rival those of reason applied to external reality.

The evolution of "rationality"

The role reason has played in human life has changed from early times. Generally, the ancients considered reason as fundamentally a religious faculty. The universe was discovered to run on mathematical regularities—the "music of the spheres"—which were discovered by reason. Perhaps, therefore, reason was a means of contemplating the ultimate reality of the universe, infinity and eternity. It seemed a means of being in tune with the transcendental. St Augustine took this Platonic concept of transcendental "Ideas" and simply incorporated it within the theistic stance of medieval Christianity. The Ideas and the mathematically regulated rules by which the universe turned were simply the "thoughts of God", he said. Reason remained a moral virtue, as a means of access to the mind of God. During this time, reason was balanced by the emotions (passions). But, increasingly, reason tended to be the method of controlling the earthy animal (bodily) nature in human beings and a way of thus turning towards the divine in contemplation.

A radical change of attitude occurred after the Middle Ages, when the authoritarianism of the Catholic Church began to wane. This brought the realization that reason could be employed in a thoroughly material way, as an instrument for living on this earth rather than for contemplation in the spiritual stratosphere. It was not just that people realized that there was a new use for reason. There were many ways in which people had used reason in their lives ever since the beginning of civilization and before. What changed was a *valuation* given to this employment of reason—a changing attitude. Bacon, Galileo, and many others had to fight hard and sometimes with great personal suffering for this change. It was perhaps as much the demand for military technology together with a reaction against the hypocrisy of the Church towards bodily and sexual indulgence in this life that did as much as the wisdom of the scientists to bring reason to the fore as the great provider of good in Western society.

The properties of reason could thus apply to the human individual. Mankind was then endowed with "rationality"—no longer an attribute monopolized by God.

Once the enormous instrumental power of rationality had been established and the modern age had progressed from the mediaeval, there was no going back, though there was a good deal of harking back to what appeared to be moral values that had been lost, and the consequent more rigid assertion of morality—often in Victorian times supported by rigorous and intricate reasoning (rather than a simple appeal to faith). This was because the prioritizing of reason involved all sorts of changes to other attitudes, with a progressive loss of personally comforting and socially stabilizing attitudes. These left a moral vacuum. The problem was this: if the church had been discredited and if reason was as much an instrument for the good of people in this life as a device for the contemplation of God, then what was there to give meaning and a sense of goodness in life? If reason now applies to material goods, what are the sources of moral good?

We will return for the moment to the more technical problems of employing rationality within a system of ethics.

Problems with rationality

The problem that Culver and Gert (1982) found with rationality was in its definition. They consider two—(1) "holding true beliefs" and (2) "maximizing the satisfaction of one's desires"—and argue that both are flawed. They also note that there is an asymmetry between rationality and irrationality:

> . . . all theories of rationality and irrationality agree that to label something as irrational is to express an unfavourable attitude towards it. Thus to say that a proposed action is irrational is to advocate that it not be acted on; and one should even avoid having irrational beliefs and desires.
>
> It is not quite so clear what is entailed by labelling something as rational . . . to call beliefs and desires rational is to advocate holding them. But this seems to be far stronger than our ordinary understanding of the concept, for almost all agree that there can be two incompatible actions that are both rational. [Culver & Gert, 1982, pp. 20–21]

In consequence, they claim that the definition of irrationality is less ambiguous and is a better criterion than that of rationality.

Even if we know what reason is, there are still problems in deciding when someone, or some decision, is rational or, in parallel, irrational. Medical ethics depends on that estimate, and this can be very fraught and uncertain in psychiatry (Edwards, 1982). One instance is the confusion in Russian psychiatry in the 1970s and 1980s between paranoid schizophrenia and political dissent (Bloch, 1981). A personal point of reference may be as dubious as that cultural example. One person's account of whether some other person is or is not rational is relative and may be personal and unreliable. Both personal and cultural reference points are suspect. Whole cultures can embody wildly irrational elements when viewed from the vantage point of another culture—such as psychiatry in the latter days of the Soviet Union, or the grip of Nazi culture that swept Germany in the 1930s, or, perhaps, a Jehovah's Witness refusing transfusion of blood.

Irrationality

The philosophical problem with rationality concerns how there can be such a thing as irrationality. The mind is conceived of, following Descartes *cogito ergo sum*, as a mechanism for cognition. It operates according to a rational proposition: a syllogism that starts with (1) a desire that is conjoined with (2) a belief about a way to satisfy the desire; the resultant (3) is a reason for action (or choice). This paradigm of rationality, a propositional logic, is held by analytic philosophy to be the basic unit of mental functioning. Given that this is supposed to be the way the mind works, then how can it be that something irrational can come out of the mind? By tradition, since the time of Aristotle, two forms of irrationality are considered by philosophers: self-deception and akrasia (Elster, 1986). Self-deception occurs when a false belief is entertained even though the person knows the true one. Akrasia is behaving in a way the person knows to be not in his best interest.

Contemporary philosophy turns to two kinds of answers: (1) the concept of a divided mind (or a second mind), and (2) psychoanalysis and its claim to understand the irrational and its sources.

The first of these, the philosophical debate about divided minds, is considered in the next chapter, and so we turn to the second of these—psychoanalysis.

Psychoanalysis of the irrational

Freud was concerned that the states of mind of the patient during analysis could be overwhelmed by emotional forces, unblocking feeling states and cultivating powerful transferences, and he believed that these could lead to impulsive and irrational decisions that the patient would later regret. Thus, in the days when psychoanalyses were shorter, Freud counselled a patient not to "take any important decisions affecting his life during the time of his treatment" (Freud, 1914g, p. 153). Rationality cannot be relied upon to be sustained during the course of a stressful treatment. The degree of rationality varies therefore with context, time, and stress.

Freud also discovered the logic of a patient's symptoms. They could be made sense of in the patient's own terms. Unconscious mental life has a logic of its own. For instance, a brief paper by Freud (1916d) argues that the character who is wrecked by success, or the character who is a criminal out of a sense of unconscious guilt, is behaving with impeccable logic: guilt demands punishment or, at the very least, a lack of success. Thus, there is a powerful logic to failing or to committing crimes for which one is caught.

Rationality turns out to be a muddled concept, if even irrationality can have a logic of its own. It is a weak and flawed criterion for such a crucial role in an ethics of psychoanalysis. A set of major problems have built up for this use of rationality:

1. The definition of rationality may be ambiguous.
2. The measurement of rationality is problematic.
3. Assessment of rationality will vary with cultural compatibility between patient and assessor.
4. Rationality varies with the intensity of emotional states, and

this may be related to the process and progress of the treatment.

5. In the unconscious, even the apparently irrational has a discernible logic.
6. It is uncertain whether rationality, a central focus for investigation by psychoanalysis, can at the same time perform such a crucial role of discrimination in the ethics of psychoanalysis.

This presents us with a catalogue of major problems in the use of "rationality" as defined in medical ethics for use in an ethics for psychoanalysis.

The rational unconscious

If, as we have just seen, there is a degree of unconscious reason in the seemingly irrational, in what does this hidden rationality consist?

There have been two strategies for answering this. One is that psychoanalysis teaches that the mind is not a unified structure; it is divided between conscious and unconscious, and therefore perhaps between deceiver and deceived (in the case of self-deception). This line of argument converges with the divided-mind hypothesis and can be followed in the next chapter.

A second strategy is the one adopted by Gardner (1993), who separates irrationality into two forms: ordinary irrationality and "psychoanalytic" irrationality.

Ordinary irrationality is structured in ordinary propositional form, such that the desire element of the syllogism is a second-order one—in the case of self-deception, a desire not to have the knowledge.[1] For example, the ordinary propositional form is:

1. a desire;
2. a belief about satisfying the desire;
3. a consequent action to gain satisfaction.

[1] Gardner adopts Frankfurt's (1976) idea of second-order mental functioning, namely the thesis that free will depends upon a second-order desire—a desire to have a desire.

And the propositional form that underlies ordinary irrationality is:

1. a desire;
2. a belief about having the desire;
3. a consequent manoeuvre to dispel the desire.

He states that akrasia can be similarly reformulated. These syllogisms weld this kind of irrationality firmly into ordinary psychology, and such irrationality is therefore philosophically unproblematic.

The second category—*psychoanalytic irrationality*—adds "heterogeneity" to the phenomenon. This is important. The unconscious and pre-propositional wish-fulfilment and phantasy form an entire second area of mental functioning, beyond ordinary propositional psychology. In this, Gardner follows Freud's description of the two principles of mental functioning: primary and secondary processes. However, pre-propositional psychology (Gardner regards it as the philosophical form of "primary process") has its own syllogistic form. In this pre-propositional world, motivations are expressed as wishes (not desires) and become, in dreams and hallucinations, imaginatively fulfilled wishes, leading to momentary satisfactions. This he elaborates with the help of the Kleinian concept of unconscious phantasy. Propositional and pre-propositional psychology, while on divergent tracks, have similar forms:

Propositional psychology:[2]
DRIVE—DESIRE—BELIEF—ACTION/CHOICE

Pre-propositional psychology:
DRIVE—WISH—WISH-FULFILMENT

When in infancy reality enters into the picture, the pre-propositional mode does not completely disappear in favour of propositional "secondary-process" thinking. It, too, may adapt to reality to become a more mature phantasy that is a pre-planning

[2] Propositional psychology is regarded as equivalent to secondary process.

(or drawing-board stage) of potential action and may become the stuff of aesthetic creativity (fantasy). This, of course, links with secondary-process thinking. Mature phantasy as well as reason combine in the latter.

But pre-propositional (primary process) thinking may remain, in part, unaffected by reality, continuing as a primitive and wish-fulfilling strand—in dreams, for instance. It then crops up from time to time as irrationality composed of wishes and their fulfilment, without beliefs rooted in reality.

Pre-propositional logic conforms to the same pattern as ordinary logic. Thus, Gardner has completed his strategy to extend ordinary psychology so that no new metaphysical assumptions have to be introduced and therefore defended. He thus encompasses this now huge and heterogeneous mental world without departing from the assumptions of ordinary psychology.[3] His claim for psychoanalysis is that being merely an extension of ordinary psychology it breaks no new philosophical ground.

Rationalization

A special form of reason is its distorted form, rationalization (Jones, 1908). In the form of rationalization, reason can give a spurious validity to the neurotic or defensive solution of conflicts. (We examine aspects of repression and splitting as the focal psychological defences in Chapter 8.) Such solutions serve to evade self-understanding.

Psychoanalysts have become sensitive from early on to the occurrence of rationalization and the way it may reinforce unconscious defences, giving rise to distortions and irrationality and dismantling insight. The construction of apparently water-tight, conscious reason is illustrated by a patient who soothed herself with a rationalization:

---

[3] See, for instance, Morton (1982) on the relation between psychoanalysis and a common-or-garden vernacular psychology. As Morton comments, there is, in any case, a strong link between the two, as so many psychoanalytic ideas have slipped easily into common use in the way we conceive each other and interpret each other's behaviours.

> When I billed a woman for a session with me that she had cancelled, she said she was glad I had done so as now she had less money to spend on smoking and on creamy cakes. At the time she was suing over a financial settlement that had previously been made in the course of a divorce.

This woman disabled her awareness of her resentment towards me, at being asked to pay for something she had not had, and avoided a potential litigious conflict with me, by creating a spurious reason (a rationalization) for agreeing with me. I might add that she never did pay for that session! Philosophically, such shallow reasoning cannot be distinguished from a truer account of her intentions. The psychoanalytic account of rationalization brings the validity of reasons to test. Philosophical ethics, addressing the basis on which people choose to act and to consent, has tended to neglect this psychoanalytic distinction between rationalization and conscious, rational decision-making (Barker & Baldwin, 1991).

Rationality is a useful tool to work out choices, but it can, equally, be exploited to paper over spurious reasons and self-deceptions. What appears on the surface to be a rational choice requires rather complex assessment. The complexities of the various forms of irrationality, together with rationalization, render the criterion for paternalism extremely problematic.

Because philosophers prize the rational, following Descartes's *cogito*, they often find the psychoanalytic probing of the individual's reason, rationality, and irrationality uncomfortable (see Hospers, 1959). In fact, contemporary philosophy is based so firmly on valid reasoning (analytical philosophy) that it delayed its acquaintance with psychoanalysis:

> [I]f Freud's ideas have, in one form or another, overrun the awareness of our age, if they have deeply influenced the minds of intellectuals of various kinds, of artists, of common people, they have barely impinged on philosophers. [Wollheim, 1974, p. ix]

An interest in Freud's theories has come late. But one of the contemporary uses of Freud by philosophers is the psychoanalytic contribution to the understanding of irrationality, in the form of the possibility of a "divided" mind or a "second" mind.

CHAPTER FOUR

The divided mind

In mining Freud and psychoanalysis as a source of ideas that might bear upon philosophical problems, those psychoanalytic ideas often become distorted in the process. Some philosophers have taken a broad view[1] and have attempted to recast the whole system of psychoanalytic ideas in more accurate philosophical language. Others have more narrow targets. I shall turn to the

[1] These studies have varied over which school of psychoanalysis they address. In the analytic philosophy tradition, Dilman (1984) and Lear (1990) have approached classical psychoanalysis and its sophisticated expression in the structural model of Freud. This rests upon the view of mind as a system for the disposing of instinctual energies, which Freud called "libido". In contrast, Wollheim (1984) has been influential in drawing philosophers' attention to the school of Melanie Klein.

A number of philosophers, on the other hand, have approached psychoanalysis in a different way. They have taken up, or extracted, certain ideas in the course of dealing with specific philosophical problems. For instance, Wittgenstein (1979) was interested in Freud's approach to symbolism and the nature of meaning. He took seriously Freud's theory of dreams as a personal coded language of images, but he was critical of Freud's positivist approach

argument that the irrational—taking self-deception as the paradigm—results from a "second mind" of some kind separated off but retaining a powerful influence.

Self-deception

Sartre (1943) found in Freud a psychologist of bad faith [*mauvaise foi*] or self-deception. He described a cleavage between objective and subjective modes: the object "for-itself" (conscious and self-conscious) or "in-itself" (thing-like). The human being has both characteristics, which cannot be resolved together. This cleavage results in a sense of futility, and yet it is in the nature of being to continue to reach for resolution of the cleavage. One false resolution is to reduce "for-itself" to "in-itself"; and this is bad faith. It is, for Sartre, the origin of self-deception.

Freud's descriptions, aimed at the objective scientific stance, were in bad faith in Sartre's terms, and patients, he claimed, were encouraged to follow false deterministic views of themselves. Sartre found severe contradictions in psychoanalytic explanations. In particular, he argued that if the mind operates deterministically (not "for-itself") in deceiving itself, then there must be some superordinate part to the mind that knows—indeed, orchestrates—the self-deception, in which case it is not deceived and operates in the "for-itself" mode. One form of philosophical explanation of irrationality (self-deception) and akrasia (acting against one's own best interests) contrasts with that of Gardner—that the mind is capable of division, and it works against itself by one part working against another. However, following Sartre's view that to postulate a part of the mind that knowingly deceives the mind is a

---

since it confuses reasons with causes (Johnston, 1989). On the other hand, Davidson (1982) attempted to clarify when causes are reasons for what they cause and when they are not—a view that Hopkins (1982) exploited to defend the basis of psychology. The psychoanalyst, Home (1966), also specified reasons as being in the realm of the human sciences and causes in that of the natural sciences. Sartre's views of self-deception and repression form a basis for this chapter.

contradiction, it has been difficult to understand philosophically how a mind can, in fact, be divided. Nevertheless, in trying to understand irrationality, the search is on for partitions in the mind.

Repression

In considering Freud's theory of the mind in separate parts, Dilman (1984) simply described the division between conscious and unconscious as the source of self-deception, arguing that

> Freud's contribution was to recognise that the ego cannot be master in its own house by the exercise of will-power through repression. Repression is what splits a person, increases inner conflict, curtails autonomy. [Dilman, 1984, p. 6]

Dilman meant that repression undermines *conscious* will-power. Nevertheless, Freud implied that the success of the psychoanalytic process in making the repressed conscious, "did not mean to deny that it can achieve a position of mastery 'in its own house'" (Dilman, 1984, p. 6). Then, with consciousness achieved, the "will" is in a position to operate autonomously. This equates the conscious with autonomous agency and the unconscious as the deterministic element in human nature.[2] In this psychoanalytic account, Dilman clearly takes self-deception as meaning the *conscious* mis-belief in the nature of what one knows. It is like forgetting a person's name, which is "on the tip of the tongue". This is a motivated forgetting, and in this sense the conscious person is deceived by his unconscious into not knowing the name of the other person. This is valid enough.

---

[2] Despite Freud's espousal of Hughlings Jackson's doctrine of concomitance, which allows the investigation of either the material brain or the psychological mind as separate spheres, Freud did seem to suggest that the ego was the seat of the will, and the unconscious (or the id) was a deterministic influence delimiting the agency of the will. This incidentally contrasts with the interactionist position of Jung. It also contrasts with Freud's position, when he theorizes his clinical material in such a way as to imply that the unconscious retains its own agency, intention, and awareness.

However, Dilman flies in the face of Sartre's criticism. Sartre's quarrel is with the concept of the unconscious as a deterministic element in the mind—as if it did not know what it is doing—that is, it is not self-reflective ("for-itself"). Freud also, taking the view that the mind operates as a whole, regarded repression as an agent that is merely unconscious but is not itself deceived. If self-deception is a real phenomenon, it needs to cover the loss of unconscious self-knowledge as well as the conscious knowledge. There is a difference between, on the one hand, the conscious mind being deceived, and, on the other, the whole mental system of conscious and unconscious being deceived.

As far as Freud's structural theory—id, ego, and superego—is concerned, all parts of the mind exist in relation to each other. Despite conflict, they operate as a whole. They know what the others are up to. The problems of understanding self-deception, using the structural model of id, ego, and superego, are probably insuperable, since the central idea of structural relatedness does not adequately lay to rest Sartre's core point that something in the mind goes on knowing that self-deception is happening.

Sub-systems

Nevertheless, despite Sartre's argument, there has still been a great deal of interest in the view of the Freudian unconscious as a "second mind". A vigorous argument has developed on the basis of sub-systems within the mind. The mind is made up of sub-systems that may act against each other. This view has been advanced by Pears (1982) and developed also by Davidson (1982), who structured the mind with sub-systems, not all of which worked together, but often in opposition.

However, it is doubtful as to whether they have confounded Sartre's objections of a divided mind. In particular, these doubts rise from the question whether a sub-system of the mind has the qualities of a person ("for-itself"). Can it have agency and self-consciousness—without consciousness? Davidson distinguished a "sub-system" from the whole of the human system of the person. In particular, he defined the sub-system as the place of "a mental cause which is not a reason for what it causes" (Davidson, 1982, p. 298). Therefore it cannot be granted that a sub-system is, in fact, also a person-like system in its own right.[3] Instead, a sub-system, as described by Davidson, is non–person-like and thus falls foul of Sartre's criticism of reducing human beings to the status of non-being ("in-itself").

The failure to combat Sartre's argument has led to further attempts to debate the idea of a divided mind. In particular, three main positions can be distinguished: (1) an argument against a divided mind, based on representation; (2) a debate explaining irrationality on the basis of the heterogeneity of the mind; and, (3) an argument for a divided mind that has recourse to empirical findings. As an extension of the latter, there is also a fourth strategy based on empirical psychoanalytic findings—the core of this book.

Representation

One might say that the mind *represents itself* as if it were divided rather than being in a true state of division. In that sense, the mind remains one, but it *represents* itself as two.[4] Thus, division is restricted to the level of the mind's image of itself, rather than as some objectified level of observation. This idea of a *mere* representation is important psychoanalytically, and Sandler particularly has attempted to address the importance of representation and self-representation as the materials with which the processes of mind operate (Sandler, 1987).

Wollheim's (1984) premise is that an individual's sense of being a person is the process of "living a life". This amounts to the creation of a narrative biographical thread through the act of living. The person's mind represents itself to itself in the form of an

[3] Arguments on philosophical grounds are given in Chapter 3 of Gardner (1993).

[4] I am grateful to Jim Hopkins (personal communication) for helping me to get this point of view clear.

autobiographical narrative or, as Wollheim puts it, an "iconic mental state"—pictures of his past imaginatively brought to mind. In this, Wollheim in effect also dismisses the need for an actually divided mind. In principle, it is possible to deduce, though Wollheim does not do so explicitly, that a person may construct a narrative of a divided self. Irrationality is then merely in the person's representation. The unity of the mind is still preserved.

The heterogeneity of mind

Certain philosophers sophisticated in psychoanalysis, notably Gardner (1993),[5] have disputed that the mind is merely a system of rational propositions. We have examined his claims in Chapter 3.[6] His argument contends that certain contents of the mind are outside the rationality system and will give rise to mental events that are not rational. Obviously, in this way, a heterogenous mind will only give rise to partly rational effects; partly there will be non-rational effects. By showing that the influence of wishes and phantasies from unconscious levels of the mind creates non-rational mental activity, it is not necessary to postulate a division in the mind such that the parts operate quite without contact or "awareness" of each other. Instead, parts of the mind are different in quality or nature and not separated by a rift. A phantasy of eating faeces[7] may not be rational in an ordinary sense, but there is a reason for it—a meaning to the madness. The action follows logically from a false belief. Segal elaborated how "Underlying

[5] Lear (1990; and 1995—his review of Gardner) supports the argument based on the heterogeneity of the mind.

[6] Gardner's case rests, he tells us, on the findings of Melanie Klein and claims that the mind has heterogeneous contents—wishes and phantasies, as well as reason. However, Gardner's reading of Klein is selective and restricted to Klein's emphasis on unconscious phantasy. He neglects the aspects of Klein's thought—splitting—which this book takes up, to show, as I shall argue, yet another category of irrationality.

[7] See for instance Abraham (1924) and my commentary on this (Hinshelwood, 1994a, pp. 21–23).

irrational action are delusions" (Segal, 1992, p. 61). The murderer of a prostitute may see in the woman an underlying delusional image of his mother as the "vehicle of obscene sexuality" (p. 59), which he is then compelled to eradicate. Given delusional beliefs, such irrationality does not therefore indicate a divided mind. It is evidence that the reality of the situation is ignored, overwhelmed from internal sources in wishes. What is crucial is that wishes overwhelm reality-testing, the capacity to see what is what. Instead of the capacity to take the reality situation into account in the form of a rational belief, wishes become supreme—that is, pre-propositional psychology—and reality is redefined.

None of this, however, rules out the possibility of a further form of irrationality, one deriving from a "second" mind. Gardner merely argues that, given the difficult philosophical problems arising from the divided mind hypothesis (such as Sartre's argument, as we have seen), it is simply not necessary on *a priori* grounds to defend the divided-mind hypothesis.

Irrationality could, however, be due to more than one process: both (1) the heterogeneous irrationalities described by Gardner and (2) splits in the mind, which, however philosophically impossible, could be empirically verified. There is room for a different kind of irrationality—one where reason, meaning, and coherence of mind are, in fact, actively disrupted. Lear (1996), for instance, drew attention to an instance of a positive disruption of the "vehicles of meaning" in Freud's Rat Man case. This kind of irrationality is the focus of the argument of this book.

Empirical findings

Gardner's argument, seeking to obviate the need for a philosophical defence of the "divided mind" on *a priori* grounds, does not cover certain situations, found empirically.

The philosophical interest in the unity (or divisibility) of the person has tended to turn to empirical findings and, in particular, to the question:

- Under what conditions could one expect to find a divided mind?

Locke's idea of the self, or mind, as a form of substance, equivalent in many respects to material substance, gave it spurious spatio-temporal attributes. It thus allowed so-called "thought experiments", in which minds can be swapped from one body to another (Shoemaker, 1963; Williams, 1970). The point is that one can consider whether one mind in a particular body would remain the same mind if it were in another body. These "experiments" were aimed at an enquiry to establish whether identity results from psychological experiences or from a bodily presence.[8]

A further step was to consider the direct manipulation, through surgery, of the brain substance—as if mind were co-extensive with the brain (Puccetti, 1973). This direction of the argument turned directly to the work, from the 1950s onwards, of the neurophysiologist, Sperry, and others. Nagel (1971), in reviewing that neurophysiological literature, was dubious about the evidence for divided identities. In answer to his question—how many minds compete if the corpus callosum is sectioned?—Nagel concluded that it is "no whole number of minds". This anticipates similar reviews and similar conclusions by Glover (1988) and Parfit (1984).

Glover (1988) took a neurophysiological starting-point by reviewing the clinical literature on split-brain patients (and other pathology)—that is, on people who had actually undergone surgery separating parts of their brain. He amassed a useful summary from neurological conditions on multiple consciousnesses. He concluded that:

> . . . the "two minds" view gives the best account of the kinds of integration and lack of integration that are found. But this is

[8] Identity is a philosophical notion that has been treated as a paradox since Plato (Russell, 1956). It might therefore be better to stick to a psychological term, such as "sense of self". However, the philosophical term "personal identity" does have those sorts of connotations that adhere to "sense of self". Swinburne (1973–1974) has argued that there is an *a priori* residual meaning to the term "personal identity" which remains after empirical description has been exhausted. Despite the attempt by analytical philosophers to pin this residuum to the ground, I shall take it that we have a correspondence between that residual quality and a "sense of self". I shall tend therefore to use the terms as equivalent in denoting that irreducible internal sense of knowing who one is.

> comparable with accepting that "minds" may have fuzzy edges, so that counting them may be a rather blurred affair. [Glover, 1988, p. 46]

Parfit (1984) also accepts evidence from these empirical findings, concluding that:

> We can come to believe that a person's mental history need not be like a canal, with only one channel, but could be like a river, occasionally having separate streams. [Parfit, 1984, p. 247]

These views rely largely on objective, empirical experiments, and the data are therefore gross in comparison with the data gained from subjective experience. Wilkes (1988) argued against this analogy, ascribing whole-person attributes to parts of persons and brains. Thought experiments, she concluded, could not address real people in this way. The spatio-temporal analogy runs thin.

Yet another step in this process has been to consider other pathological conditions—those where the division has not been a surgical but a psychic one, giving rise to multiple personalities (Mackie, 1985).

Braude (1995a) and others (e.g. Hilgard, 1986) turned to these subjective states. Instead of physical divisions of the brain, Braude has studied the phenomena of psychological divisions—multiple personality disorder. These conditions have been well known for a hundred years and were, in fact, perhaps better studied by psychiatrists a century ago than now.[9] Braude noted the extensive literature on these states at the end of the last century (for example, Myers, 1903; Pierce, 1895; Podmore, 1895; see also Oppenheim, 1985). This step reacts against the equation of mental with bodily substance, and it establishes the person as a separate immaterial substance.

---

[9] The hysterical phenomena studied by Janet (1892) were well known to Freud. Surviving interest in these phenomena depends in large measure on the case of Sally Beauchamp (Prince, 1906). Given Freud's antipathy to Janet, it is not surprising that recent interest, such as Braude's, is disdainful of psychoanalysis. For a useful account of the history of hypnosis to which these multiple personality phenomena are connected see Chapter 1 of Braude (1995a).

Despite the connection between these studies and spiritualist and paranormal phenomena, which Braude endorses, these studies are concerned with the subjectivity of being a person, and of being a person divided into many. These states would satisfy one of Sartre's conditions: that the divided parts retain person-like qualities, including self-reflection. However, Braude concluded that in the disorder of multiple personality

> . . . alters are often aware of the thoughts and behaviour of others and that they can interfere with each other as well. [Braude, 1995a, p. 104]

This brings these dissociative phenomena into the category of "repression", and there is no real separation of personalities (non-interference)—apart from the striking conscious phenomena, they are more a representation of alters. In this case the phenomenon does not pass Sartre's criteria: there is awareness of the division and the parts are not deceived. Despite their dramatic and exotic character, multiple personality disorders can therefore be included in the self-deception that Gardner called "ordinary" psychology. To mark the difference from a more truly divided mind we can consider schematically Freud's paradigm case before looking in some detail at contemporary psychoanalytic work.

The irrational fetishist

Freud (1927e, 1940e [1938]) believed that he had, rather late in the day, realized how the ego can pull itself apart through incompatible mental functions. Starting with a desire (libido), no fewer than two irrational consequences occur simultaneously (see Figure 1). The first line, on the left, exchanges the desire for a wish—that women do have penises and are not evidence of the reality of castration. That wish then receives fulfilment by hallucinating a female penis in the form of the fetish, which the ego then sexually worships. In the other line the desire is exchanged for an alternative wish—that the ego shall be exempt from castration. That wish is then fulfilled by manual masturbation of the penis.

Freud's example exhibits a split of an extreme kind in pre-propositional mental functioning (primary process). In this case,

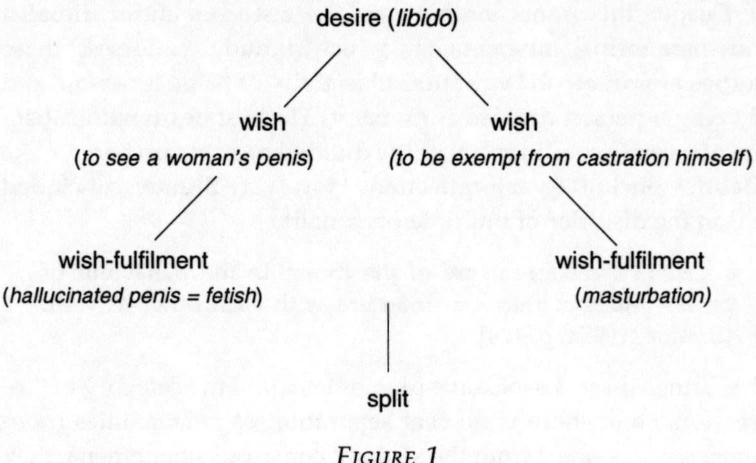

FIGURE 1

both parts of the ego continue to function, but completely out of communication with each other. Reality is denied twice over, but in different ways. It is not a heterogeneity in Gardner's terms of competing propositional and pre-positional psychologies, but two quite separate pre-propositional syllogisms.

It is the lack of communication between these two wishes and fulfilments that is the important hallmark of splitting. This contrasts with other forms of partition, such as repression or the divisions into id, ego, and superego, where the parts continue to relate to, and influence, each other. In other words, it is at the primitive levels of mental functioning where splitting can occur. This is the level where reality has not been fully grasped, and "below" the propositional level, where secondary-process rationality becomes established.

Gardner's argument, therefore, that irrationality is due to heterogeneity and not to division of the mind is not complete—on empirical grounds. The fact, therefore, that it might be possible to explain many instances of irrationality as a heterogeneity of the mind does not necessarily exclude the possibility of irrationality from a true division of the mind.

In summarizing this work, we can say that some confirmation of a divided mind comes from thought experiments and real surgical experiments on the subjective experiences of individual persons and their autobiographical narratives. Subjective experiences in highly mentally disturbed individuals also seem to suggest a division in the mind.

We can now turn to psychoanalysis for further possible—but empirical—evidence of this kind of division.

CHAPTER FIVE

Psychoanalytic evidence

Empirical findings of the subjective kind are the bread-and-butter of psychoanalytic work.[1] The arguments in defence of a divided mind, described earlier, based on repression and representation seem to fail because they imply a superordinate part of the mind acting unconsciously to orchestrate divisions—a mind, therefore, that is not itself deceived. However, that point of view contrasts with the self-action of the mind upon itself, which is claimed by many analysts (led perhaps by Kleinians) as a more fundamental layer of mental functioning and development that lies beneath repression and representation.

Freud's work largely entailed elaborating our understanding of those conflicts located in the unconscious that resulted from repression, and he dwelt on the conflicts of the Oedipal drama. But in his last work, Freud's (1940e [1938]) description of "splitting of

[1] It could be questioned whether empirical findings on the subjectivity of an "other's" interiority are to be classed with empirical findings of an objective kind as encountered in natural science, but the nature of a "science" of the subjective will not be tackled here. (See, however, O'Shaughnessy, 1994.)

the ego" was quite different from the division between cognition and emotion, or between conscious and unconscious. In his example of the fetishist, as we saw in Chapter 4, there is both a wish-fulfilling assertion that women possess a penis and therefore castration does not occur, and a simultaneous wish that castration need not be feared anyway. Both systems are in the form of a pre-propositional syllogism (drive/wish/wish-fulfilment) and can be understood as underlying (not parallel with) propositional rationality. However, there are two wishes, quite independent, leading to inconsistency/irrationality that is quite different from the irrationality within each of the pre-propositional trains of thought. It is precisely because the false beliefs do not obtrude into each other that they are to be described as split in a way that is completely different from repression. In fact, each side of the split is pre-propositional in Gardner's (1993) terms, and thus on each side repression plays its part, forming two quite separate systems that function precisely because they are not brought into contact with each other. On each side there is a lack of awareness of the other—satisfying one of Sartre's conditions—and on each side there is a full syllogism of a motivated intentional being or person—satisfying another of Sartre's points.

Later (Chapter 6), we will meet my patient, Miss J, who could recognize how her mind had fragmented—"gone through the shredder". This split state of shredding, or fragmentation, is sharply different from the moments when the parts of Patient J came back together in the form of disguised (and repressed) representations.

An emphasis on the splitting of the ego is characteristic of the approach developed by Kleinian analysts from 1946 onwards, where the mind does not merely work with representations and repression, or a manipulation of what is repressed. It operates upon itself in some way in which there is a realization of the division, without representation. In this form, the mechanism of splitting is most frequently supplemented by the mechanism of projective identification.

It is also based on what Freud referred to as the "omnipotence of thought" (Freud, 1909d)— a circumstance that, from one point of view (objectively), appears fantastical, yet has a complete reality from another (internal, or subjective) point of view. That reality he called "psychic reality", distinguishing it from the objective and positivist-styled real physical world.[2]

Forms of partition

This brief account has demonstrated that there are a number of senses in which the division of the mind can, in practice, be understood. To summarize: we can distinguish at least four forms of partition that have been discussed:

1. the partition into a set of working parts according to Freud's structural model of id, ego, and superego;
2. the barrier of repression between consciousness and the unconscious in which the two parts operate according to different rules;
3. the representation of the mind as divided;
4. a division at the pre-propositional desire/wish/wish-fulfilment level, as in Freud's description of the fetishist.[3]

In clinical practice, these various forms of division may not always be distinguished, as the psychoanalyst may not need to proceed differently with each type. Nevertheless, whatever the clinical interventions, these varieties derive from quite different phenomenological levels. In the first three of these, repression and self-representation play the key role. They thus fail to survive Sartre's argument. Because in repression self-representations remain, though they are unconscious, the agent of the process is in some sense a superordinate part of the mind, which "knows" what it is doing.

---

[2] When Freud moved from his natural science stance at the beginning of his research to establish a kind of autonomous world of psychic reality, he produced a psychologist out of his earlier neurophysiologist hat.

[3] An extension of this form of partition is Bion's (1957) description of the self-splitting of the mind—a motivated disruption of the person as a result of self-directed aggression. Observation of these extreme forms of self-disruption emerges in Freud's clinical notes on the Rat Man case (Freud, 1909d).

Examining the empirical data, as I shall in the subsequent chapters, the findings suggest that in splitting, Category 4, there is no representation, as there is with repression. In subjective experiencing, there is a significant phenomenological difference between Categories 1–3, where something missing is represented, and Category 4, which merely represents a "missingness".

If this claim, on empirical grounds, is accepted it must lead to a view of splitting (as distinct from repression) that completes the philosophers' search for partitions of the mind. Though we can have a psychoanalytic description (along with the neurological data) of what happens in such a division, philosophical problems of how it can happen may remain unresolved. However, that does not of itself invalidate empirical findings.

Thus, we have to confront a strange phenomenon: an activity of the mind, the phantasy of dividing into two (or more) parts, results in an actual occurrence of this, not merely a representation of it. The sense of something missing, consciously and unconsciously, is conjoined with a loss of awareness of what has happened. A piece of self-reflection has disappeared in the process. No knowledge remains of the location and character of that missing part. As we shall see, the awareness—self-reflection—may be gained by the mind of someone else in certain circumstances.

Omnipotence of phantasy

Such occurrences are instances of the "omnipotence of thoughts", as Freud (1909d) called it. He saw it in superstition and magical belief, but those phenomena were congruent with certain features of obsessional patients who suffer (gravely) from the anxiety that their worst hatred towards their loved ones has actually come about. The magical quality of this demands magical recompense. He observed a mechanism (undoing) in obsessional symptoms designed to undo the results of these fantastical activities. For instance, Freud's celebrated patient, the Rat Man, had ghastly fantasies of subjecting his father and also his lady-love to a torture that he had heard about during his army service, in which rats, applied to the anus of the victim, gnawed their way into the victim's body (Freud, 1909d). The patient was so aghast at the awful nature of these fantasies that he was himself tortured by his own thoughts. He suffered particularly strikingly because he could find so little to do to put right such a phenomenally cruel intrusion into other persons, and in particular into those others who were his loved ones. He believed—and actually felt—as if he were responsible for *really* applying the torture to them.

Thus the patient suffered from a belief that to think the fantasy was to have actually done it—"no sooner said than done". However, another angle to this omnipotence was described by Abraham (1924). Curiously, this was not only stranger even than the Rat Man's omnipotence, but it was also to be discovered in much more "normal" people. In this form, the fantasy was not just that it had been enacted on some other person, but that the effect had been real upon the mind of the fantasizer himself.

Concerning a bereaved man who had lost his appetite since the death of his wife, Abraham (1924) described a dream that had followed his first good evening meal some weeks after the burial. Without repeating details here (for fuller details see Hinshelwood, 1994), the man had dreamed both of a butcher's shop and of the post-mortem on his dead wife. The effect of the dream was that

> Consuming the flesh of the dead wife is made equivalent to restoring her to life. Now Freud has shown that introjecting the lost object the melancholiac does indeed recall it to life: he sets it up in his ego. [Abraham, 1924, p. 436]

In this case, the dream represented a psychic change that took place during the process of mourning. The man introjected (eating) his loved wife in his phantasy and thereby restored her to life. But not only was this a phantasy—it also "announced the fact that the work of mourning had succeeded" (p. 436). The dream represented the phantasy, but the phantasy was in itself an event on the road to actually restoring a more normal state of mind. Phantasy had real consequences.

*Ph*antasy (as opposed to *f*antasy), as it was subsequently investigated by Kleinian psychoanalysts, provides not just a content to the mind, but an instrument that restructures the mind. Processes of projection (expelling from the person) and introjection (taking into the person) are both mechanisms of the mind and at the same time effects the working of the mind. They form the very basis of judgement:

> Expressed in the language of the oldest—the oral–instinctual impulses, the judgement is: "I should like to eat this", or "I should like to spit it out"; and, put more generally: "I should like to take this into myself and to keep that out." . . . The original pleasure-ego wants to introject into itself everything that is good and to eject everything that is bad. What is bad, what is alien to the ego and what is external are, to begin with, identical. [Freud, 1925h, p. 237]

In this way, the origins of the ego are in the reordering of its experiences, so that the comforting and good are located inside and the threatening and bad outside. This was taken by Klein and her co-workers to refer also to good parts and bad parts of the self (Klein, 1946). The very shape and constituents of the person are determined in this way.

Thus, the mind, and the self, have the capacity to create changes through this activity upon the self. It is an activity charged with the drives that are embedded in the biological substratum of the phantasies—bodily ingesting and eliminating. Not only are mental contents and parts of the mind itself evacuated, but clearly the awareness of such activity may also evaporate.

The capacity to understand what is happening to the self is essential to maintaining a coherence and unity to it. In splitting, that self-reflection is lost; in repression it remains (though unconscious). Later we will see that this capacity for self-reflection is the link that joins disparate parts together.

These "omnipotent" occurrences are empirical findings from psychoanalysis, for which philosophers and ethicists may need to give a metaphysical grounding. They may seem very strange, and perhaps we accept them in extremely disturbed people, such as those having had extensive brain surgery, or perhaps those with a mental illness. We will move on in the next two chapters to examine detailed clinical evidence from psychoanalysis. We shall see that these occurrences are not restricted to such extensively disordered persons.

CHAPTER SIX

Primitive phenomena in psychoanalysis

The three phenomena that are relevant to our understanding of personal choices are known as the "primitive mechanisms"—splitting, projection, and introjection. They are studied best in the transference relationship of individual therapy. They have profound implications for understanding who is choosing what and thus create problems for the definition of personal identity. I shall describe each of the three phenomena, giving a detailed account of the clinical process that can be observed in the psychoanalytic setting.[1]

[1] The clinical material in this chapter was previously used in R. D. Hinshelwood, "Social relocation of personal identity through splitting, projection and introjection". *Philosophy, Psychiatry, Psychology* 2 (1995): 185–204 (reprinted by permission). The case material is derived from real patients, but with biographical and other details changed to ensure confidentiality.

Splitting

All kinds of parts of the mind—affects, cognition, memories, wishes, intentions—can become separated from each other. Even functions (such as understanding and perception) may become split off from consciousness and—usually temporarily—obliterated, even from the unconscious. Freud's (1940e [1938]) example was of a male fetishist who could both obliterate the belief in castration, despite the observations of a woman's lack of a penis (her castration) and, at the very same time, sustain a tenacious belief that she does have a phallus (which he excitedly adores). Neither part of the mind influences the other.

Melanie Klein employed the concept of splitting initially to account for patients in whom there appeared to be something missing in the way they related to other people. She noted a blankness of affect. For instance, a patient told her of a sense of anxiety that was afflicting him and talked of people more successful than he was himself, towards whom he experienced feelings of frustration, grievance, and envy. She continued:

> [When] I interpreted . . . that these feelings were directed against the analyst and that he wanted to destroy me, his mood changed abruptly. The tone of his voice became flat, he spoke in a slow expressionless way, and he said that he felt detached. [Klein, 1946, p. 19]

He had thus lost, suddenly, the emotional quality of his mood. A similar phenomenon is illustrated in the following example, in which the patient's mind is drastically split up. It contrasts with *repression* in the ordinary (Freudian) sense—where representation remains, though distorted by repression—which I also demonstrate in this case.

Clinical illustration: Miss J's shredded mind

This patient, who was in her mid-40s, had been in analysis for about two years. She was not seriously disturbed and was satisfactorily coping with a stressful job. When she was young, she had been close to a man who had died of a slowly progressive illness, and she had then entered a period of some disturbance of an anti-social kind. At the time of starting her analysis, she was much more stable. But she did have persisting problems—a rather chronic depressed mood, a poor relationship with her mother, and certain isolated phobias. The session prior to the one described here had ended with her feeling cross with me about an interpretation I had made the day before, in which I had suggested that she actively cultivated her chronic miserableness.

> She started this session by saying that the day before, when she had left me, she had witnessed a scene in which a woman was arguing angrily with a man in a shop. The woman had a young child in a pram. Miss J described the sense of being a bystander at the scene of the quarrel in the street. She had been disturbed about what she should do. The two people seemed on the verge of physically grappling with each other.
>
> I recalled that she had been angry with me when she left the session the day before; so, I said that I thought she wanted to talk to me about the hostile quarrel in the street outside my house yesterday because it was a way of dealing with the hostile feelings she had had towards me and had taken into the street at the end of the previous session. Her fairly friendly manner towards me suggested that the painful feelings and hostile response to me had gone out of her conscious mind, probably pretty quickly; and, indeed, she seemed to have some trouble recalling her disagreeable reaction to me at the end of the previous session. Hesitantly, she said, "Er . . . you mean, about the miserableness", and she remained thoughtful in her quiet way.
>
> I then said I thought she was struggling to recall the end of yesterday's session, and that it was very difficult because she dare not risk the hostile feelings towards me appearing in the room again today.
>
> In response to this interpretation, she was silent and unmoving for a minute or so, then she put her hand to her brow as if perplexed. She sighed in a resigned way and said: "That's a

> minefield." It confirmed that she felt in some difficulties, but it also seemed that she felt I was pressing her to remember her hostility. I was uncertain exactly what she meant. She was silent and did not enlighten me. So I asked: "What do you feel is a minefield?" There was silence for a couple more minutes, until eventually she muttered, "I've chopped that up, so I don't know what you said. It went through the shredder."

Here is an interesting situation. The patient makes attempts to deal with hostile feelings in the immediate relationship with me. First, she dealt with it after the previous session by abolishing hostile feelings from her own mind and seeing them only in a quarrel in two quite different people distant from her and me, and from whom she felt detached. She actually had words, and images to convey that a quarrel had happened yesterday; it was, however, a displaced quarrel. Then, secondly, when I brought her back to the hostility towards me, she seemed to feel somewhat pressured, and she resorted to a different method of dealing with the hostility; she did something quite drastic to her mind. She could recognize that she had chopped something up, or "shredded" it. We can see this as an effort to avoid the understanding that I offered her because it seemed as dangerous and as explosive as a minefield. This "shredding" is the patient's subjective experience of splitting.

We can see again that something has happened to the shape or structure of her mind. Something has gone out of existence. The missing parts, as I understand, are firstly her hostile feelings towards me; and, secondly, her capacity to understand the experience that she has of hostility.

> I interpreted the process I thought her mind had undergone. I suggested she had shredded my words because of the risk of blowing up at me if she had really taken them in, and that this resembled, too, how she had distanced herself from her memories of yesterday's session for the same reason. She seemed emotionally moved by this and appeared able to continue in a more fully functioning way.

To summarize the process that occurred in this session: at the beginning, a familiar process of repression conveyed something but in disguised representational form—the quarrel in the street. The experience for her at this time, of attacking me with her anger, was inconceivable consciously—partly because in the back of her mind was the experience with a fragile (ill) man who had actually died. Thus, instead of the hostility to me, she returned in a relaxed frame of mind, seemingly quite cooperative and pleasant. This implies a state of conflict in her mind: feeling hostile but feeling it is too dangerous actually to have her feelings when she is with me. The conflict, resolved by repression at that stage, represented the anger of yesterday as not anger with me but, instead, the hostile scene on the corner of my road. There was, though, some sense of involvement in the quarrel she had witnessed, as she pondered what to do. That was all that was left of *our* quarrel.

When she arrived at the session, there was a representation of *a* quarrel, which served as the return of her repressed experience with me. As is the rule with repression, it returns in disguised form. This is like the appearance in a dream of disguised contents in the form of impenetrable symbols from the unconscious.

However, when I tried to help her to remember her own anger consciously, something more drastic happened. A different kind of defence came into play—her mind went out of action, and she actually lost the capacity to process what I said, or to have her own thoughts properly. Her capacity to think appeared to have been momentarily annihilated. It was clear to me that I was a considerable problem to her at that moment. I had pressed her with my words, which expressed what she was unable to process. She could no longer repress and transform it into a disguised form—a memory, a phantasy, or whatever. In this case she, instead, destroyed what she heard, so she did not hear it. Not only had the contents disappeared, but seemingly her ability to hear and to think had also been lost—temporarily, of course. It was utterly terrifying to be in the room, as if anything could blow up without warning. Instead of her hostility to me being more clear to her, an obliterating aggression turned against her own mind.

It is processes of this latter kind that Melanie Klein called "splitting". The patient was left with a sense that something destructive had gone on in her. Certain mental functions, as well as certain contents of her mind, had simply been lost. With this mental loss she was unable to give ordinary responses and was reduced to silence. She was, as we say, "at a loss", significantly depleted in herself for that moment.[2]

Projection

The term "projection" [3] is derived from its use in the psychology of perception. For instance, activity in the retina is projected outwards into the visual field experienced as distant and outside the person. Or, when a blind man with a white stick in his hand feels certain sensations of the stick against the skin of his hand and fingers, he "projects" to the other end of the stick and assumes that there is an obstacle in his path. A pattern of sensations in his hand at one end of his stick is perceived as something he locates three feet away, at the other end of the stick. In this sense, projection can be the basis of exploring actual reality.

At another level, at which we perceive other people, the term "projection" means an inference about their characters—seeing *in* them certain expected features. Sometimes we call it "first impressions" when we sum up in our own mind the whole of the personality of another person in the moment when we first shake hands; though later we can explore whether those impressions match up to what that person is really like.

At times, the assessment of another person—including those met with in the transference relationship in a psychoanalysis—on the basis of a "first impressions" type of projection is not mitigated

---

[2] This temporary destruction of my patient's mind is not on the same scale of destruction as the schizophrenic will achieve, and on a permanent, or semi-permanent, basis (Bion, 1957; Rosenfeld, 1947). In other words, the kind of partition I am describing in my example is of the Category-4 kind (see "Forms of partition", p. 48), whereas the phenomena described by Bion and Rosenfeld, and perhaps Freud's Rat Man case (1909d), are significantly different in scope and intensity (see p. 48, fn. 3).

[3] For a systematic account of "projection" and related terms (such as projective identification), see Hinshelwood, 1989a.

by subsequent exploration of what the other person is *really* like. In these cases, a belief in those first impressions is sustained, and the other person continues to be perceived, and related to, in a distorted way. This is when projection becomes a mechanism of defence and is required as a means of avoiding pain and anxiety on the part of the projector.

More recently, however, the use of the term has been expanded. Projection is not just the perception of another person as a projection of an expected figure, but instead it can be, literally, the projection of parts of the mind (experiences or functions) of one subject into the mind of another person. This, too, may be sustained tenaciously without a respect for the reality of the other person. Melanie Klein (1946) introduced the term "projective identification" for this particular kind of projective process, which can radically distort the perception of the real personality of another person.

In this case, the projection (or projective identification) supports a splitting process as described in the last section. One part of a person's mind goes missing (splitting) and turns up as if it were part of someone else's mind. For the projecting person, however, it is not *as if*. Instead, they suffer an unshakeable belief that the other person really is as they see them. Thus, the process of splitting may not be merely the obliteration of one part of the mind of the person concerned. That split-off part can, in addition, be projected onto (and hence perceived in) someone else. It is believed to be *really* a characteristic of the other person. More normal processes of exploring the other's character are then suspended altogether under the pressure of such a violent splitting process. The reality of the other person is seriously distorted by a tenacious and untested belief. The other person really is experienced as having that perceived character, and then behaviour is modified accordingly. The subject's self and his world have changed in a way that is, to all intents and purposes, real.

Certainly, such projections can be benign enough processes, provided that they are not connected with splitting. Then we have the familiar process, with which we must all be familiar, in which we check and explore another person by trying out our own experiences as if they were someone else's—the I-know-how-you-feel kind of conversation. It can form a basis for understanding the other person. Such a process would be the basis for empathy. We put ourselves into their shoes.[4]

We are concerned here with the more malignant and defensive process, which creates persistent distortions of interpersonal perceptions, associated with splitting, resulting in a loss of self-understanding. We will now proceed to examine this phenomenon in detail with the magnifying power of the transference. In the following case, something—a dullness and depression—potentially experienced as part of the analysand, Mr F, came to be perceived by him as a feature of the analyst.

Clinical illustration: Mr F's depression

In his late 40s when he came to analysis, Mr F had had several career changes during his life which had made him feel (probably rightly) that he was not fulfilling the potential of his considerable talents, and at brief moments he could feel quite depressed about it. He had, at the same time, some professional seniority though he felt quite stuck in that career, and during the latter part of the analysis he became increasingly sought after for a series of prestigious posts. Initially his manner was quite lofty, loquacious, and bristling with vivid metaphors, which, though apt, were conveyed more for the sake of impressing me than of exploring. He frequently regarded me as grey, dull, inarticulate, and probably untalented, in deep contrast to his dramatic and colourful presentation of himself—we had come to refer to his "operatic" descriptions of his life. Clearly, his career ambitions ran foul of this unfortunate manner, and he seemed often to get himself disliked

[4] The forms of projection lie along a spectrum, ranging from severely abnormal—connected with the destruction of the mind, as with the splitting of Patient J—at one end, towards empathy, involving inserting oneself into someone else' position, at the other end. The latter involves remaining perfectly aware of one's own position at the same time, whereas the former, associated with splitting, means a severe loss of self-reflective capacity. This kind of spectrum is described and illustrated clinically in my book, *Clinical Klein* (Hinshelwood, 1994a).

in his department, and in meetings and at conferences. At the beginning of his analysis, he often interpreted the responses he elicited as jealousy and envy on the part of his untalented colleagues. Often their only talents were to form elaborate conspiracies, which, he believed, were designed to thwart his own natural advance in his career. For a long time his persistence in denigrating my own talents and articulateness created moments of impatience in me, since his view so seldom accorded, in the analytic situation, with my own evaluation of myself.

We had made some headway in helping him to address the reality of my performance as an analyst in comparison with his lofty, though caring and courteous, sympathy for my shortcomings. Shortly before the brief vignette I am about to describe, a book of mine had been published, and by chance he had become aware of it. He was shocked that, like him, I really had some academic worth—especially as the book was quite well received.

> The session had begun unusually quietly. In the past, such quietness seemed to indicate he was cross with me—I was, as it were, not worth talking to. I said something to that effect. It was not a new idea, and he briefly acknowledged it as something we already knew and that it pointed to my rather dull predictability. He then told me a dream, still in the same mood—that I needed him to brighten up the session and to give us something to talk about.
>
> He said: "In the dream, *I was with my wife, and we were away at a conference, and at the same time, it seemed, we were having a nice holiday together. Then we were visiting a church. It was broken down. The vicar was trying to get us to sing, though he realized we had come unwillingly. So he tried to get us interested by involving us in deciding on the hymns. But we made no suggestions, not even me. I felt sorry for the vicar.*"
>
> After waiting for further details, which were not forthcoming, I interpreted the dream in a way that was now familiar to us. I said that although he is well occupied in enjoying an academic conference, he feels I keep trying to interest him in a broken-down sort of analysis. He feels sorry for me and joins in, eventually, by producing a dream for me. I pointed out the

conflicting feelings he had in reducing me in his mind to this rather pathetic vicar, whilst also he had caring feelings for me. This interpretation of the dream did not go down well, and he complained at my interpretation being predictable—which it was. He also argued that there was no reason to connect the church and the vicar with myself. He implied that I was feeling sadly left-out and was trying to include myself in his dream. The vicar looked nothing like me. In fact, he carried a rather strange implement with an interesting wooden end to it. There was a knowing kind of pause after this, which might have been for me to make another predictable interpretation, perhaps about a phallic object.

Instead, I said he was trying to convey to me that we should take an interest in the woodenness of this session. I persisted that he attributes the woodenness to me, since my name has a "wooden end" as well. Therefore, I said, this link indicates that he is a lot more interested in my interpretation than he makes out. He was silent for a moment and, I thought, slightly more reflective. He then said, in a congratulatory tone, that he actually thought my interpretation had been really rather clever. At this point he seemed in some difficulties; his words were not as fluent, and he moved his legs uncomfortably.

Because my interpretation seemed to him to be clever rather than predictable or wooden, his customary view of me as dull was shaken. I described this as putting him in a difficulty and linked it up with the shock he suffered when he had discovered the book I had written. He then conveyed in a much more genuine way that he was moved by my understanding his difficulty and felt grateful. We then seemed able to proceed for a while to question where the woodenness had really come from.

For the major part of this session, there was a tenacious view of me as a rather unimpressive figure, untalented and lifeless. It came to be described as wooden. The dream had many aspects, including his use of it to reinforce his perception of me as needing to be enlivened by the products of his mind (his dream, for instance). This perception of me, held as an enduring belief, could be true about me, and that I am more dull, in fact, than I think I am. However, alternatively, it could be a projection onto me. Then, in the latter part of this session, his enduring perception of me as dull was confirmed as not completely realistic when I made a more impressive "clever" interpretation. It became possible for him to see the unreality in certain respects. He could acknowledge quite genuinely that I had a cleverness that impressed him. His momentary recognition of his previous distortion of me in my performance as an analyst, though discomforting, led also to a more reflective and less shallow kind of experience and contact with me.

The distorted view of me was needed, driven by the urgency to obliterate a "dull" and depressed side of himself. Therefore, we have a situation in which he viewed himself as persistently lively, to a dramatic, even operatic, degree; whilst I was only dull. Such polarization suggests that having divested himself of certain aspects of his own that might be depressed or lifeless, Mr F then actually re-finds them in me. Here we have a process, first of all, in which some aspect of him had been obliterated, or split off. It left him exaggeratedly lively—though in a somewhat shallow way. That splitting in which his mind is left depleted made him seem shallow. Then, secondly, that lifelessness was projected into me and sustained without exploring my abilities in a more realistic way. He needed to sustain that projection in order to support the splitting-off of a depressed and dull part of himself.

To his credit, Mr F could, with discomfort, begin a process to recognize the discrepancy between his habitual view of me and the reality that sometimes pressed in on him. It was discomforting because an implication, a little further along the road, would be that some of his own dullness needs to be recognized.

In this case, a two-fold process has been illustrated in which a split-off part of the analysand's mind was re-found in someone else—myself. We will now move on to a third process, in which the other person comes to take on the projected characteristics.

Introjection

Freud (and others) became interested in the way people's personalities can develop through contact with other people, in particular by taking on some of the characteristics of others (Abraham, 1924; Ferenczi, 1909; Freud, 1917e [1915], 1923b). It is a common observation that as they grow older, married couples grow more alike in their likes and dislikes, attitudes and behaviour, as well as in their physical appearance. Freud founded his view of the superego in the recognition that a whole gamut of moral and social attitudes and standards are absorbed by the developing child from the parents as a necessary part of his own growing up to become a social being. This process, Freud realized, is not just a question of parental prohibition. A process of internalization is set going. The parental attitudes are established inside the child and obeyed there, as they once were when embodied in the parents. One can sometimes catch a phase in childhood, when a toddler will talk aloud to himself in this way. When approaching, shall we say, one of mother's precious and fragile ornaments, we can hear him say to himself, "Mustn't touch". Mother's command has become an actual *internal* prohibition, in her words, which he carries within him. It is now part of his personality. He "talks to himself", as it were, in an internal dialogue that replicates talk with mother.

The theory of internalized objects has become fundamental to much of the more recent development of psychoanalytic theory and practice (see Hinshelwood, 1994a). Klein expanded this understanding of internalization processes—or introjection, as they came to be called. Typical is the transference/countertransference relationship, in which the analyst introjects the projection that the analysand makes onto him. In many instances the patient's projection meets an aspect of the analyst's personality that responds. For instance, in the last example, Mr F's continually denigrating attitude towards me as predictable and dull was difficult to bear, as it inevitably touched on self-doubts that I have at times about my mind being lively and capable of good analytic work, and I could begin at times to wonder whether he was right.

These kinds of reactions that occur in the analyst are often troublesome. However, they may also be revealing. Paula Heimann represented this in the following way:

> My thesis is that the analyst's emotional response to his patient within the analytic situation represents one of the most important tools of his work. The analyst's counter-transference is an instrument of research into the patient's unconscious. [Heimann, 1950, p. 74]

> The analytic situation is a relationship between two people. What distinguishes this relationship from others is not the presence of feelings in one partner, the patient, and their absence in the other, the analyst, but the *degree* of feeling the analyst experiences and the *use* he makes of his feelings. . . . The aim of the analyst's own analysis is not to turn him into a mechanical brain which can produce interpretations on the basis of a purely intellectual procedure, but to enable him to *sustain* his feelings as opposed to discharging them like the patient. [Heimann, 1960, p. 152]

The analyst is, first and foremost, a person who feels and experiences. This means he takes in from his patient a certain impact that the patient makes on him. Money-Kyrle (1956) has provided a detailed analysis of the vicissitudes of this relationship between the analyst's mind and what is projected into it. Brenman-Pick (1985) also meticulously illustrated the problems of the analyst in disentangling his own experiences from those the patient arouses. This technical aspect of the practice of psychoanalysis has become important. What the analysand can evoke in the analyst is likely to accord with the projections that he has made onto the analyst.

In the following case material I describe how the patient's impact on my mind led to my behaviour in the session which did tend to conform to the projection the patient had made into me.

Clinical illustration: Miss J's worried analyst

I shall return to my patient, Miss J, whom I described in the first clinical example—concerning splitting. It will be recalled that she had undergone an explosive process in which the part of her mind capable of hearing and thinking about my words had been temporarily annihilated—"shredded", as she called it. The patient had annihilated the part of her that could articulate what she felt, and even that part which could experience what she felt. This process left her unconnected to her own feelings, experiences, and memories.

I will take up the session where we left it in the earlier illustration of splitting.

> At that point, I felt considerable anxiety at the severity of what happened. And I registered, in my own mind, my alarm at the momentary disintegration of her mind. I found myself struggling with several things: notably, my sense of responsibility for what had happened, and a wish to put right whatever had gone wrong as a result of what I had said.
>
> She had talked of "shredding" her awareness of her hostility. It had been said in a thoroughly matter-of-fact way, so that it acquired a curious blandness that had a provocative effect on me. That is to say, something as serious as the "shredding" of her mind, passed off so blandly by her, magnified my alarm—and, indeed, caused some irritation.
>
> In this way, her blandness coincided with an actual state of alarm in my mind. In addition, I began to feel, at this point, irritated at her seeming indifference.
>
> I said that I thought she felt a destructive quarrel with me had gone on in her own thoughts, inside her head, and in order to deal with it she had not only shredded her awareness of it, but had also attributed the hostility to me. Then, having, as it were, made me responsible for the hostility and its effects, she feared for "my" hostility—and my awareness of it.
>
> Her mood changed, and she was then restless. Her blandness had disappeared. She seemed near tears, but she said nothing for a minute or so. Then she told me, quite moved now, that the couple in the street who were having a row had a baby with them. As she had passed, the baby had looked at her as if terrified, wanting comfort from her. She wanted to reach out and pick the baby up. She said that that might have stopped the parents quarrelling.

A very complex process was going on here. The analysand's awareness of herself, her hostility, and her fear of its severity had disappeared from her own mind, and she had become bland and indifferent. But her capacity to be aware of these feelings, and her sense of alarm and responsibility, had not disappeared altogether, since I actually came to experience some of these feelings: I felt the alarm of something violent happening, the responsibility for it, and a degree of hostility (or at least irritation).

For a brief period, feelings were carried by me that resembled hers. One could say that missing from one place, and found in another, a process of relocation had occurred. Her feelings, split off, were projected into me—but, more, I introjected them. I had been invoked—and partly provoked—to actually have those feelings and that awareness. My mind was in this instance actually induced to operate on her behalf. I experienced the alarm that she had lost; I did feel the responsibility; and I felt the urge to know what had happened.

It was not unreasonable for me to have had the feelings I describe, at least to a degree. Phenomena occurring in the transference can be alarming, and there was a sense in which, as analyst, I was responsible. But what happened was, to a degree, out of proportion. As an analyst, I knew that these processes, far from being destructive, were necessary if we were to make progress. Thus, my irritation was, in my role as analyst, groundless. Furthermore, as far as the analysand was concerned, the appearance of these feelings in me coincided with their disappearance in her.

Thus what happened was that my feelings could be made to function for hers—mine were employed by the patient. I was responsive to a kind of provocation which, I believe, indicated her unconscious intention that I carry them. Moreover, there is a dislocation of the awareness of the feelings. That capacity for being self-aware, and curious, was also lost and, I believe, tethered in some way to my own curiosity. She freed herself from suffering certain of her feelings, on the expectation that I would experience them instead. And also without conscious intent, I introjected those feelings to lie in correspondence with my own and to enhance them. Her projection conveniently met with an aspect of myself. Moreover, I retained also, as analyst, a curiosity about those feelings, whilst she had lost her capacity for curiosity and self-reflection.

In this process, then, my experience had been modified—it had been shifted out of true with my actual character. I had responded in accord with the analysand's projections. Through introjection, I had literally taken on that part of the identity of the analysand which was anxious, fearful of being destructive, and at the same time hostile.

In the event, I managed to restore the situation. As reported, I brought some of those feelings and an awareness to a verbal (and conscious) form—my interpretation. In response to my putting these feelings into words, she, too, could then use verbal means to express how she had felt as a terrified baby needing a maternal arm to pick her up for comforting. Her method of telling me about these things—a reversion to the external incident (as she had done originally in the session)—was imaginative recall. The narrative metaphor she constructed around the baby indicated that her mind was by then working much better again. Its shredded, fragmented blankness had been replaced by new memories and a fantasy about comforting the baby. This expressed something of the process that she felt she had herself just gone through with me: a frightened baby that needs reaching out to. And when I, as her analyst, had in a psychological sense been able to reach out and grasp, in words, that terrified part of her, she recognized the disguised need to be comforted and represented it in the fantasy of the terrified baby.

In the latter part of this sequence, then, the obliterated part of her mind had become restored to her, the evidence being that she could resume her capacity to have a fantasy and represent something of the baby restored to comforting arms. She could feel, and she could know she was feeling. And her account was vivid, emotional, and now coherent instead of shredded. She had resumed a process of repression instead of annihilation (splitting). But now she knew she was talking about the hostility, both in the shop and also in the consulting room. This response is of the kind the psychoanalyst regards as indicative of the correctness of his interpretations and as reconstitutive of the patient's mind.

* * *

These observations of the processes of splitting, projection, and introjection have been described in detail because they indicate how aspects of mind are not lodged individually in one person—even where less disturbed people (and their analysts) are concerned. They constitute empirical evidence for divided minds, and a category of irrationality not as yet properly discussed in philosophical and ethical literature. I shall follow this further in the next chapter with everyday occurrences between people which lend themselves to interpretation in terms of these processes; in Part Two, I return to the problem of informed consent when these processes operate.

CHAPTER SEVEN

The primitive phenomena in everyday life

The phenomena displaying depletion or growth of the mind are made to appear clear in the amplifying field of transference in the psychoanalytic setting. Having first spotted them in individual psychoanalytic work, we can, in fact, find them again in other, more everyday social situations. Such psychoanalytic observations would have little merit, or effectiveness, unless they corresponded to what happens when people engage every day in their ordinary lives as well as in the transference.

In this chapter I describe, first of all, occurrences indicating splitting, projection, and introjection taken from a non-psychoanalytic setting (a therapeutic community meeting), and later from other non-clinical settings.

Clinical illustration: Ellen's persecution

The following example[1] comes from a community meeting of all staff and patients of a day hospital. Though the meeting had the task of looking at community issues in a conscious and business-like way, the intention was also to display how unconscious processes of the group invade and disturb the conscious functioning of the community, in the same way as the transference disturbs the individual setting of a psychoanalysis. The way the community works together was considered from the unconscious point of view as well as the conscious. In this example, a meeting gradually took up a particular form as a result of unconscious processes locking together in a group dynamic. The meeting moved from a consideration of the conscious issues, for the individuals and the group, towards a dramatization of deeply personal issues of one of the members, Ellen. She was largely unaware, consciously, of these issues and considered herself to be dealing simply with a community matter. The example shows how one person's distress can be externalized to become an interpersonal issue, and it indicates how others are also involved in this externalization process themselves, whilst joining in with the dramatization for their own internal reasons. In this collective drama, processes of projection and introjection move parts of the individuals' minds around the group.

In the community meeting, Ellen was normally a leading figure in the practical discussions about hospital organization. But in recent weeks she had become increasingly distressed, tearful, and rather impenetrably miserable. In the therapeutic work she had often complained about her authoritarian father.

> On this occasion, after contributing in her usual way to the community meeting, Ellen changed fairly suddenly, to report herself as the sad victim of an unwarranted attack that had happened the previous night. At the time, she was staying in the small in-patient unit of four beds which provided a 24-hour back-up for patients who were in temporary crisis during the

---

[1] This example was previously published in my book *What Happens in Groups* (1987a).

course of their treatment in the day hospital. In the evening, she had come back for her supper with two friends. These friends were also attending the day hospital, but they were not resident in the in-patient unit and so were not entitled to the meal. Ellen was then "attacked", she complained, by the night-nurse in charge of the unit, for asking them to supper. She reported that she was told off again by Susan, the nurse who was in charge the following morning.

On the surface, Ellen conveyed that she was bringing usefully to the attention of the meeting an event of unwarranted harshness, which should be an issue about the management of the hospital for all to discuss.

However, Susan was present at the meeting. She gave a less harsh version of the occurrence and disputed Ellen's picture of the victimization by one of her night colleagues.

It emerged that Ellen had not, in fact, known about the regulations concerning who could eat a meal in the evening in the unit. She had been living there for only a couple of days. She felt deeply innocent and was becoming distressed again in the meeting. She took on the role of the victim who had been unjustly condemned. She cried and cried in the meeting and implored Susan not to criticize her so. For Susan, it had been necessary to explain the supper regulations to Ellen. Yet everything Susan said in an effort to explain, Ellen took as searing criticism, and she responded to it with wounded crying.

The meeting gained momentum, faced with Ellen's tortured responses. A righteous indignation against the night-nurse now developed, as others responded to Ellen's distress. The night-nurse was pictured as neurotically unfit for her job. Ellen remained, however, tearfully hurt. She believed herself to be still under attack—first by the night-nurse, and now continued by Susan. She was, indeed, suffering deeply in front of our eyes.

Ellen had come to believe that there really was an evil authority that had victimized her the previous night, and she found it again the next day. However, the reality of the hospital and its staff made it seem unlikely she had, in fact, been attacked the night before, as she had said, any more than she was actually being "attacked" in the meeting. These experiences of attack came from inside Ellen. She, however, had to insist that this harsh controlling figure actually *was* the night-nurse outside, rather than an internal figure (such as her memory of her authoritarian father). The night-nurse and then the nurse on duty in the morning were real external authorities, upholding the social standards of the community. Ellen had accomplished this process by means of the mechanisms of splitting and projection—first splitting off an internal harsh and authoritarian side of her and obliterating its existence so that she was *only* a persecuted victim; and, then, to reinforce the freedom she had achieved inside her, secondarily projecting this figure into others in the social group around her.

> Despite the considerable support she was beginning to get from other patients, it appeared nearly impossible to focus Ellen's attention on her own role in all this. Susan's firm but quite fair manner of explaining had not apparently been correctly perceived by Ellen. There was a move by one or two people in the meeting to look into Ellen's own contribution to the event the night before, based on Ellen's rather masochistic need to be unhappy. Ellen skilfully countered any of those tentative attempts to look into her own potential for filling a victim role by cowering away into her tears, as if the meeting were now pursuing the same attack.

Susan, the nurse, confronting her there in the meeting, did not seem to the others to be the attacking, punitive figure that Ellen perceived. But that could not be acknowledged by Ellen. She needed to escape her own internal self-punishment (or guilt) through an external recreation. Ellen's persistence was desperate, in spite of efforts by others to look at the reality and to achieve a more sophisticated insight. By this stage, Ellen had projected, not only her superego, but also her mature thinking function. This had been lost by projection and re-emerged as the thinking of other members of the community. More and more depleted and weakened in this way, she felt more at risk and vulnerable to her persecutor.

> Eventually, a rather impatient member of the meeting began to question Ellen, in a crisp way that showed his impatience with her determined suffering. By taking up a role that could clearly be seen as harshly "inquisitorial", he gratified Ellen's need for a complementary role to her one as victim. Led by the "inquisitor" and Ellen, the meeting polarized into two camps—for or against "the victim".

Thus, one member of the meeting had finally introjected the severe critical figure that Ellen sought to project.

This meeting illustrates the process of one person's distress turning into communal distress. Ellen could, with her successful social skills, employ the social context in a way similar to the patient who sets up a transference in the setting of a psychoanalysis. Ellen's unhappiness was made manifest in an outward preoccupation with a critical authority. As with a psychoanalysis, some controlling part of Ellen's mind was obliterated from her internal life. We might call it her superego. And then she was able to use the social context of the meeting to rediscover this figure—the superego—but in the staff of the hospital. (On the common occurrence of unconscious guilt, see Freud, 1917e [1915], 1924c; Klein, 1933.)

On the other side, there are introjective processes. The members of the community did strive to understand the problem—a struggle for insight that Ellen had, temporarily, given up. The meeting (at least its members) had introjected this struggle to understand and actually performed it for Ellen—as the victim, being unreasonably persecuted for wrongdoing, whilst trying to understand what was going on. Her own persistence in splitting her mind with projections of parts of it was met with eventual introjections by others willing to enact the dramatic lash of unsympathetic questions. Ellen had achieved a spectacular result. The entire meeting had turned into a dramatization of her internal state of mind

Although, for the sake of clarity, I have presented this group meeting as if it were dominated simply by Ellen's distress and her need to divide and externalize in the way I describe, the complete picture is, of course, much more complex. The other members of the meeting do not simply play passive roles in Ellen's drama.

They take up their positions for their own reasons—and frequently become deeply identified with those roles through the operation of the same processes of splitting, projection, and introjection. For instance, the inquisitor's own personality is important. He was a rigid, middle-aged man who had lost at least two managerial jobs because of his inflexibility—on one occasion because of his harshness in an educational establishment. One can see that his own rigid internal management was being evaded by splitting off and obliterating some rather vulnerable part of himself, and then projecting it into Ellen (as he had done previously, with those in his charge at work). And he had found a willing "introjector" in Ellen to play out in dramatized form the matching internal persecution on the stage of the meeting.

The rest of the community meeting could become involved in a similar way. Thus the identity of an individual member is based on a role being unconsciously negotiated through the processes of splitting, projection, and introjection. We have here a complex situation, made up of many individual instances of these defensive processes, which results in the majority of the members adopting only partial identities of themselves: (1) a rather righteous but persecuted victim, (2) an equally righteous persecutor, and (3) a thoughtful mature (perhaps disengaged) function. None of these participants is fully him- or herself. For that transient period of the meeting, they become distorted. That dramatized encounter depleted the members of crucial aspects of their identity.

This setting is not a psychoanalysis, but it reveals as a theatrical drama the phenomena of splitting, projection, and introjection as we have described them within the psychoanalytic setting. Being a therapeutic community, it still has the features of a therapeutic method, with disturbed people. Thus we might now look at some ways in which everyday life, outside therapy, can come to be construed by these phenomena.

Everyday non-clinical contexts

Splitting, projection, and introjection can be discerned in a wide variety of everyday social contexts.

Thus, the common experience of an ordinary crowd suggests similar depleting processes of the self (Moscovici, 1981; Nye, 1975). It has long been recognized that in groups an individual may suspend certain parts of his mind. Typically, the individual in a large crowd—from a lynching mob to football fans—temporarily loses a moral part of himself. Buford (1991) described how enthralling that liberation within a group is: ". . . with numbers there are no laws" (p. 64). Many of those members of a football crowd who commit delinquent or even murderous acts when together are ordinary, responsible citizens in other circumstances. Their moral conscience is split off when in a collective, just as readily as they become disinhibited with alcohol (indeed, the two are often mixed). The individual turns a blind eye to the moral implications of what he has done;[2] he is rendered morally blind by splitting off his conscience.

Quite ordinary people, when under stress, may seek to deal with a sense of guilt by splitting, supported by projection. In order to avoid guilt, they blame other people. This may occur dramatically in bereavement: a grieving relative may project (unjustified) guilt onto others—for instance doctors, nurses, or other professionals who had some real responsibility in the dying process. They may end up suing them not only in order to gain financial compensation for loss, but also to gain relief from intolerable guilt by projection into the professionals, with the ultimate confirmation in a court of law. At a more ordinary level, if I am cross with someone else, I might say in ordinary language, "I shall give him a piece of my mind". Or take two motorists who have bumped into each other: typically, they produce accusations and counteraccusations, in a crescendo of mutual recrimination and blame. In this instance, each one is hotly, sometimes violently, rejecting any blame and locating it in the other person. Sometimes it is projected into the other person with the added force of a physical punch, or even stabbing! Here two people are each establishing that any blame is *in* the other person. And each person is deeply engaged in proving that he is not tainted with guilt or blame himself. Rage on the road

[2] There is here a set of occurrences within the social organization that replicates a retreat into a haven within an internal organization as described by Steiner (1982)

is frequently a projective contest of blaming the other with escalating energy that can eventually reach murderous proportions.

Conran (1985) compared the process during the admission to a mental hospital with that occurring in the admission of an ill person to a general hospital. He described a psychotic patient's admission to a mental hospital, in which the patient divests herself of her own responsibility for herself by a massive splitting of her personality—more-or-less as if she were divesting herself of her clothes and parading naked in the street. Through this abandonment of self-control and responsibility, the patient forces into others her own control of herself. Conran contrasted this, interestingly, with something remarkably similar when a physically ill patient with appendicitis "puts himself in the hands" of his surgeon. The doctor engages the patient in choices and decisions, but the man cannot reach the doctor's level of communication. He eventually tells the doctor to make the decisions for him, since the removal of anxiety into those around renders him unable to reach an adult level of communication or decision. Instead, the hospital then contains the patients' projections. A general hospital may often have to introject the projected rational decision-making function of a patient, just as a mental hospital has to do.

In both cases—one psychotic and one mentally quite normal—a dispersal of the patient's state of mind goes so far as to deplete him. However, there is a difference—one that I will emphasize later. At this point, let us note the more benign quality to the loss of the personal capacities of the appendicitis patient, almost consciously negotiated and, it seems, temporary. The "normality" of the process occurring in the patient with appendicitis seems very familiar, but Conran prompts us to recognize ourselves in an ordinary situation where processes somewhat similar to that occurring in psychosis are taking place.

One can see that relinquishing control of oneself can be a normal enough process—and often an adaptive one. Another setting is created when travelling in an aircraft. Passengers allow themselves to be shepherded together in quite a passive way, strapped into chairs, with a plastic table in front of them, on which is put an individual tray of food. Such a procedure, practical in the circumstances, can also recapitulate the experience of the feeding infant, such that large numbers of people regress to the trusting and dependent posture of the infant strapped into a high-chair. They pass their more capable abilities to look after themselves into the cabin crew (as surely as their baggage has been booked in and removed to the cargo hold). As we know, not everyone can manage this, and some will experience the situation in maladaptive ways (leading, for example, to panic and a phobia of flying).

Another, and familiar, situation is that of a married couple. Main (1975) gave a vivid description of the process by which each partner adopts a role that expresses something for the other. It is worth repeating in full:

> A wife for instance may force her husband to own feared and unwanted aggressive and dominating aspects of herself and will then fear and respect him. He in turn may come to feel aggressive and dominating towards her, not only because of his own resources but because of hers, which are forced into him. But more: for reasons of his own he may despise and disown certain timid aspects of his personality and by projective identification force these into his wife and despise her accordingly. She may thus be left not only with timid unaggressive parts of herself but having in addition to contain his. Certain pairs come to live in such locked systems. [Main, 1975, p. 101]

Two people may thus live in a mutual system of splitting and projecting with a confidence that the other will introject.

In another dimension in the family, consider a common situation: a teenage girl says, for example, "Dad, I'm going to stay out till two o'clock tomorrow morning. And I'm going to that disco, the one which was busted for drugs"; and then she waits, apparently innocently unaware, for Dad to say something. Her announcement is likely to have made Dad rather anxious. Dad, having his daughter's best interest at heart, will dutifully get worried and tend to admonish and advise good sense about getting home early, about what company to keep, and so on. The teenager, although perfectly capable of assessing the risks for herself, has blissfully shed this, for the time being. Instead of feeling anxious, she has engaged with a specific part of her father, which allows her to split off and lose a capacity for mature judgement.

She can project it into her father because she knows he will introject the worry and will respond in a certain worried way; this is the responsible and protective father in him.

It is not that the teenager is unable to judge the risks involved in her plan for the evening. On the contrary, it is precisely because she once "knew" the risks that she can engage her father in worrying about them, rather than suffer these worries herself. It is common enough for adolescents, poised between childhood protection and adult responsibility, to find it difficult at first to bear the worries that adult independence throws up. In this illustration, the parent is functioning to hold or "contain" the adolescent's anxiety for her. We can see that there is a defensive quality to the adolescent projecting her worries into her father and leaving him to introject and suffer them instead of her. She is defending herself against a worry that could be too great for her, with her limited experience and development. But the effect is that she loses (temporarily) a significant part of herself—her emerging adult capacity to judge, and to worry about her judgements.

In a sense, the concept of two people carrying out significant mental functions for each other is no more extraordinary than that of a physical division of labour between people, within couples, or in the workplace. But this division of labour in the intimate functions of personality has implications for accepted notions of "individuality", "personal identity", and professional ethics. In Part Two I return to these implications.

PART TWO

THE PROBLEMS OF AUTONOMY

CHAPTER EIGHT

Resolving conflicts: repression and splitting

If the person is divided, then, when it comes to consent to treatment, which part of the person is it that makes the choice? Even more difficult, if one part is for the time being located in someone else—in particular the psychoanalyst—"who" should make the choice? We need now to look at aspects of choice and choosing from a psychoanalytic point of view.

A person can make a conscious choice between two (or more) alternatives. We can say, if it is helpful, that his mind is divided between the two. Colloquially, he is "in two minds". Ordinarily, when we say that a person is "in two minds" about something, we mean that he can see two sides to an issue. A student may have to decide between going to visit his parents on their anniversary or to continue swatting for an imminent examination. He has choices and has to "make up his mind"—that is to say, he has to decide between those alternatives. It is a perfectly familiar aspect of life. Often resolving difficult, conscious conflict counts as part of the satisfaction in life.

A person with a choice to make is in a state of conflict. He will continue consciously in that state until he makes his decision—and some time afterwards he may continue to review the decision with satisfaction, alarm, or regret. However, this is a trivial example of a divided mind, since the person, in fact, operates as a whole. It is not his mind that is divided, but merely his interests. He knows his own conflict, and even in the longer term he will remain conscious of the alternatives from which he made his choice. The alternative he has given up continues in his awareness, and it may require, often, some emotional "work" to let go of it. He remains, to his conscious knowledge, the person who has accommodated both alternatives and decided between them.

However, this common account is not the only possible version of the story. Psychoanalysis has contributed others. An alternative case would be the person who represses the fact that he had a choice at all—that is, he denies that he has had to give up one alternative. The student we have just mentioned might visit his parents whilst pretending that he did not need to revise for his examinations. If such pretence convinces him, then consciously he can believe that he has only one significant alternative. Our student could persuade himself with a conscious rationalization to the effect that he has no need to continue further revision work as he knows enough—but then a hint of what is now unconscious may crop up as he takes one of his books to read whilst he is travelling on the train. In that case the emotion, the anxiety of the examination, has become unconscious, is denied, and allows a spurious reason to be constructed.

This denial is often more explicit over feelings. A bereaved spouse may describe her deceased partner as wholly good, even though they had frequent rows and she could become extremely frustrated or intolerant of him. Such a denial of the bad feelings in favour of a one-sided good perception of the partner is just as much a kind of division of the person as repressing one of two alternative choices of action.

Unconscious conflict

Though a considerable intuitive understanding of an unconscious mind existed before Freud (Ellenberger, 1970), he systematized the knowledge of this hidden aspect of the mind and developed a rigorous method for investigating it, at first through dream analysis (Freud, 1900a), and later with his method of free association and transference (Freud, 1915a). All his theories were based on the results of these methods. Central to them was the recognition that a person's unconscious might be in conflict with his conscious interest, wishes, and intentions. Such unconscious impulses intrude without awareness of their source and, indeed, without a full awareness of the state of conflict. This is illustrated by the following example from my practice:

> A patient became distressed over an interpretation in which I suggested that in his view I, like his wife, seemed to be quite neurotic and therefore unhelpful to him. At the following session he brought a dream after watching a wild-life programme on television in which an insect devoured its mate. In the dream *a vivid picture was displayed in the sky as if from a magic lantern onto the underside of the clouds. It was a picture of a large tower-block crumbling around his feet. It collapsed because it was made with many flaws. He was not afraid.*

In this case, the distress felt by my patient about my own mental condition (he associated the tower-block to me, as there is a famous one near my house) was converted into pictures in a dream that could represent in disguised—and therefore emotionally muted—ways a dangerous collapse he actually feared in me (or in his wife). In the process of the dream the disguise indicates the work of repression. The outcome is a picture of the problem in which the terrifying eat-or-be-eaten conflict is no longer recognizable in consciousness.

What, then, has happened?

It is helpful in examining the possible answers to determine the various points of view from which an answer could be given.

1. First of all, the simplest situation is one where the conscious choice of the subject coincides with some outside point of view of a disinterested observer. Both subject and observer consciously recognize two alternatives that formed the choice.

2. However, when we come to the situation in which some alternative has disappeared (repressed), then a discrepancy occurs between the two points of view. Consciously, the person would claim to be single-minded in his decision. To another person—say, the child of the bereaved mother, who witnessed the many rows between his mother and father—some hypocrisy or insincerity would appear to have affected the mourning. From outside, the person has distorted his own visible self.
3. The unconscious level is a third vantage point. The unconscious may have two states:
   - 3a. First, the unconscious may be quite aware of the alternative that no longer appears in consciousness. This is, then, a case of repression. What is missing from consciousness appears in the unconscious and can be, potentially, represented in disguised form, say in a dream or in unconsciously motivated behaviour. The bereaved wife may, then, have unexplained nightmares about a violent anonymous man. In this case the unconscious contents conform with the awareness of the child in recognizing, outside consciousness, that only a distorted set of feelings is being described during the mourning. These feelings conflict, therefore, with the conscious awareness.
   - 3b. Second, at the unconscious level there is the possibility that the unconscious bears no representation or trace of the lost alternative, even though an external observer or relative might be very clear about it (splitting). Then a drastic revision of self-reflection has occurred: some content has disappeared completely from this mind, from both the conscious and the unconscious. In this case, the unconscious awareness does not conform to that of an observer. It may be represented as a gap in the subject's own mind, or it may make a reappearance unexpectedly in the form of another person's state of mind (projection and introjection).

Let us concentrate for a moment on this last method of resolving conflict. The student might telephone his father and in some hardly appreciated way provoke an argument in which the father demands peremptorily that his son should visit as a matter of filial duty. The son can then respond with innocent reasonableness and ample, unpolluted justification that he has his examinations to prepare for. He has in this case split off his sense of duty. It reappears in the father, who represents it for the son in the ensuing argument. The son, then, retreating from the telephone encounter, can feel wholly justified that his father is completely unreasonable. His father's collusion in the quarrel (which his father may have entered into for his own reasons) enables the student to believe that a wish to be present on the occasion of his parents' anniversary is entirely within his father. He himself is no longer in conflict about that wish; he is simply in conflict with his father. The student is thus rendered conflict-free, in the sense of not being in two minds, even unconsciously.

In the latter case, the conflict is not rendered unconscious, it is simply wiped out. In addition, the processes by which it is so obliterated are themselves deleted from self-reflection. Klein (1946) described a conscious experience of blankness and loss of meaning (see Chapter 6); Guntrip (1968) described a pervading sense of futility. These processes are now believed to be more primitive than repression and to underlie it. The psychoanalytic observations of Fairbairn (1944), Klein (1946), and others (Rosenfeld, 1947; Segal, 1950) indicate that the mind can be split up in a much more radical way than the repression of certain mental contents. Instead, the conflict disappears altogether because one side of the conflict is obliterated (split off), and perceived in someone else, or even actually represented by this other person—processes examined closely in Chapters 6 and 7.

Melanie Klein remarked of one such patient in psychoanalysis:

> It was not only that parts of her personality did not co-operate with me; they did not seem to co-operate with each other. [Klein, 1946, p. 17]

The parts of a person that separate from each other assume a kind of independence—as separate as two strangers might be. In fact, an internal part of one person is actually perceived in someone else, who, like the father of the student, takes it in and plays that part of the subject. The student's father embodies the son's wish—which joins with his own—and he enacts it by putting on a pressure of an intensity that is in accord with their joint wish.

In the first of these states (3a), repression, there is an awareness of the partition of the mind, though it is an unconscious awareness. The mind is therefore operating as a whole in seeing its partition. In the second (3b), there is a true split in the structure of the mind. Self-reflection is radically impeded. At best, the unconscious and the conscious mind might have some sense of a blankness, an awareness of something missing.

These different states—splitting and repression—are observed and distinguishable in the psychoanalytic setting. In repression, certain contents remain, unconsciously, as an active influence manifested in disguised forms (dreams, slips of the tongue, symptoms, images, fantasies, and so forth). Splitting, on the other hand, results in a very altered structure of the mind, not really a division of contents—the separated parts no longer influence each other. These distortions of structure correspond to early forms of functioning of the mind in the development of the normal infant, but they also occur in extreme form in the functioning of the minds of those who are mentally ill (in particular the psychotic and those with severe personality disorders). However, in everyday life they may also radically distort that person's capacity to make judgements and to function rationally. What, now, about the judgement involved in consenting to treatment?

Consenting and changing

Holmes and Lindley (1989), in their defence of psychotherapy as a liberal, freedom-enhancing practice, commence with the assertion that "Cooperation is the essence of psychotherapy" (Holmes & Lindley, 1989, p. vii). At the same time, psychoanalytic practice is founded on the view that the essence of psychoanalysis is resistance. That is to say, patients resist conscious knowledge of what is unconscious. Resistance is the form taken by repression within a psychoanalytic treatment. The patient reacts unconsciously against the efforts of the analyst to investigate his mind—a resistance against the uncovering of what is repressed. For instance, a patient of mine reported a dream:

> When I asked him to tell me what a figure in the dream reminded him of, he said, "Nothing. He reminds me of no one at all." And he promptly went off to sleep for some minutes, until I said something, and he woke with a start and some embarrassment, having forgotten my question and his answer.

The cooperation (i.e. consent) normally expected was refused or "resisted". My sleeping patient's resistance was represented dramatically by the very flagrant act of becoming temporarily unconscious in sleep. Unconsciously, a resistance to the psychoanalysis has taken, it seems, a dominant position.

Instead of consenting in the normal way—by comparing the pros and cons—Mr F separated the pros from the cons and projected, as it happens, the pros. He thus ensured that the decision remained unconcluded. His choice was, as it were, to make no choice, because it became one between him and me—between what I thought he needed and what he thought he did.

As Freud indicated, the psychoanalytic work of helping the patient to know himself better often does not proceed in a way that really counts. This man bluntly disagreed with me at a conscious level and struck despair in me.

However, a patient's resistance is not necessarily so blatant. Freud commented that a patient may "not receive [our knowledge] *instead of* his unconscious material but *beside* it" (Freud, 1916–17, p. 436). Here a resistance occurs that is concealed behind a seemingly rational cooperation. When resistance surfaces strongly, it can take on a quite conscious form—as when the patient leaves treatment. Then the cooperation (consent) to psychoanalytic understanding is split off.

In the longer term in a psychoanalytic treatment, progress can be indicated by the overcoming of resistance and by the patient's response at an unconscious level, *as well as* the conscious level, to the communications from the analyst.[1] The psychoanalyst is thus

---

[1] Overall, the patient can expect to be assisted in recovering and sorting out the various parts of himself that have "gone missing" as well as the impact of other's projections that seem to impinge on him from the interpersonal arena. We examine this process as "integration", or achieving "integrity", in Chapter 11.

the prime agent overcoming resistance in the patient to what will do him good. But we have seen that this effective technical operation contains an ethical pitfall. It implies something like a paternalism. To progress with this problem we will look in more detail at an illustration, from the psychoanalytic setting, of the distortions of consent that occur in a psychoanalysis.

CHAPTER NINE

Splitting and informed consent

The problem that splitting creates for psychoanalytic ethics is greater than that caused by repression. With repression, there is a conflict between the conscious and the unconscious. Usually—though not always—the positive intent, or consent, is conscious, and the resistance is unconscious. With splitting, the process of autonomous choice and consent within the transference relationship is rendered more uncertain and more confused, since it becomes a conflict between patient and analyst.

In a sense, the patient's resistance means that he has *unconsciously* withdrawn consent, and by means of projection he has "consented" to an analyst whom he expects to cooperate with him by arranging the conflict between them (instead of within the patient himself). Conflicts over the treatment itself then raise the urgent question:

- What, therefore, is the status of the patient's consent?

It seems arbitrary to take only the conscious intent, when an opposing unconscious intent (to resist) is active, or even dominant at times.

Clinical illustration: Miss C's self-treatment

I shall begin an attempt to disentangle this dual position with a further clinical example.[1]

> A patient, Miss C, in her mid-30s, came for problems with her relations with men. She had a successful career of an intellectual kind. As a child, she had felt a bitter resentment towards her father when he had returned from military service and, shortly thereafter, a little brother had arrived. Soon after starting her analysis, she decided to marry a man who made no sexual demands on her. He had a career in the same academic field. She contracted such a marriage as a way (unconsciously) of solving her difficulties. Her relationship with him was fruitful intellectually but not sexually.

In a way, Patient C had found her own form of cure—an asexual marriage to a man agreeable to such a relationship. That cure, however, does not correspond to the sort normally anticipated by psychoanalysis. I had been led at the outset to believe that she wanted some understanding of her problems in order to make changes in herself and her life. She and I had commenced the analysis on the assumption that she wished to be able to have an enriched sexual life. It seemed an unsatisfactory result from a psychoanalytic point of view to engage in such a "celibate marriage", even though as her psychoanalyst I could understand how satisfactory an evasive solution to her problem might seem. Two aspects were in conflict—a conscious consent to psychoanalysis (she was well informed about psychoanalysis) and a contrary wish to solve her difficulties in her own way through evasion.

Freud always counselled patients not to make major life decisions during the course of their psychoanalysis. He believed that just this kind of decision was in danger of being made as a result of

---

[1] This clinical material was previously used in my paper, "Social relocation of personal identity through splitting, projection and introjection" (*Philosophy, Psychiatry, Psychology* 2, 1995: 185–204; reprinted by permission). The case material is derived from real patients, but with biographical and other details changed to ensure confidentiality.

a resistance to psychoanalytic exploration. Thus, should I have advised her that she should not embark on the marriage—as Freud might have done? Had I proceeded thus, I would, in terms of standard professional ethics, have resorted to paternalism and overridden, or attempted to override, her own decision. My effort would be the result of what I knew and she did not (consciously). On what grounds could I have assumed such a paternalistic attitude? In fact, I did not step into a paternalistic role of this kind, and Patient C did go ahead with the marriage.

But I was then faced with a further problem: should the psychoanalysis continue? If she had, in her own way, found a cure—though not a psychoanalytic one—I should perhaps accept that her consent to psychoanalytic treatment was withdrawn and thus terminate the psychoanalysis. And to terminate at this point raises the question: was it a failure? Or, for whom was it a failure? In her terms, she had come with a problem—her worry about her problem with men. She solved this by curing her worry, not her problem, and she did so by causing me to have the worry instead of her. A psychoanalytic success would be to restore her mind (its worried part) to her.

To terminate would also seem to act paternalistically. The patient continued coming in order to use my mind to cure her worrying.

> The patient consciously thought very highly of me and my interpretations. She continued to come. But, contrary to expectations, my interpretations rarely moved her. They did not touch feelings that were problematic for her. She always agreed with me and thought about all I said. Often she would start one session by recapping where we had got to in the previous one. There was an intellectual quality about it. When I pointed out such processes, she agreed pleasantly.

Her cooperativeness was very similar to Freud's description of the fate of conscious knowledge, intellectual and conscious. But it seemed that she still very much wanted to continue to see me. Consent to something was still very evident. Thus, the question arose:

- To what is the patient consenting?

Did she come in order to gain an ineffective, conscious knowledge? Is she still in some way intent on making that a deeper knowledge that could truly affect her sexual life? If the latter were true, it seemed a very hidden intent. In the next short piece of material I convey my dawning awareness of the vicissitudes of her wish to come and work at her problems with me:

> Though I felt that the psychoanalysis did not seem to progress much and the issues were repetitive, she began to report a persistent theme. This was a difficulty with her work colleagues. They pursued their work without cooperating with her. One day she told me about her timetable at her place of work. It worried her, because she wanted to make sure she could continue to come to her analytic sessions, but she could not make other people aware of her need to safeguard her sessions. She felt some anxiety. I said she felt that there were work colleagues who did not really listen in to the worries she tried to discuss with them; and that she felt me to be rather indifferent to her worries in a similar way. I said she wished for someone who could be like a mother who would have nothing else on her mind but to attend to these worries. I said that also she felt, in a contradictory way, that I was good at listening, and she wanted to continue to come. She agreed with my interpretation and seemed pleased with it and applied the idea of a listening mother, in a chatty way, to the characters of her colleagues at work.

This material suggested to me that she was conveying a real anxiety, for once, about getting cooperation going, but that she also felt that I did not listen in to some significant issue—the failure of cooperation.

However, by this time, I was wearily familiar with interpretations that seemed to say something to the point about her hopes and disappointments but fell to the fate of her easy, chatty response. She had appeared pleased with the interpretation I had given, and yet it did not move her, nor touch her at all deeply, as might have been expected if it was an accurate interpretation. I felt, on occasions like this, that what I had said had not been correct at all. I found I tried very hard to, as it were, get through to her. And repeatedly I felt I failed, despite persistent approval from her.

> Gradually, I began to realize that the material I should be paying attention to was just those experiences that I was having with her, and not so much the content of her chatty descriptions. I noticed my deep frustration, and the lively wish to help that was at the bottom of my frustration. That wish to help her to change was as important a part of the material for interpretation as the free associations she actually gave me. I could see that it was not so much the content of my interpretations that impressed her. Instead, it was the fact that I made an interpretation at all. She took it that if I made an interpretation, it indicated that I had an absorbing interest in her; she responded with her especially admiring chat. We were, it seemed, engaged on establishing a narcissistic arrangement between us, a mutual admiration. I was to be cast as a mother who not only listens but does so with undying approval. She is a child, as it were, who can feel herself to be the apple of her mother's eye.

That arrangement allocated different roles between us in the transference. In one sense, she had put onto me the character of a doting mother privileged to admire my idealized child whilst expecting nothing of her.[2] One could say, as an initial hypothesis, that she harked back to the days when she was an only child and had her mother's attention all to herself. She required me actually to recreate that experience for her.

There was a good deal more to my feelings than those of a doting mother, however. In fact, I found that, contrary to the role I

---

[2] Technically, this is an example of the "projection of an internal object" (her mother) into an external one, and thus implies important shades of difference, for psychoanalysts, from projection of parts of the self. The latter is often called "projective identification". However, following Spillius (1988), I have not distinguished between "projection" and "projective identification", in order to avoid confusion. Definitions and distinctions between the two terms can be found in my *Dictionary of Kleinian Thought* (Hinshelwood, 1989a). In this instance, the object (mother) she found in me was one who was the recipient of parts of the patient, in particular the worry about her.

had been allotted, I did not always feel admiring of her. I had felt increasing frustration. I was worried about the progress of her analysis. Indeed, there occurred to me a view that I was being unethical in continuing to try to give treatment and to continue to bill her for a fee, when she was not intent on a psychoanalysis at all—in fact, this experience has been one reason for addressing myself to many of these ethical questions.

Thus, were the feelings of concern about the analysis itself also countertransference feelings that might be useful? I came to the conclusion that they were. I believed that the emerging theme of work colleagues who did not cooperate was the beginning of a disturbing awareness of her own frustrations that did penetrate beyond her surface chattiness. Those brief moments I noted with relief. But the point for our present purposes is that this intelligent patient did not, on the whole, experience her *own* concern about the progress of the psychoanalysis. Instead, it was *I* who seemed to harbour—and with some intensity—those feelings of concern and enquiry.

This conclusion about the countertransference is complex. It is not merely that my countertransference experience derives from repression, where I could have been playing a part in recreating an early relationship—the doting mother, as it seemed. That was only part of the countertransference. I seemed, in addition, to play a part that her own mind should be playing—having the worries she should be having for herself (via splitting and projection). The implication is that I functioned, mostly, as the one who worried about her, *instead* of her worrying about herself. Rather than worry about herself, she abolished worrying from her mind and left it to me to worry for us both. This hypothesis was strengthened when she reported the following dream:

> In the dream, *she had parked her car, not in the usual place near her house, but around the corner outside a shop. While she was parked there some men came along, complained that she was in the way, and bumped the car out of the way, doing some damage to it. She complained in the shop about the damage and was given some money.*

The dream conveyed that she had actually been moved to a new position, represented by the new parking place. In terms of the problem of the psychoanalysis, I could take it that she was communicating about a new psychological position, one that suggested her need to come and shop for something that she needed from me (a more conventional form of consent). This differed from the usual position in which she came, oblivious to her needs whilst, she believed, she charmed me, in the role of the doting mother. This movement to a new, needy position—one where she might worry for herself about what she needed—was, however, not easy for her and made her feel persecuted, since she had recognized things that were normally unnoticed by her. To recognize through this disguised representation in the dream that she "shops" from me, as it were, in the session results in some damage to herself. The damage is the loss of her preferred mutual admiration arrangement. The representation in the dream—however disguised—is itself an important indication that she is no longer so split and can represent herself.

She has regained, though in an unconscious form, something of herself that had been split off and lost. What she had regained was a view that she needed to shop for something from me. If she has to realize this, even unconsciously, then she feels not very admirable and thus damaged by her new position. It is another moment when something troubling breaks through her surface and returns to her to disrupt her life. In one sense, it recreates the intrusion into her life of the men in her childhood—her father and her brother. However, in a very different way it represents the intrusion back into her life of her own worries and concerns about herself that she had parked for so long in me. The latter intrusion, felt by her in a paranoid way, led to a grievance—the demand for monetary recompense. I was drawn to this theme—the central place that movement occupied in the dream—by my own preoccupations with how immovable the patient was. My own prolonged wish to move her could be linked with her own lost worries—momentarily regained here in the form of the dream. I was strengthened in my view that the splitting process was the more important by her response to my interpretation:

> I interpreted that she felt a grievance towards me because I seemed often to threaten to move her emotionally by the interpretations that I made. I referred to a moment in the previous

> session when she had felt quite a strong response to something I had said. She was thoughtful for a moment during a silence that was unusual for this patient. Then she said, with a quite unprecedented bitterness, "I hate those sorts of interpretations". She continued, though in a vein that seemed quite thoughtful, "But it is true that my father once told me I was aggrieved about something. I don't remember what it was, now."

The quality of her bitter response, though brief, was quite different from those chatty ones I was accustomed to. There was a charge of real emotion. It was a remarkable response in that it conveyed a deep cleft in her wishes—on the one hand, a hatred of my efforts to describe and explain; on the other hand, an effort on her own part to find a link with what I had said and to acknowledge a sense of being moved on one occasion at least, as she was by her father when he intruded into her relationship with her mother.

Detailed scrutiny of this process of splitting off a part of herself suggests a crucial point. What she lost was her worry, and this was a part of her that would normally form the basis of her wish (motivation) for psychoanalysis. In an important and significant sense what was split off was her wish for treatment, and therefore her consent. In addition, she hated it when she re-found it—in me. It is the process involving splitting and projection of that consenting part of herself into me, and my playing that part at least for a while, that so complicates the ethical issue here.

Something is going on in the actual process of a psychoanalysis that is quite different from what is normally acknowledged by standard medical ethics. The ordinary autonomous cooperation expected in a professional setting is simply not forthcoming in any simple way. We shall see that there are a number of arguments that can be used, though unsuccessfully, to support a psychoanalytic paternalism—that is, to continue a psychoanalytic treatment despite these resistances and these oddly split forms of withdrawal of consent. This means that consent to psychoanalysis is greatly complicated by these unconscious (transference) components unrecognized in the apparently conscious decision to consent.

CHAPTER TEN

Psychoanalytic paternalism

It is commonly joked that a patient becomes dependent on the psychoanalyst. Freud himself originally thought that there was a process whereby a patient, inevitably, fell in love with the analyst (Freud, 1895d), and he coined the term "transference" for this. It is not an autonomous choice in the normal sense (Freud, 1905e [1901]). In those early days of the practice of psychoanalysis, Freud cultivated these positive feelings, which he thought essential to overcome resistance. However, the impulse to recreate, unconsciously, past forms of relationship (typically, the love for the parents transferred onto the analyst) cannot really represent an autonomous consent. Consent in this sense is not "informed consent"; it is not based on a knowledge about the present therapeutic intention and procedure.

Consent is a curious and muddied issue if it is impelled by such powerful elements from the transference. On the other hand, transference to the analyst is the object of study in psychoanalysis. Zetzel (1956) described the "treatment alliance" as separate from the transference. In this sense, it is possible to separate consent that is given at a conscious level from transference love at the unconscious level. However, such a belief in the separation of conscious from unconscious is not now (even if it was then) accepted as realistic. The intrusions of the unconscious into conscious decisions have been known ever since Freud's warning that patients should not make important life decisions during their analysis (Freud, 1915a). The debate over the possibility of an area of functioning that is transference-free has been lively.

> Segal stressed Klein's concept of the transference as "a total situation". In this view, transference and the underlying stream of fantasy which it reflects are not occasional occurrences. They are continuous phenomena, central to the analytic process. [Levine, 1992, pp. 814–815]

Crucially, the analyst has to answer the question:

- Should the analyst respect the resistance to his work, as a withdrawal of consent?

Since the nature of psychoanalysis ensures that resistance is the rule at some point in all analyses, we would on the whole prevent psychoanalytic practice altogether if we honoured the patient's resistance by ceasing the work of analysis.

In a case treated by surgery under anaesthesia, the patient is required to give a conscious signed agreement beforehand for an operation that will be conducted while he is unconscious. The operation is explained so that he understands, as far as is possible, what he is agreeing to. If, during an operation, the surgeon discovers a condition, not anticipated beforehand, that entails immediate surgical correction, he must have obtained consent prior to the patient becoming unconscious. If he goes ahead to do further surgery without having explained this beforehand, he is guilty of unethical practice. Is this similar to the psychoanalyst going ahead on his own judgement of what is necessary when he finds the patient no longer predisposed to the methods of psychoanalysis—for instance, when negative transference (i.e. resistance and defences) emerges?

Transference and consent

Early on, Freud (1905e [1901]) described negative transference as well as the contrasting love for the analyst. Psychoanalysis, as practised today, tends to avoid intervening in the conflict between the two in favour of observing the conflict and understanding it and its unconscious roots. We now have the ability to observe and understand extremely fine and subtle details in the transference/countertransference relationship (Joseph, 1989). It gives a very specific picture of that particular patient's characteristic ways of relating, in the past and in the present. It is the prime source of psychoanalytic knowledge about the patient and ultimately of the patient's self-knowledge, since it reveals—in the form, as it were, of a second edition—that which is hidden. As Freud put it:

> What are transferences? They are new editions or facsimiles of the impulses and phantasies which are aroused and made conscious during the process of analysis; but they have this peculiarity, which is characteristic for their species, that they replace some earlier person by the person of the physician. [Freud, 1905e [1901], p. 118]

In the more contemporary psychoanalytic stance, consent implies the intention to discover, consciously, knowledge about just those unconscious relationships. The psychoanalyst proceeds by describing, as a kind of narrative, how the patient's mind comes to be broken up. If it tallies with something actually going on in the patient, it will become an arresting and moving experience for both. In this descriptive activity the psychoanalyst forms an alliance to learn and develop knowledge—a "K"-link, as Bion called it (see Chapter 12).

Psychoanalytic progress enables the patient to be less trapped within the emotional force of the transference feelings, through knowing something about them. In the instances I have described,[1] the patient's "intention" is to *enact* that split. We saw this dramatically with Ellen, in the example of the therapeutic community

---

[1] Though there are other forms of transference, based on representation, I have chosen the "worst-case scenario" for testing the ethics of psychoanalysis.

meeting (Chapter 7), and we also noted it in the transference/countertransference of Mr F's analysis (Chapter 6), and with Miss C (Chapter 9). Those patients sought the psychoanalyst's willingness to create, as a reality, a situation in which the patient does not contain a certain part of his mind, but the analyst does instead. If this succeeds, psychoanalysts call it "collusion", and both analyst and analysand often slip into this. Of course, this situation *can*, with adequate reflection, prove extraordinarily revealing of the arrangement that the patient demands, as I have shown in my cases.

Thus what, then, are the ethics of this radical disjunction between the intentions of the patient and those of the analyst? The patient seems to seek a conflict with the analyst over consent. The analyst seeks a knowledge of this conflict and a depth of understanding of it. In a sense, the patient consents to a collusion that dismantles his coherent personality. He cannot make his decisions out of a proper balance of mind, and, as a result of the dismantling of his personality, he cannot be aware of the severe imbalance he has achieved in his own mind. In the psychoanalytic setting, therefore, the analyst's position is slightly better for understanding the proper balance of mind in which the patient might be able to make his decisions.

In this situation, the psychoanalyst has to decline the patient's request to play out a splitting—that is, he should not collude in the patient's own form of cure. This is the rule of abstinence for the analyst. He must stick to description rather than active, suggestive prescription. It is also in the application of this austere rule that the transference intensifies and, thus amplified, gives such a good magnification to these subtle unconscious processes.

Instead, stepping back and engaging in a description seems like a paternalistic overturning of the patient's actual wishes. If the psychoanalyst tries to avoid becoming the patient's split-off consent to treatment, he risks a "therapeutic ambition", as Freud (1912e) called it. Becoming involved in the patient's decision and choice—in either direction—enacts, as it were, a sort of innocent bystander caught up in a fight.

Some possible ethical arguments for paternalism

Therefore, on what ethical basis should the analyst continue with the treatment? The psychoanalyst has a choice of several positions that he can take, and we will briefly review these now.

1. *The prior-agreement argument*

> *"The patient has given his prior consent to be treated, and the psychoanalyst must continuc, come what may."*

This argument runs into difficulties. The patient does not have the capacity to conceive, at the outset, what will befall him, in the way that a surgical patient can anticipate something of what may happen to him. In a slightly provoked moment, Bion said, about a particular insightless patient:

> I can try to get a consulting room and the conditions in which to work, but after that I would certainly not be prepared to analyse whoever happens to come. I would have no right to analyse them. . . . I would certainly not take the risk of starting to analyse and give interpretations to such a person. I should consider that I was liable at once to have an action for damages brought against me. It would be just as serious as a surgeon starting to operate on a patient without the necessary authority. [Bion, 1974, pp. 168–169]

To be aware of the technicalities of a surgical operation when one is unconscious is different from being aware of an unconscious wish. The surgical patient may be ignorant of the complexity and procedures of the treatment he faces when unconscious. This is different from psychoanalysis, where we expect changes to be made *in* the unconscious. Awareness of what is to be changed is resisted. That is different from ignorance. The unconscious cannot be explained to the patient to any useful degree. The nature of the process, the effects of the unconscious parts of the patient's own mind, and the unfolding drama of the transference relationship cannot really be understood prior to treatment at all. We cannot rely on the patient consciously to understand what his unconscious will do—it is, after all, unconscious! Proper conscious understanding by the psychoanalytic patient would have to wait at least until the completion of the psychoanalysis! Also, we may expect changes that are completely contrary to his own expectations. Nor can he properly comprehend before his treatment that it will include analysis of his consent to it! It is not a fully informed consent.

2. *The pragmatic argument*

"It works, therefore it is right."

This is a pragmatic philosophy—it has a fine history in science and technology—but when it comes to the human sciences, it causes an intuitive unease. Can a psychoanalysis continue just because it is known to work? Doubts are stirred. The problem is converted into: "Who decides if it is working?" And we return to the same conflictual position about what "working" means to the patient and the analyst.

Arguments 3 and 4 may be regarded as sub-categories of the pragmatic argument.

3. *The intertemporal (later-understanding) argument*

"The patient will come to understand, through the process of the treatment itself, what he has consented to."

Any superficial form of consent at the outset can deepen as part of the development of the psychoanalysis. We can tell ourselves that in the end the patient will be grateful to us for getting him through the negative transference. We would then be justified in ploughing on, regardless of his withdrawal of consent.

However, we only have to recall that Winston Smith, in Orwell's *Nineteen Eighty-Four*, was "treated", so that he wanted to love Big Brother in the end. The patient's eventual agreement cannot, therefore, provide a water-tight guarantee.

4. *The adaptational (professional paternalism) argument*

> *"The patient is out of key with his immediate social relations and needs to be brought into a more adaptive relationship."*

The patient cannot comprehend, either consciously or unconsciously, what that relationship would be—that is his problem. The psychoanalyst might therefore decide that he should act paternalistically by disregarding both conscious and unconscious commitment to treatment on the basis that it is all shot through with transference love and hate. In other words, when it comes to a psychoanalysis, the analyst must take a paternalistic stance as surely as the psychiatrist must with a psychotic patient. The problem is that it would not seem valid to assume that everyone in psychoanalytic treatment is to be compared to a psychotic.

5. *The on-going consent argument*

> *"The psychoanalytic patient can get off the couch and leave treatment if his dissent is strong enough."*

Some patients do—in contrast to the unconscious patient on the operating table. So, if he comes, it can, therefore, be assumed that he wants treatment, and this rescues the psychoanalytic treatment from the risk of unacceptable influencing. But very often the relations of power and authority within the consulting room mitigate very strongly against this kind of "defiance", and patients become immobilized, as if transfixed, upon the couch until the end of each session, when the psychoanalyst tells them to go. For periods, the patient in psychoanalysis may subjugate himself, like a hypnotic patient. And this lasts until these unconscious processes that deplete the patient's personality have been adequately dealt with in the process of the treatment. These arguments—and others—become particularly complicated when the psychoanalysis is conducted for training purposes.

In addition, we have seen that a patient's action in leaving treatment may quite possibly not be purely self-protective against an abusing psychoanalyst. It is equally possible that this action is a discharge of unconscious phantasy and energy in an action (acting-out) from unconscious motives, of which the patient is not fully aware. This staying or leaving cannot express reasoned and informed consent (see, for instance, Freud's Dora case—Freud, 1905e [1901]).

6. *The rational consciousness argument*

> *"In the conflict between the patient's wishes and those of the psychoanalyst, we should accept the conscious one. No weight should be put on the patient's resistance at all, on the grounds that it is unconscious."*

The patient's conscious consent is all that counts ethically. The problem with this argument is that the psychoanalyst enters the patient's conflict and weighs down on one side, thus enacting—and non-verbally confirming—the patient's split, when, in fact, his job is not to confuse that issue but to raise the conflict itself to the patient's conscious knowledge.

7. *The balance-of-forces argument*

> *"The psychoanalyst should honour the strongest side to the patient's conflict—the conscious consent or the unconscious withdrawal of consent—and proceed accordingly."*

He would have to discount, as far as possible, any rationalizations that the patient may put up. He would have to take account of the interpretations of the patient's unconscious intentions and consent. However, this is ruled out on the grounds of impracticality because the balance of forces changes, as we have seen, with time and stress and often on a very short time-scale. If the analyst takes this position, he seems to renounce his role of promoting knowledge about the relationship with the patient, and he removes himself to a position of reacting to the conflict in the patient.

Unresolved paternalism

These arguments all seem flawed on either ethical or technical grounds. If the psychoanalyst's aim is that the patient should know his own mind better than before the analysis, can that be achieved by the *analyst* knowing better what the patient should think and decide? If the psychoanalyst knows *for* the patient, does this in the long run contribute to the patient knowing better for himself? It becomes a paradox.

How, then, can a psychoanalyst proceed on the grounds that certain kinds of objections (non-consent) should not be acceded to? The psychoanalyst does seem to be ethically permitted on some basis—indeed, obliged—to continue with his work. Does this overriding of the patient's non-consent bring the psychoanalyst's activity near the surgeon's or the psychiatrist's—or, instead, near the torturer's intent to proceed against his victim's protests?

Psychoanalysis started as a medical treatment when paternalism was more the order of the day in professional practice—though admittedly in higher social circles the aristocratic patient prescribed what treatment was wanted, and the doctor was employed to perform it. However, as democratic attitudes in the twentieth century have percolated into professional work, the nature of informed and free choice has become progressively stressed. Psychoanalysis has, meanwhile, failed to keep an eye on the particular problems of paternalism that have evolved. A number of arguments appear to be implicit in the way psychoanalysts respond in practice. However, it is precisely the number of arguments that suggests that none really does the trick. The suspicion is that they might, therefore, be the rationalizations of an uneasy profession. If a single good argument is elusive, then many weak candidates substitute.

At the outset, Freud's intention to get the patient to express rather than to make suggestions to him left the field of orthodox medical approaches. However, his model of the mind as divided into interacting parts, some of which are unconscious, created a problem that has never been adequately addressed. In particular, should the analyst take note merely of the conscious agreement of the patient, or should he in some way consider the overall intentions of the whole of his patient, which may be arranged in the form of an unconscious conflict? These are two possible positions. At the outset of a treatment it is difficult for the analyst to take the whole of the patient's mind into account, as it is largely as unknown to him as it is to the patient until the analysis has got under way. On the other hand, if he does not take the patient's unconscious into account and relies solely on the conscious intentions expressed by his patient, he takes a deeply unpsychoanalytic stance. Moreover, he is at risk of colluding with various unconscious manoeuvres of the patient (and of himself). This is a stance that is also increasingly difficult to maintain as pressures build up in society that throw suspicion on the analyst unconsciously exploiting the patient. Patient interest groups are more established, and the phenomenon of "false memory syndrome" has thrust to the fore the helplessness of the psychoanalyst and psychotherapist in the face of repressed material; often it is very difficult to distinguish between what is retrieved from the unconscious and what is introduced there by suggestion.

This is bad enough, but when it comes to later developments in the psychoanalytic theory of the mind and of psychoanalytic practice, matters become a step worse still. This is the set of problems that we are considering here. The concepts of paternalism and autonomy have become seriously confused and inadequate when the subject of the patient is dissolved into separate parts that are dispersed within the interpersonal field of the psychoanalytic setting. Not only are both analyst and patient contending with the patient's unconscious, but the analyst now has to struggle also with the repressed areas of the analyst's unconscious, as well as with the way the patient has specifically dissolved the expected boundaries between these areas through the use of primitive psychological mechanisms.

It is in order to grapple with this multiply compounded problem that we turn now for some assistance to the notion of integration and examine one way in which some of these disadvantages could be resolved and can result in an eventual revision of professional ethics.

CHAPTER ELEVEN

Integration

Something like a paternalistic act is involved in psychoanalysis, but it is an act of a special kind. It is an "act" of learning, rather than of doing. I propose that this is the crucial difference. I will return to the rather complicated action in Patient C's dream of her car being moved (Chapter 9). Her learning about worries and about her needs was pictured as a physical "act" of moving her. It pointed to her experience of some internal movement—a psychological shift within her make-up. It looked as if she were at the point of reaching a more realistic appreciation of the help she had come to seek from me. However, the dream indicated that, though a shift, it was not a simple experience for the patient. From the psychoanalytic point of view, the patient was able to recognize a need for help (i.e. a shop that could provide for her). But at the same time, for her, the experience was transformed again from one of "being helped" to a rather paranoid view of being interfered with and damaged, for which she was due some compensation.

It seemed as if the help was not what she wanted. Yet there is a sense, of course, in which in another part of her mind it *is* what she wanted. Thus the shift was one of balance between two aspects of herself:

1. a part of her that felt helpless and seemed out of touch with others (mother, husband, psychoanalyst) who could be with her in this way;
2. a part of her that took a very different approach, to help herself by recruiting others (mother, husband, psychoanalyst) to gratify her need for admiration (not help), and one that could be quite paranoid if that illusion was not forthcoming—or was damaged.

The part of Patient C that could represent the move in the dream did, in fact, see, and give importance to, a kind of shopping and needing. And that part was no longer lodged in me but could be (unconsciously) given sufficient importance in her—important enough, in fact, for her to dream about it. For so long, her wanting to change had become my wanting her to change, and she had separated out the parts of herself into roles allotted between us. The dream suggests that, at last, both parts could now exist together in *her* mind. The fact of representing her conflict in the dream suggests that this process of splitting had changed back for the moment towards a repression that could now exist within the patient's mind, if only in a form distorted into a disguising dream.

The aim of a psychoanalysis is that the individual should be able gradually to regain for himself the lost parts of his personality:

> It is only by linking again and again later experiences with earlier ones and *vice versa*, it is only by consistently exploiting this interplay that present and past can come together in the patient's mind. This is one aspect of the process of integration which, as the analysis progresses, encompasses the whole of the patient's mental life. When anxiety and guilt diminish and love and hate can be better synthesized, splitting processes as well as repressions lessen while the ego gains in strength and coherence. [Klein, 1952, p. 56]

Through linking together conflicting parts of himself, new resolutions of old conflicts can take place.[1]

This describes a step in the *integration* of a personality. It is an act of learning and knowing—not of "doing".

These interpersonal processes affect very deep elements of the personalities of analyst and analysand on both conscious and unconscious levels. Within the interpersonal dimension, we have two alternative possibilities: either the process may deplete their personalities and, as it were, spread them out and share them interpersonally; or, equally, the personalities may become more integrated and reconstructed in the interpersonal dimension.

In the example of a psychoanalytic patient such as Miss C (Chapter 9), commencing a psychoanalysis put her personality at risk. Parts of her, such as the capacity to be responsible, were given up to another personality: the psychoanalyst, myself. In effect, she lost her own functioning as an integrated person. This is not the intention of psychoanalysis. It is, however, a risk. Nevertheless, it is through the very occurrence of this risk that the fault-lines in her personality could be plotted and the task of integration begun. Despite the short-term loss of integration, the over-all long-term *intention* is to bring the parts of the patient together. In this, the psychoanalyst resembles the surgeon operating on his patient with appendicitis, wounding the patient with an intent to heal. This points to a possible criterion of ethical practice.

- Principle of integration:

  Those practices are ethically beneficent that aim to minimize the distortions of identity and interpersonal spreading, and those are unethical that aim to fragment the personality and to enhance the interpersonal spreading.

Various professional settings may be set out on a scale of *intention*. On the one hand, there is the wish to minimize (or reverse) the

[1] This account implies that a psychological process is at the root of integration, and it is thus distinct from Glover's (1988) theories. He looks to neural mechanisms in the brain—"In the case of the unity of consciousness at one time, those mechanisms are likely to involve the kinds of neural links which are severed in the split-brain patients" (p. 55). Relations between neural links and the psychological struggle for personal integration are not easy to grasp.

coming-apart of the patient's personality and its interpersonal spreading (as in a psychoanalysis), while at the other end of the scale is a wish to enhance actively the distortion of the personality and to deplete and redistribute personality attributes. The latter end of the scale would seem to accommodate brainwashing and torture, and we investigate this in Chapter 19. Somewhere along this scale we can place other psychotherapies, mistakes, unprofessional therapies, unconscious collusions, and occurrences in various everyday settings. These differences of intention allow us to distinguish the actions of the professional: whether his practice is beneficent and therapeutic or whether it is malevolent and anti-therapeutic. I am introducing that distinction as the *principle of integration*.

The therapeutic process aims to set into reverse the splitting, projection, and dispersal of parts of a personality that have been relocated within the interpersonal social field. The patient's introjection of what he has previously projected into the analyst is an important basis for the contemporary theory of the therapeutic action of psychoanalysis (see "Containing" in Hinshelwood, 1989a). In the case of Patient C (Chapter 9), what was projected into the analyst was the very motivation for treatment. She had lost it, and it was re-found in me. This could in the course of time come to reside back in her as the evidence of her dream. Such an eventual introjection by the patient does become a real enhancement of her mind again, despite the painful experiences it might invoke in its train.

Integration and autonomy

Berlin (1958) considers the "strength of the personality" as central to personal autonomy. That view is not far removed from the idea of integration. He implies something we might call "integrity". The internal cohesive personality that contains a stable and consistent core of himself and has a flexible independence of mind is, in ordinary language, regarded as having integrity.[2] It may, in fact, be

[2] Storr (1960) has, before me, linked the problems of integrity with the disrupting processes of projection and introjection.

a better term to employ of a personality with these characteristics than is "autonomy" or even Berlin's term "internal autonomy". Thus, autonomy is, in fact, linked with integration. That individual is the most autonomous who can make balanced choices between all his options, one who will desist from dismantling his mind in the evasion of choice. To do so he must carry his own diversities and address his conflicts within himself as far as possible—in other words, he is the most autonomous who is most integrated. In this sense, integration is a necessary condition for autonomy.

If integration is the technical effect that psychoanalysis seeks, I shall argue that it can also be the mark of ethical responsibility that the psychoanalyst upholds. To promote such re-introjections and mental enrichment is, at the least, one distinguishing criterion from brainwashing. In other words "integration" can be, happily, both a technical and an ethical aim of psychoanalysis. (In Chapter 14 I consider the promotion of a technical principle to a principle of ethics.)

The notion of integration can also dissolve the confusion over "whose autonomy" and "whose paternalism" is in play when a patient has drawn an analyst into being a certain aspect of his own decision-making function. Redrawing the boundaries between them can become a tussle and, as we saw in Chapter 10, is ethically unsatisfactory. If we focus on what is happening to the integration of the partners in the system of splitting, projection, and introjection, then the confusion is no longer a philosophical problem to sort out but a confusion motivated by one (or both) individuals for them to sort out—the ethics demands a principle of integration rather than wrestling so strenuously to preserve the individual's autonomy.

Integration and the irrational

By addressing the impact of the processes of splitting, projection, and introjection on the integration of the mind, we can arrive at a more consistent measure of the irrational as well. Rationality (or irrationality) is not then simply to be gauged in comparison to someone else's rationality. If the principle of integration is applied, then an assessment of rationality is based on the negotiation over who is required to do the thinking and deciding. The person is most rational if he has available, *in his own mind*, his own capacity to think and to choose. Only then is he able to choose *autonomously* and rationally. In that sense, rationality, like autonomy, is dependent on integration, because both autonomy and rationality are themselves compromised by the degree of splitting, or supported by the degree of integration of the minds of the persons involved.

The criterion for estimating the validity of the interpretations of these activities is their effect in the immediate aftermath of being offered to the patient. In other words, a shift in the tendency for the patient to have more aspects of his mind available for use—that is, the reconstruction of the patient's mind in the immediate aftermath of the interpretation—indicates the degree of accuracy of the interpretation. Not only is this a criterion of validity, it is also effecting a significant therapeutic change of mental structure. This new awareness is the means by which minds can change.

Conceptual problems

Integration has significant advantages over the concepts of autonomy and rationality, though it may also generate some problems. Briefly, we address these advantages and disadvantages.

Problems with autonomy

The numerous problems with autonomy can be clarified through the use of the principle of integration. If the mind is divided within itself, integration makes clear an ethical approach as the one to enhance the re-integration rather than choosing between the unintegrated parts. Viewing the mind as integrated overcomes the conflict of the autonomy of conscious and unconscious parts of the mind. We can accept division and work towards its integration.

The inevitability of conflict between psychoanalyst and patient is not really over "whose autonomy" is to be dominant (though this is how it comes to view in standard professional ethics). The analyst will attempt to link the conflicting parts of the patient that have been split apart by describing in an "act of learning" the projected conflict; the intention is to restore some integration in the patient. Conflict between persons can now be checked to ascertain how much it is an externalized intra-psychic conflict that has been dealt with by splitting and projection (and with a corresponding introjection by some other mind). The principle of integration deals with an internal conflict of aims, between long-term and short-term, by pointing to an ethical act that will bring together the conflicting parts, or at the very least not push them further apart.

One of the difficulties of the word "autonomy" is that it implies a freedom from all outside influence, though this conflicts, as Holmes and Lindley (1989) have stressed, with the psychotherapeutic concept of realistic dependence; and they contend that autonomy is compatible with an idea of mutual interdependence. In fact, psychoanalysts would argue that mutual dependence would come about through the integration of both mature and dependent parts of the person. Autonomous functioning *with* others is, we have seen, clearly based on the degree of underlying integration. And integration is the core idea here.

Conformity to a cultural set of norms (including norms about autonomy) is problematic for the concept of personal autonomy, but the question becomes clearer if the choice of conforming to external expectations and adapting to society is assessed on its psychodynamic effects in terms of splitting off a part of the mind into "society".[3]

Rationality and consistency

The crucial criterion—rationality—is dependent on the state of integration, which is, therefore, fundamental. Integration also enriches the philosophical understanding of irrationality. If philosophers have, on the basis of the evidence from psychoanalysis, to discard the unitary model of the mind, then different parts of

[3] Society then subsequently represents some important part of the person, in the manner in which the hypnotist becomes a certain part of the hypnotized subject. Forms of nationalism, patriotism, racism, and cultural supremacy may be the outcome of this kind of projection into various aspects of one's own "society"; perhaps specifically it is narcissistic parts of the subject.

the mind contribute irregularly, or inconsistently, to rational processes of thought (and these depend on interpersonal and projective opportunities, as well as internal sources).

For instance, Freud's patient, the Rat Man, is an extreme example of the inconsistency that can arise. He complained that his mind was continually subjected to extraneous thoughts intruding upon his preoccupations.

> Just as he was up to his eyes in work [studying], he thought: "You might manage to obey the command to take your examination at the earliest moment in October. But if you received the command to cut your throat, what then?" He at once became aware that this command had already been given, and was hurrying to the cupboard to fetch his razor when he thought: "No, it's not so simple as that. You must go and kill the old woman." Upon that, he fell to the ground, beside himself with horror,—who was it who gave him this command? [Freud, 1909d, pp. 259–260]

This form of irrationality is very bizarre, but the intrusion of akratic and self-deceiving thoughts illustrates in gross form the kinds of inconsistencies that occur if split-off parts of the mind return abruptly to consciousness. Coherence in the person's train of thought is vulnerable to being interrupted when parts of the mind appear to go out of existence altogether, or return. The patient's mind specifically disrupts its own work, even using words themselves to effect this disruption (Lear, 1996).

We could then assess this core idea of rationality—or its converse, irrationality—in terms of consistency or inconsistency in thought. And, thus, rationality's dependence on integration may be rendered more measurable. The more integrated a person, the more he can sustain a *consistent* point of view and train of thought. His thoughts will be more consistent with each other (internal cohesion) and over time (temporal continuity). Consistency, based on integration—indeed, perhaps synonymous with it—may be more visible or measurable than rationality itself (or irrationality). Rationality is thus replaced by integration, which is then the implicit determinant of ethical paternalism, distinguishing it from unethical influencing, manipulation, and control.

Problems with the principle of integration

These advantages to the notion of integration in dispelling some of the problems of rationality and autonomy are balanced by certain disadvantages.

There is no claim that integration is an absolute principle, so it may come into contact with other moral principles; therefore, ordinary moral dilemmas still arise. As with many ethical principles, integration may be difficult to measure. However, using the observable characteristic of consistency may make it easier to measure than overall happiness (utilitarianism) or measuring the degree of rationality (standard medical ethics).

The philosophical problem discussed in Chapter 4 is also involved here. It is disputed whether a divided mind can be encompassed in the ordinary metaphysical assumptions that govern other psychologies—and this is the case despite the long acquaintance with multiple personalities since Janet (1982), Morton Prince (1906), and the psychoanalytic work on schizophrenics of the 1950s and 1960s. These are based on the primitive psychological mechanisms. Forms of a self-directed aggression (splitting) or, alternatively, integration—the bridging function of the "K"-link (Bion, 1962)—comprise phantasies that have an actual concrete effect on the functioning, structure, and identity of a mind (see p. 49).

A degree of complexity is introduced in the application of the principle of integration, since professional practices often allow a serious depletion of the patient—as, for instance, when admitting a patient to mental hospital on a compulsory order. We have seen that we must add in the *intentions* of the professional (unconscious as well as conscious), and not simply the effects of his actions.

Despite these problems encountered in the theory and in the use of a principle of integration, it is the claim of this work that it performs better than do the derived notions of autonomy and rationality. In Chapter 12 we consider the way in which integration works psychoanalytically and further implications of an "act" of knowing.

CHAPTER TWELVE

Self-reflection

The processes of splitting, projection, and introjection are phantasy activities expressed in the form of mechanisms. Psychoanalysts regard them as the engines that drive the development of mind (or its distortion and dismantling), and we have briefly discussed the omnipotence of phantasy (Chapter 5). The effects of interpretations to reconstitute a mind suggest a process of how minds might develop in the first place. When an analyst makes an interpretation, the patient takes in something from the analyst. This reverses the projection that has taken something out of a structural part of the patient's mind, but it can, therefore, represent a possible process by which the mind begins to accumulate skills and faculties.

Freud (1923b) made use of this introjective concept to explain the development of a moral conscience—the superego. He described the three-year-old child's task of having to give up its erotic interest in its parents. This loss requires mourning, and Freud described the child as internalizing these adults in the ordinary way that loss is dealt with (cf. "Mourning and Melancholia", Freud, 1917e [1915]). The parents become internal models for the child and supply it with grown-up standards and behaviour of its own.

This process illustrates a specific kind of introjection, one that is also an important part of the therapeutic process. In this stage of the process, the analysand introjects something himself—and is not merely projecting something of himself into the analyst. What he introjects is a part of the analyst's mental function—his capacity to understand the patient. This is the other half of a loop—or oscillation, as Money-Kyrle (1956) described it. A cycle exists, composed of projections from patient into analyst, followed by the introjection by the patient of something from the analyst in reply. This cycle is matched, in the analyst, as he introjects something of the patient, recognizes what it is, and reprojects it into the patient:

> . . . there is a fairly rapid oscillation between introjection and projection. As the patient speaks, the analyst will, as it were, become introjectively identified with him, and having understood him inside, will reproject him and interpret. [Money-Kyrle, 1956, p. 331]

Crucial to this process is the analyst's recognition. If the analyst can understand the anxiety of the moment and the way it is being dealt with, then the patient may also understand that process. In that sense, the patient may introject a piece of understanding about himself and thus be enabled to preserve a greater "presence of mind" about what is happening to him. In this form of introjection it is not split from, nor disappears from, the analyst. That is crucial: the process does not depend on some damaging effect upon one of the minds.[1]

As a lost part of the mind, hitherto separated, returns, a third element is created, a further piece of structure. That is an enhancement of self-reflection. Thus, returning to my present examples, Patient J (Chapter 6), who shredded her mind, could, after my verbal interpretation, subsequently use words. She could also con-

---

[1] It contrasts with a book-keeping model of interaction—one person's loss is another's gain—a point of view implicit in Freud's original theory of the economics of the libido. It is also contrasts with the economic theory of the "zero-sum game".

struct an imaginative fantasy—quite distinct from her habitual splitting-up of her mind—to indicate her own recognition of herself as a frightened baby. Introjection of this kind, in which enhanced self-reflection and understanding is acquired, is similar to the processes whereby, in development, children's identities are formed in part by introjecting aspects of parental and other significant figures.

Something significantly more than merely intellectual understanding is involved. An interpretation is not just using a piece of theory to make sense (or make sense to the analyst). Theory is a piece of knowing that, used at the right moment, can change something. If correct, it can change things by accruing a piece of self-knowledge. And that has a function: it is the glue that achieves integration. It is the offer of what is called a "K"-link (Bion, 1962).

Knowing and growth

Bion (1962) described the mind as constructed simply of links of various kinds—a form of latter-day associationist psychology. Thinking is the act of "putting two and two together", and the result is the mind—or the mind is an apparatus that develops under a pressure for dealing with thoughts. "K" stands for a link characterized by knowing and being known. The capacity for self-reflection makes a link between separate parts of the self. Accruing a piece of self-knowledge has a function; it is the glue of integration, a bridge. In this descriptive activity the psychoanalyst is crucial. He forms an alliance to learn and to develop knowledge. That alliance, as a "K"-link, is important. Bion also described more kinds of links, termed "L" and "H"—links of love and of hate, respectively.

It is the "K"-link with the psychoanalyst that is crucial. It is one in which the patient/client has to learn from the experience of being known by the analyst. He can accrue old and new parts of the self. The psychoanalyst's tool for building these therapeutic bridges—"K"-links—is the interpretation. This link has many forms—first, a link between parts of a single mind, second, between analyst and patient, and, finally, at various higher levels of collectivities of human beings.

The "K"-link, in an analysis, is a strict one—to form a bond with the patient that establishes a mutual effort to enquire and learn. Of course, we know that both patient and analyst lapse from time to time. In Bion's view, they revert to an activity that might be grouped under "L" or "H", such as either reassurance or admonishing. In this sense, the analyst has transgressed the rule of abstinence (see p. 153). Knowledge of what is happening in any therapeutic setting is difficult to gain. Even in the psychoanalytic setting, analyst and patient can engage in suggestive and extractive exchanges that disrupt and redistribute elements of mind and the self (identity), so that each becomes less of a person. Such happenings blind the participants. Bion commented:

> The analyst feels he is being manipulated so as to be playing a part in someone else's phantasy—or he would do if it were not for what in recollection I can only call a temporary loss of insight. [Bion, 1961, p. 149]

The arresting moment in the description is the recognition of loss of insight. To recognize a loss of insight is in itself paradoxical. Knowledge of such a loss of knowledge is not given to everyone! Generally, people are caught up in this process of playing parts for each other without insight—and, in addition, without any insight that insight has been lost. Though this applies to group therapy—as in the clinical illustration of Ellen in Chapter 6—it is equally true of individuals.

However, the analyst's capacity when fully functioning is to understand—even to understand these lapses when they have happened—and thus to create a "K"-link of being known. In the form of a bridge between splits, the analyst performs his unique therapeutic beneficence by imparting knowledge in the form of growth (learning). The psychoanalyst's tool for building therapeutic bridges, "K"-links, is the interpretation. However, that takes place in the context of another link—that between the analyst and the patient. And in that context both are exposed to observation and to self-reflection.

In contrast to the bridge built by a piece of self-knowledge, there is a use of deceit. In many respects, it damages the minds of both deceiver and deceived. Neither is fully aware of the forces acting upon himself. The link between the two is then replaced by a "minus-K"-link, one that dismantles bridges. The link between parts of the mind is obliterated, and the link between people can be visibly destroyed (Hinshelwood, 1994b)

Introjecting new capacities constitutes psychological growth, but the self-understanding in a psychoanalysis is a step beyond just an intellectual enlightenment. To understanding is added a new (or extended) structure—the capacity to understand oneself. Learning involves knowledge plus growth.

If there is only intellectual understanding, then not much of significance happens; as Freud commented:

> *Our* knowledge about the unconscious material is not equivalent to *his* knowledge; if we communicate our knowledge to him, he does not receive it *instead of* his unconscious material but *beside* it; and that makes very little change in it. [Freud, 1916–17, p. 436][2]

In the case of interpreting splitting, we can see what else must happen. The knowledge must impinge upon the split itself, to form the bridge across a split. That involves an extended (or restored) self-knowledge and self-reflection:

> When an infant has an intolerable anxiety, he deals with it by projecting it into mother. The mother's response is to acknowledge this anxiety and do whatever is necessary to relieve the infant's distress. The infant's perception is that he has projected something intolerable into his object, but the object is capable of containing it and dealing with it. He can then reintroject not only his original anxiety but an anxiety modified by having been contained. He also introjects an object capable of containing and dealing with anxiety. [Segal, 1975, pp. 134–135]

Segal goes on to contrast the mother who

> . . . may be unable to bear the infant's projected anxiety and he may introject an experience of even greater terror than the one he projected. [Segal, 1975, p. 135]

---

[2] Samuel Johnson once claimed, "Knowledge without integrity is dangerous and dreadful".

These two kinds of alternative interactions between the baby and mother resemble those I have been describing. In the first, it is acquiring an object inside (as a superego gets inside) that gives the experience of being known and thus of self-understanding, in contrast to the "minus-K"-link, in which "being known" is abolished and the experience degenerates to an incoherent nameless dread. Self-understanding is severely truncated at a site where it really matters.

Thus growth is driven by forces other than reason. Though reason has its part to play in recognizing the splits and repressions that need bridging, real internal change is in the structure of the mind. Parts come together, and bridges between parts are made through internalizing something capable of understanding them. The end point is that the patient has inside him his own greater capacity for self-reflection and of being known.

"An act of learning or an act of moving?"—this seems to be a question that is posed by the dream of Patient C (Chapter 9), when being "moved" by my interpretations was, instead, pictured by her as being moved on by brutal men who damaged her. This dichotomy can have more general implications than merely those for my patient. From one point of view, she has been able to learn usefully; from another, also expressed in the dream, it is an act as brutally abusive as physical coercion. In one sense, the psychoanalyst's aim was beginning to succeed—a reversal of the patient's separation into parts was starting to come about. But—was it an act of learning, or was it a coercive act of pushing her around?

I am arguing that, despite the patient's dream picture, an act of learning is rescued from coercion by the particular movement involved in acquiring self-knowledge. Implicit in that is an enhancing of the capacity for self-reflection: my patient had acquired some increased self-knowledge about her neediness (her need to shop), and, in addition, in knowing this, she could picture it to herself and could picture the distortions she made. Having achieved this dream picture, we can say that she is now in the condition that Sartre described: she is no longer self-deceiving—for some part of her knows how in this instance she can employ a grievance. Then the distortion of her knowledge into damage-deserving compensation is no longer self-deception, since she knows it well enough to represent it in her dream.

Bridging

The spatial metaphor of mind in which parts separate from each other or come together again suggests psychological distance. In these instances, the psychological distances are, in fact, created through physical distances between the separate individuals who carry different mental functions.[3]

To recapture an understanding of what is happening entails a recapture of lost parts of the self. The capacity to know oneself and allow oneself to be known (even by oneself) has specific integrating and therapeutic properties. And we can grant that this capacity to overcome splitting occurs in ordinary life. It drives the urge to maturity every bit as much as the primitive mechanisms occurring in everyday life fuel ignorance—in the form of prejudice, scapegoating, and psychopathologies.

We have ordinary knowledge of ourselves—even unconscious knowledge—without the benefits of psychoanalysis. The knowledge may be inarticulate and unspoken. Indeed, language and culture may deprive us of explicit means of expression. Nevertheless, at all sorts of levels, a certain amount of intuitive understanding, half-appreciated, hardly articulated, takes place, perhaps continuously in everyday life. And that understanding is not necessarily less potent than is the explicit psychoanalytic sort. It may

[3] Interestingly, another conceptualization of distance in mental space was offered by Ezriel (1951). He found psychological displacement of this kind concretely expressed in images of physical distance. Interpretation of that separation and the reasons for it enables the patient to test the reality of the analyst in the room. Ezriel mentions a patient who "started a session by unconsciously giving vent to hostile feelings towards me in the form of an attack upon the Government. After my interpretation he criticized the Clinic. The object of his attack had thus moved nearer my consulting room, from Whitehall to the Tavistock Clinic" (Ezriel, 1951, p. 33). The interpretation closed the distance between the patient and the explicit object of attack (the analyst). In this example the distance is represented; it therefore suggests the mechanism of repression, using symbols disguised in the unconscious. In contrast, in the case of splitting (the key process in the present argument), the separation of the parts is enacted in actual physical distance between patient and analyst, who have become the different parts of the patient's mind.

achieve great aesthetic value in art, literature, and music, despite a lack of words.

Psychoanalytic knowing is itself no more a quantum of information than is any piece of literature. In order to know another person, we need to communicate. And to communicate means engaging in being known—which, in turn, means knowing what part of ourselves we want to get across.

Communication

The negotiated transfer of something from one mind into another's is a part of everyday communication. Ordinary conversation is the transfer of experience with the punch of felt emotion. It is not simply the transfer of information. The speaker's experience is an emotional one, and the listener will attend to it to the degree that the speaker is able to retain within his words a vivid "feel" of the experience. No information is passed simply on its own. Without that relish provided by the speaker's experience, the listener will call it dry or dull, and attention will wander. In ordinary conversation there is a hunger for the transfer of experience from one person to another. Even at the highest level of academic lecturing, without a degree of emotional richness to move the listener, understanding and learning are stunted.

In this human model we are not talking about a "downloading", as might occur between computers. Human beings give each other experiences and seek them from each other—even the experience of tragedy is offered and sought. In this very ordinary, ubiquitous, and quotidian activity we see something of the transfer of minds. In this case, of course, we do not mean that there is a serious wound to the identity of the speaker and listener. The crucial distinction is that the speaker, whilst intending to put his experience into the mind of the listener, retains awareness that it is his experience; and the listener, whilst having (or rather identifying with) the experience that the speaker is relating, has no doubts about it being the listener's experience. In other words, something like projection is happening, without the splitting.

This is a link between two minds. And it differs, I claim, from a link between two computers. The latter may send and receive quanta of information, bytes and megabytes. But minds know each other and are known by each other. To know that one is known is an altogether different experience from acquiring a set of facts.

The interpretative function of the analyst is of this category. When making an interpretation, he attempts to put into his patient something of his thoughts and his pleasure in creativity. But whilst he is doing this, he in no way loses sight of the fact that what he puts across to the patient is, in fact, his thinking. And he retains this knowledge by recognizing that the patient is knowing his mind. However much it may become part of the patient's thinking in the future and an important experience, it does not become split off from the analyst.

The importance for the argument here is that a kind of transfer of parts of the mind (not just the proliferation of information) occurs in a conscious fashion. Or, to put it slightly differently, these illustrations demonstrate the particular conscious quality of everyday transfer between minds. It is not a knowledge in words, or one that is thought explicitly about, except in a psychoanalysis. But its non-verbal quality does not stop it being knowledge. It is the potential for it to be raised to a level at which conscious attention can be applied that is its crucial property.[4]

The capacity to know and to reason out knowledge (i.e. learning) is the mark of being human. It is the mark of becoming mature. Being irrational might therefore be held to be connected with aspects of the primitive mechanisms that dismantle the mind; and irrationality in particular is to do with a fault in self-reflection. I have shown the mind to separate and to come together again with a correlated variation in the capacity for self-reflection and self-knowledge. An individual's judgement and behaviour are susceptible to interpersonal influences (and therefore coercion), and this should make us wary of our patient's vulnerability. A person's choice to change is disconcertingly complex and unexpectedly in-

---

[4] The reason the transfer between minds is not thought about explicitly and contained within a verbal discourse is probably simply custom—our society does not provide words for it, and the means therefore to discuss it. This may be less true in other cultures.

volves an intricate interchange with other people's minds. The choice to change by splitting and dismantling the mind, and to distort and impede self-knowledge, or to change by bringing together, is not easily apparent to the would-be helper. The helper's position is, therefore, an equally complex one. We shall, therefore, now go back to re-examine the nature of professional ethics in the light of these empirical findings and their implications.

PART THREE

THE ETHICS OF INFLUENCING

CHAPTER THIRTEEN

Professional practices

The contention of this book is that, on balance, the advantages of the principle of integration as it has been empirically defined in psychoanalysis are considerably in advance of the notion of autonomy, with its ancillary concept of rationality. And many of the problems have been addressed, with partial solutions. We will turn now from these general issues to examine how they inform our understanding of actual practices. I want to re-examine the methods of influencing briefly touched on previously and to assess them in relation to the principle of integration. This will lead on to a verdict on psychoanalysis.

We must recognize that all influencing exists within a social and interpersonal context. As human beings, we of course influence each other in many ways all of the time, and psychoanalysis would not exist if the interpersonal setting in the consulting room—some aspect or other of it—did not have an effect on at least one of the participants. We have shown that in any meeting of two people, each influences (sometimes drastically) the other's state of mind. The following passage vividly describes the innocence of ordinary influence, and that such ordinariness is part of the impact of a psychoanalytic encounter:

> When two personalities meet, an emotional storm is created. If they make a sufficient contact to be aware of each other, or even to be *un*aware of each other, an emotional state is produced by the conjunction of these two individuals, these two personalities, and the resulting disturbance is hardly likely to be something which could be regarded as necessarily an improvement on the state of affairs had they never met at all. But since they have met, and since this emotional storm has occurred, then the two parties to this storm may decide to "make the best of a bad job". What this means in analysis is this.
>
> The analysand comes into contact with the analyst by coming to the consulting room and engaging in what he thinks is a conversation which he hopes to benefit by in some way: likewise the analyst probably expects some benefit to occur—to both parties. The analysand or the analyst says something. The curious thing about this is that it has an effect, it disturbs two people. This would also be true if nothing was said, if they remained silent. . . . The result of remaining silent, or the result of intervening with a remark, or even saying: "Good morning" or: "Good evening", again sets up what appears to me to be an emotional storm. What that emotional storm is one does not immediately know, but the problem is, how to make the best of it; this means a capacity to turn the circumstance—as I choose to call it for the moment—to good account. Neither the patient nor the analysand is obliged to do that; the analysand may not be willing or able to turn it to good account. His aim may be quite different. I can recall an experience in which the patient was anxious that I should conform to his state of mind, a state of mind to which I did not want to conform. The patient was anxious to arouse powerful emotions in me such that I felt angry, frustrated, disappointed, so that I could not think clearly. I therefore had to choose between "appearing" to be a benevolent person, or "appearing" to remain calm and clear thinking; but acting a part is incompatible with being sincere. In such a situation the analyst is attempting to bring a state of mind, and indeed an inspiration, of a kind that would in *his* opinion be beneficent and an improvement on the patient's existing state of mind. That interference can be resented by the patient whose retort can be

> to arouse powerful feelings in the analyst and to make it difficult for the analyst to think clearly. [Bion, 1979]

Strictly speaking, there is nothing specifically psychoanalytic about the incident described in this quotation. What is psychoanalytic is the way Bion tried to think about it and attempted to describe this interaction in laborious detail.

On the whole, psychoanalysts are, not surprisingly, sensitive to the suggestion that they are involved in a coercive influence on their patients. Many analysts would even take exception to the word "influence". Yet they most certainly do have an effect on them in some way. Thus, we need a term that will cover the field of phenomena in which one person has an effect on another—whether it is within a psychoanalysis or not, and whether it is beneficial or malign. Therefore I shall use "influence" for want of a better word to indicate the effects that one person has upon another, including those a psychoanalyst has on his patient, and use it to indicate both beneficial or malign influences.

If a person is rendered a less coherent individual, or self—someone who is mentally ill, or is in some intoxicated state, or has, we believe, been subjected to some unethical practice such as brainwashing—we would normally tend to consider it an abnormal state.

The psychoanalyst's special efforts are devoted to the development of knowledge, particularly knowledge of that emotional meeting often referred to as insight. As we saw in Chapter 12, the influence of a psychoanalysis is the development of the patient's knowledge of himself. But increasingly psychoanalysts are aware that their work with their patients is a process of developing their knowledge of themselves as well—at least, developing a knowledge of themselves when with their patient. In contemporary psychoanalysis, that knowledge is interpersonally discovered, and elucidating the patient's knowledge of his own transference involves "working through in the countertransference" (Brenman-Pick, 1985; Heimann, 1950; Money-Kyrle, 1956).

But there are other ways of approaching an interaction, ways with a more definite intention of influencing an outcome to the meeting: advising, manipulating, deceiving, hypnotizing, and so on. Psychoanalytic interpretation relies upon understanding. I shall first review the spectrum of possible approaches to exerting influence. Not all methods are morally acceptable, and we must keep in mind the balance between technical efficiency and an ethical validity.

Suggestion and hypnosis

In the early part of his career, Freud toyed with hypnosis and other methods based on suggestion. Freud developed his idea of the repressed unconscious directly from his own early experiments, which he had learned from the French work on hypnosis. He visited Charcot in Paris and Bernheim in Nancy during the 1880s. Suggestive therapies were being further developed by Pierre Janet (1892) in France and by Morton Prince (1906) in the United States. However, Freud moved away from suggestive methods and came to make a radical distinction between psychoanalysis and suggestion—precipitating a great rivalry prior to the First World War between suggestive therapies and psychoanalysis as the orthodox practice of psychotherapy (Hinshelwood, 1991). Suggestive therapies rely on correcting incorrect ideas, attitudes, emotions, or behaviour in the disordered patient who was regarded, in the late nineteenth century, as suffering from a degenerative mental, and probably physical, condition. Thus it was a correctional method aimed at delaying the inevitable degeneration. This contrasted with Freud's view that the state was not degenerative, it was merely unconscious. Suggestion aims to override the patient's degenerate mental function by substituting the therapist's functioning. The special link with the therapist—the "erotic tie", according to Freud—does not undo the condition. Instead, suggestion reinforces defences by diverting libido onto the physician and his suggestions—that is, his suggestions become sexually desired objects. And through such desire the physician can assert his powerful corrective influence.

The passivity of the patient in the suggestive therapies contrasts with the patient as agent, cooperating in his own treatment.

Freud viewed hypnosis as a method in which the doctor came to replace certain important parts of the patient's own mental apparatus (Freud, 1921c). The hypnotist's influence came from substituting himself for the most influential parts of the patient. rendering the latter passive and, in important ways, depleted of himself. In relating it to the phenomenon of falling in love, Freud wrote:

> The object has, so to speak, consumed the ego . . . it is impoverished, it has surrendered itself to the object, it has substituted the object for its own most important constituent. . . . There is the same humble subjection, the same compliance, the same absence of criticism, towards the hypnotist. [Freud, 1921c, pp. 113-114]

Freud's pointed way of describing this abject state indicates that it was more than just a method that he found technically limited; it conveys an ethical aversion to subjection and compliance of this kind. This giving-up something of the self to the hypnotist was a danger inherent in having loving feelings at all.

Hypnosis and other suggestive therapies are limited by the effects on the integration of the patient's mind. Technically effective in certain respects (Karle & Boys, 1987)—for example, negative suggestion for the removal of specific symptoms or positive suggestion for best performance in specific events—the corrections invoked in the patient's thinking do indicate a special relation of the power of one mind over another.[1] The patient is temporarily depleted of certain aspects of his own mind. The hypnotist takes them over. The hypnotist must use the authority of his position as a significant element in the patient's own internal conflicts and adjustments between the various parts of his mind. In other words, his "internal" autonomy becomes dominated by an external authority. Part of the patient—his capacity to make his own decisions—is relocated away from him. It is in the hypnotist, who, by introjection, takes on the role. At some point the direction

---

[1] Interestingly, hypnotism can be used in an analogous way to psychoanalysis; suggestions can be introduced under hypnosis to induce the patient to recall and express forgotten memories (e.g. Erikson, 1939). The problem with this is the danger that specific "memories" may be introduced by the hypnotist in his eager search for them and the patient's excessively compliant study when in a trance. One example may be the so-called "false memory syndrome" especially connected with the recovery of memories of sexual abuse in childhood (Sinason, 1997).

of the arrow is reversed by the hypnotist, and he returns to the patient a decision he has made, a suggestion implanted into the patient's conscious or unconscious mind.

In some respects, this to-and-fro interchange of parts of the contents of the two persons resembles the exchange in a psychoanalysis.[2] The crucial distinction is that what the hypnotist puts back into the patient's mind is a decision he has made, a decision of the hypnotist in his psychodynamic role as that patient's own capacity for judgement (this amounts to Argument 6, p. 104). In other words, the contemporary psychoanalytic view of primitive processes dramatizing internal states describes what is happening at levels beneath the surface one of hypnotism. Psychoanalysis tends to focus on just the sort of thing—displacing aspects of the patient—that is occurring in a hypnotic treatment. However, that which, in hypnosis, is the treatment is in psychoanalysis the material for joint study.

At the deeper levels, parts of the mind of the patient (and often of the analyst) are exchanged between them in a way that is characteristic of the patient. In hypnosis, it is jointly agreed to establish a particular pattern of exchange that is characteristic of the treatment (hypnosis). This is more akin to a surgical treatment negotiated, say, in a case of appendicitis, and particular patterns may encourage the transitoriness of the psychic exchange. Mostly patients recover and "collect themselves" after being in a hypnotic trance. But, of course, it may not be like that, and hypnotists are extremely wary of taking on patients who seek these dramatizations on a more long-term basis—those with more serious mental disturbances.

---

[2] This to-and-fro occurs in everyday life as a basis for the most trivial conversation to the most serious debate. Continually, people open themselves to varying degrees to receive what is presented from another person's mind, and they will return something from their own. This is not merely a communication of verbal information—which would make for conversation being unacceptably tedious. Nobody can conduct a satisfactory conversation, however trivial, without an emotional impact—"putting something of themselves into it", we tend to say. In fact, the most trivial of informational contents can be loaded with the most vital interest—the "sweet nothings" that lovers whisper in each other's ears (see p. 123).

We can grant ethical validity to this temporary division of mind in hypnosis in so far as the hypnotist has the intention of ending this division and returning the capacity of judgement properly to his patient at the end of the session. He must do all this unconsciously, since neither he nor the patient is properly aware of what is happening, nor does he have the conscious technical means to do anything about these unconscious processes if they go awry.

Hypnosis, therefore, carries a risk and a limitation: the ethical risk is that the hypnotist or the patient will unconsciously resist returning the parts of their minds to their proper places, and the technical limitation is that hypnosis can only address the relatively minor disorders of mind and is at a loss to address these primitive processes, which it can only exploit.

Advice

The psychoanalyst is constrained from forms of influence that are not interpretative. Nevertheless, at times simply advising the patient on the best course of action may seem obviously the influence that needs to be exerted. However, "Educative ambition is of as little use as therapeutic ambition" wrote Freud cynically (1912e, p. 119; and see p. 100). Eschewing ambition by the psychoanalyst is grounded in the view that ambition clouds the capacity to receive the patient's communications. In fact, as mentioned, the patient is also enjoined not to follow up certain ambitions (Freud, 1914g). This professional rule concerning important decisions became less possible to sustain when psychoanalyses grew longer, especially after the First World War, as treatments changed from dream analysis to the analysis of character (Abraham, 1919; Freud, 1917e [1915]; Reich, 1933) or of the ego (Anna Freud, 1936). Later, after the Second World War, the understanding of the analyst's own part in creating the interaction (countertransference) led to a more complex understanding of the nature of advice in the setting—examined, for instance, in my case of Patient C (Chapter 9). Nevertheless, advice is a stock-in-trade of the helping professions in general, and the backbone of supportive therapy and counselling, even when the practice is informed by psychoanalytic understanding.

In a professional context of any kind, advice is invited by the client. However, because of certain exaggerated views about the greater expertise of the professional, it can also be greatly overrated, especially as far as advice on personal problems of feelings and relationships is concerned.

In the light of the principle of integration, the issues concerning the giving of professional advice become clearer. Taking on the role of an advisor who knows more allows the possibility of a serious division of labour. To enact the roles of the one who knows and the one who does not can have attractions for both partners, especially if the stakes are high. In general medicine, the bedside manner of the doctor is important as just such a means of giving faith in the near-almighty power of the doctor to a patient who is frightened about his illness and for whom death inevitably looms menacingly behind it. There is nothing that a patient wants more than a magically effective doctor, one who can defy death itself. Something similar will present itself in the encounter between a lawyer and his client. The priest makes a very explicit claim to be near to the Almighty.

All these situations allow a division of labour in which both parties may be very happy to acknowledge an overly neat division between the helpful and the helpless. As Main devastatingly puts it, the "helpful will unconsciously *require* others to be helpless while the helpless will *require* others to be helpful" (Main, 1975, p. 61; these processes of institutionalization are described in greater detail in Chapter 15, p. 172).The gain for the professional is that he can feel, with this unconscious assistance from his patient/client, that he has achieved his professional claim and status for which he has striven. In a way, all are happy. None of this—the unconscious psychodynamics—negates the fact that the professional may well know more than the client. However, the extreme states of helper and helped that are unconsciously achieved threaten the mental integration and stability of both and therefore their capacity to use their own capabilities realistically. A typical division of the personalities builds up—the patient becomes depleted of his knowledge, power, and agency, while the helping advisor becomes enhanced in these respects.

Knowledge of these occurrences is usually hazy, but generally there is a profound suspicion of "experts", and, much as they are wanted, they are also denigrated and satirized. The belief that professionals can abuse their power is rife and gives rise to a plethora of users' groups that attract, in numbers and solidarity, a counterweight to the power of professional expertise. Such suspicions are warranted at the unconscious psychodynamic level, where there is the power to seduce into an unbalanced relationship (see Chapter 15). The depletion of the power of the patient/client does need to be counterbalanced. However, that depletion is not caused simply by the overweening ambition and power-seeking of the professional. The cause may exist, but it cannot be truly effective without general gains to *both* sides of the professional encounter—the patient/client as well as the professional.

In a psychoanalytic treatment, advice does not have a central place. Instead, central to the psychoanalytic process is knowledge of this division of labour, a knowledge of the extremes of the roles—and then of the ensuing suspicion and its sequelae. It could be argued that the psychoanalyst's work is, indeed, one of advice—but one of a specific kind of advice. It is advice on just these kinds of polarizations that we might find in the advisory relationship itself. However, such a role is not the kind of advice that clients usually expect. It is a "K"-link in which the patient/client has to learn from the experience of being known rather than from being advised (see Chapter 12). There is here a fine distinction between knowledge passed on from one person to another in the form of, shall we say, a textbook, and the informing of an experience that is happening in the immediate here-and-now, textbook or no. To require the patient to learn about the process itself prompts him to accept a responsibility and a research project on his own mental state.

There are two risks that arise from this analysis of the advisory situation. One is that a reliance on the technicalities of passing on expert knowledge without a deeper understanding of the processes of influence involved leads to vulnerable people becoming depleted. The other is that psychodynamically anti-expertise movements can develop towards dismantling the helpfulness of the professional even *within* its realistic limits.

Manipulation and deceit

The cultivation of certain aspects of the helping relationship could be manoeuvred or manipulated in ways that do not make known to the patient what is happening to him. There is, for instance, something rather unsettling about the following passage, written some 75 years ago, about establishing a psychoanalytic treatment of a ten-year-old boy:

> He had so far as his anxiety was concerned a partial insight into the malady, and a certain desire to get rid of it and of his inhibitions. But for his main symptoms, his rages, it was rather the contrary. Of them he was unmistakably proud, regarding them as something which distinguished him from others, and he enjoyed the worry they caused his parents. He thus felt himself in a certain sense at one with this symptom, and probably at the time would have resisted any attempt to rid himself of it with analytical help. But here I ambushed him in a not very honest way. I resolved to embroil him with that part of his nature. I made him describe the outbreaks as often as they came and showed myself concerned and thoughtful. I enquired how far in such states he was yet master of his actions at all, and compared his fits of rage with those of a madman who would be beyond my help. At that he was startled and rather frightened, for to be regarded as mad naturally did not chime with his ambitions . . . the symptom finally, as I had intended, turned from a treasured possession into a disturbing foreign body. [Anna Freud, 1946, pp. 11–12]

This passage from Anna Freud's 1926 lectures on child psychoanalysis recommends engineering, or manipulating, a positive, cooperative transference to the psychoanalyst at the outset of treatment.[3] To "ambush him in a not very honest way" is preparatory work that is no longer deemed necessary (Geleerd, 1963), but 75 years ago psychoanalytic influence was believed to rest in the

[3] The nature of consent in child psychotherapy is, of course, further complicated, since the child's autonomy is not regarded as equivalent to that of the adult. Below the age of consent, a parent/guardian must make the decision. However, a principle of integration may apply equally to ethical acts with children and with adults.

power of the patient's positive transference—and that had to be gained at any price. Feelings of love for the analyst were thought to be the force that would overcome the resistance of the patient's unconscious to knowing certain unknown aspects of himself. This raises classical questions of means and ends. The claim to ambushing as an integral part of therapy suggests that notions of freedom and honesty carried different weight in the early part of this century.

From a technical point of view, one could argue that if a psychoanalysis is concerned with the patient developing a greater awareness and openness in himself towards reality and truth, this is hardly served by a "not very honest" method. But the uneasiness about these methods is not really on technical grounds of effectiveness but on ethical ones. It is a moral issue which makes for the unease about dishonesty. Although such ruses are not now employed, it remains for us to disentangle why the simple effectiveness of Anna Freud's method was not enough, and why we require more than technical effectiveness—and more than the pragmatic argument (see p. 102).

How do the technical and the moral interact?

Manipulative and deceitful influencing, as in the example reported by Anna Freud, feels intuitively unethical. However, it is difficult to track down what it is that feels wrong, because in this case the outcome, in Anna Freud's terms, was beneficent—the child patient did, in the end, accept the benefits of treatment.

However, this technical supremacy, justifying an intuitively unethical professional relationship, is sufficiently strong that some contemporary therapists (though no longer psychoanalysts) do employ dishonestly based practices. For example, certain family therapists use paradoxes that depend for their technical effectiveness upon deceiving the patient (Cade, 1979; Watzlawick, Weakland, & Fisch, 1974). This has recently been much debated (Collier, 1987; Holmes & Lindley, 1989; Lindley, 1987; Treacher, 1987; Walrond-Skinner, 1987). The basis for justifying deceit is the intertemporal argument (see Chapter 10, p. 102)—in the long run, the patient will be better, however deceived in the short term; long-term ends in this case are considered to justify the immediate dishonest means.

If, however, we refer back to the principle of integration, the ethical validity of these arguments—the pragmatic argument and its intertemporal sub-category—may become clearer. The unease about the pragmatic argument is shown by the use of deceit and what it does to the mind of the patient. He is not fully aware of the forces acting upon himself. The psychodynamics of this consist in a relationship between a client and his helper who does not offer understanding, learning, or knowledge. Knowledge is at severe risk of becoming deceit, and the "K"-link between therapist and patient is replaced by a "minus-K"-link.

There is in these instances a process that dismantles the links that hold minds together—the self-reflection of knowing and being known. Though this dismantling is intentional for a brief period whilst the therapeutic session is in progress, in the longer term such connections and links should be restored. In this way the therapist will be in line with the principle of integration if his intention is restorative. However, if he does not understand these unconscious processes, there is a risk that he plays with fire, and one or both of the partners may be burned.

We are now in a position to turn to a form of influence where there is no ultimate intention to restore the mind of the subject.

Coercion

Extreme forms of coercion comprise the Chinese system of brainwashing and the methods of torture of other totalitarian regimes. Brainwashing is a specific form of psychological duress applied as a means of imposing specifically the State values and attitudes towards the individual. It comprises two elements: confession and re-education (Lifton, 1961). Disorientation in space and time as well as of psychology and relationships is manipulated to provide extremes of disorder in the external conditions. Lifton studied the victims of this form of torture and described vividly the difficulty they had in regaining minds of their own. He described the task of the survivors "as mastery through restoration of integrity" (p. 223).

There is a body of psychoanalytic description of torture. The methods involving extreme forms of deprivation and pain to the body differ, but the intentions and effects are similar to brainwashing, being the dismantling of the person's integrity of mind. Torture, like brainwashing, does not just impose a particular point of view or elicit a specific act or confession—it destroys the person:

> It seeks to provoke breaches in the identity, i.e. in the sense of internal cohesion and continuity . . . the torturer's aim is to destroy thought and identity. [Amati, 1987, p. 112]

Vinar (1989) has described, in slow motion as it were, the progressive destruction of a person under torture. The terms "demolition" and "dereliction" are used to describe the resulting devastated personality. Particularly prominent in this process is the removal of the capacity for thinking (Puget, 1988a, 1988b; Vinar, 1989). Reyes (1989) refers to the loss of the capacity for discrimination, and Amati (1987) to the loss of the capacity both for discrimination and for responsibility. Kestenberg (1991) described disturbances in the experience of past, present, and future, with subsequent unrealistic attempts at reconstruction of continuity of life and experience, and Reyes described enduring loss of reality:

> There was here less of a delusional denial of reality than an attempt at making possible the simultaneous co-existence of two mutually exclusive realities: one where the catastrophic event had happened and one where it had not. [Reyes, 1989, p. 192]

Parts of the self split apart, as in Freud's example (see pp. 43–44). Those that particularly connect the person to reality are under attack and go out of existence under successful coercion. The person is finally reduced to nothing but a relation to his body (Vinar, 1989) or to his bodily needs (Amati, 1987):

> Starting with the intensity of the physical pain, sensory deprivation, obscurity, blind-folding, the breaking of all effective and affective links with the personal world which was loved, the subject finally arrives at the constant presence of a painful body, hurting, broken, totally at the mercy of the torturer; all other perceptions of the world which are not centred on the present experiences cease to exist. We call this moment: *the demolition*. [Vinar, 1989, p. 359]

The loss of so many parts of the personality leads to a state of violent depletion. In this demolished state, desperate attempts are made to recover the sense of the "self" and to survive as a person. The final demolition can be put off by recourse to internal resources—"you get strength from hatred" (Amati, 1987, p. 100): "The indignity he felt at the iniquity and the brutality of these methods [beating, suspension, drowning, electric shocks] helped his resistance" (Vinar, 1989, p. 355). However, these internal resources to survive as a person are limited, and the subject turns to external resources—foremost amongst them an attempted bond with the torturer (Kuleshnyk, 1984): "The imperative to repair the psychic catastrophe drives a search for the restitution of a lost world in the 'other'. Yet in this search, the only available 'other' is the torturer" (Vinar, 1989, p. 360); ". . . the highly abusive torturer offers himself as the only possible sustaining object" (Amati, 1987, p. 108). At this point, the torturer's work is complete. The victim's personality is largely obliterated and evacuated into the torturer, who becomes the whole world for the victim, comparable to the infatuated relation between lovers for whom the loved one is everything (Freud, 1921c; see p. 133), and also that between the hypnotist and his client and, in the transference, at times between the psychoanalyst and his patient.

This torturer–tortured relation describes in many instances the splitting apart of the personality (Ricon and Borgnia, quoted in Puget, 1988b, p. 121). The torturer is not necessarily in a more psychically healthy state than his victim; he is just more fortunate:

> "When he was violating me, I kept thinking that he was even more violated than I." Yes, these people are more violated than Irma. They are mutilated split people, technically and coldly divorced from their feelings incapable of any discrimination in life other than the one permitted them by authority or by the hierarchical order in which they operate. [Amati, 1987, p. 104]

It would not be a surprise to find that the instigators of others' splitting are themselves highly damaged by splitting. Lifton (1982; see also Dicks, 1972), particularly, described a similar splitting:

> . . . there is one overall mechanism, that which I call "doubling," within which all the others operated. It includes compartmentalization or "splitting" of various elements of the psyche, so that one could both participate actively in the kill-

> ing and remain tender in one's family relationships. [Lifton, 1982, p. 296]

Aspects of the torturer also come to be divided and obliterated whilst "on the job"—notably, the human capacities to feel, to empathize, to care, and perhaps to fear. Some of these will end up in the victim, though others are relegated to the torturer's ideology elsewhere.

The aim of violent coercion and torture is the destruction of the person; it is the passport to the victim's re-entry into the State's corporately organized mentality. And this is the important key: the psychological dismemberment of the victim describes the division of his mind in a way that is analogous to, though not completely identical with, the process we have described.

Intuitively, these forms of extreme state-organized coercion seem completely wrong. But such intuitions are probably not universal; for instance, they would not be part of the thought-process of the torturer himself, or of his political masters. The torturer would, however, have difficulty in showing that his actions benefit his victim, except in the adaptational sense, since his concerns are to benefit the State. The latter might itself constitute an argument that would go something like this: it is good to coerce individuals into accepting the authority of the State, because if all accept certain principles (say, ideas concerning race; or concerning economics), then everyone will benefit in some specified way (a purified race and culture; or a non-exploitative social system). This is a utilitarian argument, and the ethical justification for the organized violence depends on maintaining that the specified aims are, in fact, beneficial to everyone. In the two instances given, the utilitarian argument has simply proved technically ineffective: the achievement of a purified Aryan race in Nazi Germany did not in the end prove a possibility; equally, the use of economic measures to create a non-exploitative system in the Soviet Union collapsed in the end. The cynical endpoint is that the victim will, in fact, be happy once brainwashed, and thus accepting, and adapting to, the reality of superior force.

Leaving aside their ethical validity, technically these aims proved unattainable. They did not work. In principle, it is conceivable that a utilitarian argument of this kind could be effective technically, and countless science-fiction stories have imagined possibilities. But, apart from putting those arguments *for* coercion to the test technically, the question is:

- Do we have cogent ethical arguments that torture is wrong?

These processes are versions of those that occur in the individual relationship between psychoanalyst and patient. What are the differences?

The differences are twofold. In the first place, the relocation of parts of the person is not achieved collusively. It is instigated by the oppressor and, we suppose, resisted by the victim. There is not always resistance, as the Stockholm syndrome attests, where the victim becomes attached to the threatening terrorists. This, too, is recognized in the clinical descriptions of "a search for the restitution of a lost world in the 'other'. Yet in this search, the only available 'other' is the torturer" (Vinar, 1989, p. 360). This depletion is quite consciously forced on the person, not, as in most everyday and professional encounters, negotiated between the partners.

The second difference is that the effects are lasting and intended to be so. There is no pretence that this is an interim stage, from which the victim will regain his lost aspects—the capacities for thinking, discrimination, responsibility, and to appreciate reality. The state of the person is very like the end-result of processes of institutionalization of incarcerated mental hospital patients (Chapter 15). Instead of a move to ensure an adequate "K"-link, the reverse occurs. What the victim is required to "know" is not self-reflective. He must "know" only what his torturer knows about him, about the torture, and about the reality around them.

The demolition of personalities involved in torture suggests strongly that disintegration is the aim—not merely the taking-over of their autonomy. General social processes ordinarily found in groups (such as the therapeutic community described in Chapter 7) may coerce individuals into certain identities, stripping them severely of important personal functions and depleting them into one-dimensional stereotypes. It must be true that we all do operate in this way at times, especially when we consider people in the abstract—say, those from another culture, whom we do not know sufficiently in a direct way.

In those societies where this kind of influence is raised to a much more consciously deliberate method of controlling minds, the branches of the State administration dedicated to organized violence and political oppression have developed their methods out of the "technical neutrality" of social psychology. That is, they work and are methods of operating upon people as the means to other ends. The relationship between torturer and victim operates on the victim not as an end in himself, but as a means to support the State. The ethical principle that a beneficent act involves an intention to support or enhance a person's integration is severely breached by torture. This seems a strong case.

Having reviewed how various forms of influencing work with regard to the principle of integration, we now need to examine psychoanalytic practice.

CHAPTER FOURTEEN

The verdict on psychoanalysis

On the road to discovering what sort of moral practice psychoanalysis is, we have inspected other forms of influencing people. Each time we have addressed a particular method of influence, we have found a complex, interwoven pattern of technical effectiveness and ethical validities. The psychoanalytic practice of interpretation is no exception, and psychoanalysis veers between being a scientific and a moral activity.

Implicitly, Freud's discussion of his method, however much he emphasized the scientific aspects, in fact addressed moral categories, including the patient's agency. In contrast to the suggestive therapies aimed at correction, psychoanalysis aimed at expression, especially emotional expression (catharsis). Freud started with

> . . . the assumption that my patients knew everything that was of any pathogenic significance and that it was only a question of obliging them to communicate it. [Freud, 1895d, p. 110]

Their disordered ideas, attitudes, behaviour, or feelings derived from the blocking-up of excessive mental energy, which could, in theory and in practice, be unblocked. When blocked, this libido then seeps around the edges, as it were, to form apparently unrelated symptoms. Such a blockage could then be undone by psychoanalytic understanding provoking a catharsis—a ventilation of feelings. These early views set the direction within psychoanalysis for a particular attitude to the patient's agency. It absolves the analyst from correctional activity upon the patient's mind. The patient is required, instead, to be active in producing his thoughts and ultimately of revealing his unconscious. Ironically, in spite of advocating a more active role for the patient, Freud is known to have been characteristically very directive in urging the patient into revealing his thoughts (Wortis, 1954). However, Freud pressed his patients in a different manner from the suggestive therapists. He required self-revelation according to the "fundamental rule"—to speak everything that comes to mind, uncensored, however shaming, in other words, "free association". Freud's influence was to press patients into self-knowing. And he believed this to be a completely different influence from that of implanting new thoughts.

Freud emphasized the contrast between *suggestion* and *expression*, and thereby he founded, inadvertently, a non-instrumental technique. He had not originally intended to do so. In fact, he rejected the hypnotic method, because instrumentally it was too weak for him. He believed that the suggestive therapies had a low or impaired technical effectiveness. Hypnotic suggestion was unreliable and ineffective, or at best it brought only temporary respite from the symptom, which either returned or was replaced by another symptom. Moreover:

> When I found that, in spite of all my efforts, I could not succeed in bringing more than a fraction of my patients into a hypnotic state, I determined to give up hypnosis and to make the cathartic procedure independent of it. Since I was not able to alter the mental state of the majority of my patients, I set about working with them in the *normal* state. [Freud, 1910a [1909], p. 22]

Freud viewed hypnosis as a method in which the doctor came to replace certain important parts of the patient's own mental apparatus (Freud, 1921c). The relative passivity versus agency of the patient seems not to have been an issue with which Freud dealt explicitly, though he was well aware of the contrasting active and passive impulses in human beings. It is, therefore, implicitly and unwittingly that he hit upon his method of obliging the patient to become an agent in knowing himself.

A moral practice

The patient's active role in self-knowledge is a psychoanalytic value and, like medicine, psychoanalysis is a moral activity—to do good for the patient. Moral practices are governed by a code of practice. Some codes may be very short and general, like the crux of the Hippocratic oath: *primum non nocere* (firstly, do no harm); but often they are merely a set of quite low-level rules: "do not sexually exploit the client".

However, psychoanalysis is in a unique position, since, as a sympathetic sociologist has admiringly said, psychoanalysis offers

> . . . a view of human beings which in an intense and unusual way assumes them to be moral in their fundamental nature. It also—and in close relation to this—assumes them to be constituted as social beings in a primary and continuing dependency with others. . . . Theory is impregnated with moral categories. [Rustin, 1991, pp. 19–20]

If human beings as agents are fundamentally moral in nature, then psychoanalysis is not only a moral activity with a patient, but also a study of a subject with morals. In other words, a practice that inevitably concerns a person's moral nature cannot be morally neutral. It is a moral practice.

Another way of approaching a very similar position is Fulford's examination of psychiatric activity. A moral activity constitutes a discrimination between good action and bad action. He argues that such evaluations deeply permeate mental health in general, and terms such as "illness" and "disease" are value judgements:

> Mental illness . . . [is] shown actually to reflect the evaluative logical properties of its constituents (anxiety, sadness and so on). [Fulford, 1989, p. 258]

Fulford reviews two attitudes to mental illness: First is Szasz's (1961) scepticism towards the concept of "mental illness": he complains that the concept is erroneously based on a weak analogy with physical illness, whereas he argues that the analogy is invalid, as there is *no* relation to physical illness. Second, the defenders of the concept of "mental illness", such as Kendall (1975) and Boorse (1975), maintain that illness is a scientific category, and "mental illness" should be shorn of its primitive emotional evaluations in the way that "physical illness" has been. Fulford quarrels with both positions and calls the views of both the sceptics and the defenders "the conventional view", because both are founded on two basic themes:

> . . . first, that the conceptual structure of medicine is essentially factual in nature, and, second, this is so because a biological-scientific concept of "disease", defined in terms of a (supposedly) value-free concept of "dysfunction", is logically central to medicine. The theories of Szasz, Kendall and Boorse, it will be recalled, were all built on these two themes. But the corresponding basic themes . . . are (in the sense of the term as it has been used here) the reverse of these. They are, first that the conceptual structure of medicine is essentially evaluative (rather than factual) in nature, and, second, that the particular kind of value which is expressed by medical terms is derived via "illness" (rather than "disease") from "failure of action" (rather than "failure of function"). [Fulford, 1989, p. 260]

In other words, Fulford is arguing that we need to move to an ethics-based view of medicine as a whole, aimed to benefit agents who act, and away from a value-free science-based view. Both Rustin and Fulford are arguing that the moral essentials of human nature—in the ideas of agency, intention, and primary evaluations of good/bad—require that both psychoanalysis and medicine have to be regarded as moral activities in themselves. This position is implicit in much of Freud's own work, despite his overt allegiance to a quest for a scientific psychology.

Psychoanalysis is not only a practice that must observe ethical principles, it is also one that works with moral categories themselves, as Rustin and Fulford argue that psychoanalysis and psychiatry must. But, in addition, in important ways a psychoanalytic treatment is an analysis of the moral attitudes and practices of the patient. This tricorn nature of psychoanalysis suggests that it is a paradigm of a moral practice. One aspect of this complex moral status, which is focal here, is that an activity that might be encompassed by expressing and knowing is central to combining both technical effectiveness and ethical validity. An "act" of learning, knowing, or expressing is ontologically distinct from an act of doing, suggesting, and psychologically manipulating, because of the role of self-reflection, a function that is embedded in the specific psychoanalytic tool, interpretation. We look now at this technique against the backdrop of the moral/ethical injunction of beneficence.

Psychoanalytic interpretation

We will start with the *technical competence* of interpretation. There is a notion of a psychoanalytic treatment going steadily along, with the patient observing the *fundamental rule*. This means that the patient must say whatever comes into his head freely and frankly without internal censorship, the psychoanalyst discovering the links between the various pieces in this stream of consciousness. In this model of free association and interpretation, the patient indicates to the psychoanalyst, in disguised form, those things that he does not know consciously and, in particular, would especially not like to know about himself. But this model is a bland fiction. No psychoanalysis proceeds for more than the briefest moments in that fashion. In fact, something radically different and more troubling happens.

From the earliest days, psychoanalysis consisted largely of dream analysis. Free association illumined elements of dreams. Cooperation in this was supposed to depend on the patient's love (for the analyst), deployed to overcome the resistance against knowing the unconscious. However, it became clear that things could go embarrassingly wrong with that process. In the later months of 1899, Freud started a psychoanalysis with a patient known as Dora. He embarked on this, according to Ernest Jones's biography (Jones, 1953–1957), with the intention of conducting and recording an exemplary psychoanalysis of a hysteric that could serve as a model of his method to demonstrate to his students and confound his critics.

In fact, Dora left this exemplary treatment prematurely after only three months, greatly to poor Freud's surprise and dismay. Perhaps it is to his credit that he did publish this case in the end, despite failure. But he did not do so for five years, and not until he had understood and had learned something very important: that Dora had used the psychoanalysis in a way that was quite different from the one that Freud had intended. She sought the satisfaction of revenge against men of a certain kind—a category that included her father and into which she came to put Freud himself. Her revenge was to disappoint him by turning away from his treatment (Freud, 1905e [1901]).[1] Not much learning or knowing resulted. However, Freud realized that, nevertheless, there was still a form of expression embedded in the relationship.

Resistance and reliving

Dora's method of dealing with Freud enabled him to realize (though in Dora's case too late) that she was reliving with him an early situation of pain and revenge. This discovery about Dora became, in Freud's hands, a discovery about the way in which "forgotten" (repressed) memories return, not as conscious recall, not necessarily as dream symbols, but instead in the form of insightless re-enactments with substitute objects, especially with the person of the psychoanalyst (Freud, 1914g). This problematic dramatization, therefore, has a status similar to that of symptoms and dreams, all expressions of problems not consciously appreciated but unconsciously active (i.e. determining life, attitudes, and behaviour). Freud was confronted with the full weight and seriousness of the *transference*.

Subsequently, the history of the development of the technique of psychoanalysis has been largely a continuous working-over of this paradoxical situation; learning about the patient can occur

[1] A good deal has been written of the conflict between this female patient and certain abusive paternalistic attitudes that Freud represented in the analysis (Lakoff & Coyne, 1993).

maximally when something goes wrong in the ideal model of the psychoanalytic process; it is a *via negativa*. This was elegantly described by Anna Freud:

> Even today many beginners in analysis have an idea that it is essential to succeed in inducing their patients really and invariably to give all their associations without modification or inhibition, i.e. to obey implicitly the fundamental rule of analysis. . . . The fundamental rule can never be followed beyond a certain point. The ego keeps silent for a time and the id derivatives make use of this pause to force their way into consciousness. The analyst hastens to catch their utterances. The ego bestirs itself again, repudiates the attitude of passive tolerance which it has been compelled to assume, and by means of one or other of its customary defence mechanisms intervenes in the flow of associations. The patient transgresses the fundamental rule of analysis, or, as we say, he puts up resistances. . . . The observer's attention is now diverted from the associations to the resistances, i.e. from the content of the id to the activity of the ego. The analyst has the opportunity of witnessing, then and there, the putting into operation by the latter of one of those defensive measures. [A. Freud, 1936, pp. 13–14]

This explicitly describes the paradox: that the psychoanalyst stands not just for a particular procedure, and that frequently a conflict with the patient's unconscious over this arises, but the conflict itself is also of importance as a key element in the process of learning and the discovery of the unconscious.

Anna Freud states quite explicitly that technically it is when the patient breaks the fundamental rule that the psychoanalyst then has the best opportunity for scrutinizing the defences. It is when things go wrong that the psychoanalysis is at its most productive. And yet those moments of deeper realization are the ones that go most against the patient's own deep intentions. In discussing this, Anna Freud realized that much of the patient is not in alliance with the analyst:

> In the analysis of the ego's defensive operations there is, of course, no such community of aim. The unconscious elements in the ego have no inclination to become conscious and derive no advantage from doing so. [Anna Freud, 1936, p. 14]

This absence of a "community of aim" between patient and analyst is a curious but potentially risky situation for both. We have seen the technical reasons why this is therapeutically advantageous, and the implications for psychoanalytic "technique" have been extensively discussed over a long period of time (see, for example, Fenichel, 1938; Glover, 1955; Greenson, 1967).

The mutative interpretation

The terms in which Anna Freud couched her description are different from those mainly used today. However, the more contemporary approach to thinking about psychoanalytic technique stems from about the same time as Anna Freud was writing the passage quoted above. James Strachey (1934) described the psychoanalyst as operating in a unique way that will not have been experienced by the patient previously. In particular, the psychoanalyst will resist playing the parts that the patient expects. The analyst's technical operation is to stand against his patient's perceptions, expectations, and requirements—the rule of abstinence for the psychoanalyst—as Freud had refused to play the part of Dora's older lover.

The rule of abstinence enjoins the analyst to refrain from active or gratifying responses to the patient:

> . . . the patient's need and longing should be allowed to persist in her, in order that they may serve as forces impelling her to do work and make changes, and that we must be aware of appeasing those forces by means of surrogates. [Freud, 1915a, p. 165]

Quite unconsciously, the theory has it, under the pressure of frustration, the patient will come to see the psychoanalyst as a mother-figure or a father-figure, either of which will in the patient's perception assume an unnaturally good or an unnaturally bad form. These perceptions have transferred over from childhood and such primitive, "archaic" objects which the patient perceives in the psychoanalyst cloud his judgement. It is the psychoanalyst's job not to play along with them but, instead, in a balanced fashion, to describe what is happening.

It is through this description and therefore the restraint of action that the patient is enabled to change. He is enabled to see, and know, a new kind of figure that is not in the mould of these archaic perceptions. The psychoanalyst comes to be seen in a more realistic way, as a balanced figure, neither unrealistically good, soothing, gratifying, nor unrealistically bad, harsh, critical, or punitive, and the patient can see himself in a new reality—his psychic reality, in which he lives with his archaic perceptions and objects.

Thus, the psychoanalyst represents a figure that can begin to reflect on these archaic burdens that the patient carries with him. Instead of simply carrying, and reacting to, these figures, the patient can acquire for himself a more balanced and reflective attitude towards them, based on the form of his psychoanalyst's interpretive function. Internally, he acquires a reflective function by an act of introjection. That is, the patient takes into his mind a figure from the external world—his learning, knowing analyst—not a "doing" helper. The patient can then have within him the crucial link between knowing about himself and having the experience of being known.

Ethical interpretations

So much for the technical effectiveness of psychoanalysis; what about its ethical validity? We need now to tackle psychoanalysis itself.

- Is psychoanalysis ethically valid, as measured against the principle of integration?

Since greater integration is the technical aim of psychoanalysis, it would seem to accord with integration as an ethical principle. However, there is a major problem: to use the discoveries of psychoanalysis, which are so replete with psychoanalytic values, as a yardstick for other methods of influence, including other therapies, may turn out to be dubious to a greater or lesser degree. But to use it as an ethical measure of psychoanalysis itself is highly dubious, leading merely to circularity—thus: prioritizing "integration" that has emerged from psychoanalytic work is bound to lead to the conclusion that psychoanalytic work is therefore ethical, because it promotes integration!

Surprisingly, this criticism can be met. Enhancing integration enables the patient to develop precisely those characteristics that are central to moral conduct. The person who is more integrated has (1) more of the precondition for autonomy, (2) more of the precondition for rationality, and (3) can better hold together intrapsychically the various choices he has to make, including consent. This is a crucial point, since it cites integration as a route upon which a person must travel to become a moral being. It is a short step, therefore, to transpose "integration" from a technical aim of treatment into a principle that underlies moral conduct. Thus, to enhance a person's integration is a beneficent act; but it is a specific kind of beneficence in that it enhances that person's moral being. This makes it different from the technical aims of many other kinds of therapy, which aim at simply reducing symptoms or suffering. These are beneficent aims, but they intervene in a different way in the subject's life. Enhancing integration, on the other hand, intervenes in a person's moral nature itself. It is in this sense that the beneficent act of enhancing integration is a candidate for becoming an ethical principle, in a way that most treatment aims of various psychotherapies cannot be.

There is a very explicit connection between the technical aim of a psychoanalysis—to enhance "integration"— and "preserving the autonomy of the individual". Even if the ethical aim were retained as the patient's autonomy, integration is a technical means towards that ethical end (autonomy). In this sense, promoting integration carries the ethical load that autonomy has always borne.

Intuitively, integration of a person seems to be an ethical good, and it performs as well as, if not better than, autonomy as a criterion in professional ethics of all kinds, not just psychoanalysis. To test the principle of integration as a criterion for deciding upon psychoanalysis, we must ask whether it can perform as an ethical principle to point to an unethical psychoanalysis. I have frequently pointed to moments when an analytic process is ethically going wrong—and going wrong precisely because it has allowed a patient to become split and depleted.

In fact, the technical aim of psychoanalysis—integration—is so powerful a principle underlying ethical practices that it accords psychoanalysis a special place amongst moral practices in general. It may perhaps even be *the* moral practice.

Because the technical/moral concept of integration is also an interpersonal one, it can define right and wrong action of one person upon another. Therefore in the analytic setting of two people, enhancement of integration is a technical accomplishment to be performed upon a patient, but it is also an ethical restraint upon the performer. Thus it can describe and evaluate both the functioning of the patient *and* the functioning of the psychoanalyst, making it a candidate for being the core of the professional ethics of psychoanalysis.

Therapy or coercion? Psychoanalysis at its best, and often even when it deviates, is distinctly therapy rather than coercion, even though it has both similarities to and differences from brainwashing. The similarities are that:

1. the same processes of splitting and projection come into play;
2. they can both result in a depleted personality;
3. there is an intense relationship between both participants;
4. that relationship is intensified, and often prolonged by a "spreading" between them of parts of their personalities.

Psychoanalysis differs from coercion in that:

1. the psychoanalyst *intends* to bring those splits together again and attempts through understanding to create a "K"-link; the torturer, in contrast, intends the opposite: he dismantles any coherent understanding, especially self-understanding, in his victim and thereby creates a "minus-K"-link;
2. it is not the *intention* of the psychoanalyst to promote splitting;
3. usually any splitting that does occur is transitory and reversible in psychoanalysis.
4. splitting is usually at the instigation of the patient, in contrast to the torturer, who *instigates* the splitting, against the intentions of the victim.

These differences are clear-cut. Together, they form an ethical litmus paper.

Moral practice

Psychoanalytic work described so far demonstrates that the human mind is in a constant dynamic of forming and losing its coherence. This occurs through the activity of phantasy, especially those phantasies involved in splitting, projection, and introjection. The coherence of the mind is governed by the self-reflective capacity to know parts of the mind or, alternatively, to obliterate knowledge. There is little that can be known—even about anyone else—that does not involve a degree of self-knowledge. If we give interpretations to someone who is intent on other things—such as re-experiencing primitive relationships in the transference—does an interpretation *force* knowledge on someone? In other words:

- Can a person be coerced into knowledge?

The act of learning involves self-reflection. It cannot be *done to* someone else. There is no way of getting around the patient as the active agent in that process. This is different from doing something, for example, in the course of an operation on a patient under anaesthetic. This is closely linked to the difference between treating the patient technically as a physical body that is subject to the laws of natural science and as a subject within human science—a subject that has an agency (in terms of professional ethics, their autonomy), a being "for-itself".

Though giving self-knowledge is "doing something to" another person's mind, it cannot be effective without that mind's agency in his own self-knowledge. He has to reflect on himself. Otherwise, as Freud said, "he does not receive it *instead of* his unconscious material but *beside* it" (Freud, 1916–17, p. 436), and that makes very little difference. When it comes to self-knowledge and self-reflection, agency has to be preserved, otherwise it is merely knowingness (a close relative perhaps of rationalization). The risk, then, when knowingness replaces self-reflection, is that the mind is dismantled by punching a hole in self-reflection.

Thus doing something to another's mind falls into separate categories:

1. those psychic events that change minds by relocation and redistribution;
2. those events that are knowledge of relocation and redistribution and provide some power to stand against the first category.

There is an asymmetry in that the dismantling of a mind can be an act of doing, whilst in contrast integration is ethically different, based on the agency of the subject, who becomes an equal "doer". We might call the first category "psychic *acts*" and the second "psychic *facts*". At times we may find ourselves doing a psychic act to someone—colluding with some primitive mechanism—whilst at the same time knowing a psychic fact with them—making an interpretation of that act. Thus there is a contradiction in the idea that an interpretation is simply paternalistic. The attempt to create a bridge, a "K"-link, does, certainly, go against the patient's intentions of sustaining a comforting split within himself and appear paternalistic. As, for example, with my patient, Miss C (Chapter 9): there may be good grounds for her to hold to her own intentions of establishing a setting in which a doting mother admires her whilst privately and uncomfortably worrying on her behalf. Once she has achieved this distribution within the analytic setting, she is likely to suffer a great deal less discomfort, responsibility, urgency, and tension. This appears very sensible. Under standard medical ethics, there would be good grounds for avoiding interpretations that override the patient's current (and in this case, enduring) autonomous choice.

But the analyst proceeds towards an integrating interpretation; he invites something as well as overriding the patient's preference paternalistically. He invites cooperation in being known. Although in one sense this is a coercive act, at the same time it offers the chance (though not the certainty) of her becoming a more whole and thus a more autonomous and rational person—through the awareness of the act of dividing herself.

There is a difference between an act of treatment upon a non-consenting patient that overrides his power and autonomy (a psychic act) and an interpretation that directly puts into his hands the wherewithal (a psychic fact) to augment his own power and autonomy through being more integrated within himself. Thus there is an ethical asymmetry between a psychic act of, say, suggestion (or even torture) upon a patient who is thereby depleted in his own autonomy of thought and an interpretation of a psychic fact that can augment his own power and autonomy.

There is a paradoxical quality to this—coercing someone into knowledge in order to make him more autonomous. It resembles the paradox of empowerment—powerfully instructing people to assert their own power! To eliminate the contradiction, we have to remove "knowing psychic facts" from the same category as "doing psychic acts". Learning that includes the agency of self-reflection is different from the unreflective act of redistributing minds. Introducing someone to knowledge about themselves is ethically a quite different occurrence from reorganizing the contents (or structure) of his mind outside conscious knowledge. In this way, the technical operation of giving an interpretation is nuanced ethically.

We have, however, not finally put to rest all debate over the power that experts and professionals have over us. We will proceed, then, to discuss ethical professionals.

CHAPTER FIFTEEN

Professions and power

Crudely speaking , a distinction is normally made between activities upon the inanimate world and those that engage with the world of human beings. Wittgenstein (1979) made a distinction for the *human* sciences: asking people for reasons is not the same as looking for causes. The former (reasons) is an interest in the other person and his intentions; engaging with them is evaluated as good or bad, beneficent or maleficent. The latter (causes)—looking for scientific determinants of behaviour[1]—is based largely on natural science and technology and regarded as ethically neutral or value-free. A "technology" means the instrumental, the *cause/effect principle*: if *this* occurs, then *that* happens. This contrasts with the ethical impulse, the *intention/effect principle:* I should do *this* because I want *that* to happen.

[1] This distinction corresponds to Sartre's "in-itself" or "for-itself" dichotomy. Both the person having reasons and the one existing "for-himself" can be said to acknowledge the agency of the person, which drops from the conceptions of biological scientists and experimental psychologists.

Such a distinction between natural and human science is crude because clearly there are ethical implications to the way that natural science uses and exploits the inanimate and the non-human world. The knowledge of the instrumental (cause/effect) is at the same time governed by judgements of an ethical kind (intention/effect). Knowledge of what will happen must be tempered by intentions of both "wanting" and "should". Equally, there are aspects of the human "sciences" that are technological—for instance, experimental psychology, or the practice of economics, or medical therapeutics.

Values and technology

It follows that the attempt to exert an influence on the object of study differs between the natural sciences and the human sciences. In the natural sciences it is referred to as a technology; in the human sciences it is unfortunately variably referred to as technique or practice (or praxis).

Though there is both technology and practice in human sciences, it would seem clearer to restrict ourselves to the term "practice" for the influence exerted in the human sciences; and so I shall call those efforts "moral practices". However, there is not a proper dichotomy between technical operations and ethical principles. In fact, they converge, and moreover such a convergence is a necessary condition for human science. It is not the same in natural science, where ethical considerations can be separated out. Whether this separation is legitimate or not, in practice it is successfully accomplished, and it has led to a great freeing of natural science, for the good and for the bad. Ethical considerations come in when we consider what to do with the results of natural science.

In the human sciences—and in this I mean to include all categories of human sciences: not merely psychoanalysis, but medicine, social work, and so on—ethical principles are embedded in the practice itself. To have a good therapeutic "technique" is to realize ethical principles in practice, and to approach a person ethically is, in a sense, therapeutic. This is because a moral practice is about the "good" or "right" way of living with others, of relating to them, of being with them. A moral practice cannot eschew that "being-with" element. The ends are not distinct from the means.[2] Therefore moral practices—including psychoanalysis (and all forms of psychotherapy and therapy)—are, by nature, complicated. The psychoanalytic phenomena that arise between professional and client add to the complexity. This is unfortunate, but not to be shirked.

The intention to have an effect on someone else is a feature of virtually all human interaction (see the earlier discussion on communication, p. 123). But certain more formalized activities of this kind and, in particular, professional practices—including education, law, religious ministry, medicine, and also, of course, psychological and psychoanalytic help—aim to help individuals with their own interests. There is also another category of formalized moral practices—including economics, social policy, and politics—that attempt to create a beneficial balance between individuals with their own strivings and the collective in which they are embedded. I would, therefore, restrict my term "moral practice" to these two formalized categories of influences—professional and political—upon human beings.[3]

---

[2] Implicit in the account given earlier (p. 2) of the infant's blissful love for the mother is an indication of the "other" as an end in itself and not just a means to satisfaction by her. It suggests that the convergence of a means and an end in the object is apparent from the beginning. Trouble—the specifically human struggle—begins in life when one and the same object ceases to be both end and means (this is a way of restating the problem of the depressive position). For instance, when an infant feeds for its needs from mother, the mother is not simply a means for the infant to satisfy its needs (end). She is also a loved object that is valued in her own right as the source of satisfaction (means) and as the recipient of the infant's generous gratitude (end). The pain of the depressive position can seriously disrupt this happy union of means with end as the mother fails at times to satisfy needs and becomes a hated object; her value to the infant is then not at all an end in itself. Maturation through the depressive position entails struggling to sustain the valuation of persons as ends despite their moments of failure as means.

[3] These categories—the professional (moral practices in relation to individuals) and the political (moral practices upon the collective)—are not separated in any simple way, since all individuals exist within human collectives.

As far as the political realm is concerned, there seem to be rough-and-ready rules that define an ethical boundary between acceptable and unacceptable influence, although these may vary from country to country, that is to say from political system to political system. In this country, deceptions, *ad hominem* attacks on opponents, and the buying of the might of the advertising industry tend to be accepted, if reluctantly. And we would largely agree that political oppression and censorship, physical torture, psychological intimidation, and financial bribery are unethical methods of influence. These are rather *ad hoc* categories.

In the professional world, there may be similar *ad hoc* rules and categories. Explanation, teaching, respectful persuasion, reasoned argument, and psychotherapeutic interpretation would count as rightful methods. But there are grey areas, and the privacy of a professional practice, together with the special and complex relations of power that attend a psychoanalytic treatment, seem to make it imperative that we should be as clear as possible about the borderline between what is ethically correct and what is unethical in the influence that is exerted on the patient. If we intuitively agree with these categories, then are they merely arbitrary and relative to the society we live in, or can we know that they are ethically quite distinct categories?

Ethical suspicions

I have emphasized the curious situation in which a conflict with the patient—refraining from colluding with the transference—may lead to considerable therapeutic benefit. The technical procedure goes ahead on the basis that we learn from lapses, like the engineer testing the strength of a material by measuring the load at which it breaks. However, there is a difference: this is not a case of a break in some inanimate material, it is a break in the "community of aim" between two people, as Anna Freud (1936, p. 14; see chapter 14, p. 152) put it. This is the point where our ethical problem arose. Should one of the participants continue exerting his influence, as if the community of aim were still intact? Technically, this makes sense. We touched on a plethora of arguments for the ethical validity of this psychoanalytic paternalism: the prior-agreement argument, the pragmatic argument, the intertemporal (later-understanding) argument, the adaptational (professional paternalism) argument, the on-going consent argument, the rational consciousness argument, the balance-of-forces argument (see Chapter 10). The mere variety of arguments led to a suspicion that no single argument is any good. The sense of an argumentativeness, instead of a single good argument, then provokes the actual suspicion that psychoanalysis might really, after all, be coercive.

Power-relations

It is true that a patient in analysis will have to join the analyst in certain beliefs and values, such as a belief that the unconscious exists and that it is beneficial to know about it.

However, there is a common assumption that the process of an analysis is an implicit conversion of the patient to the analyst's point of view, to his belief system and his philosophy of life.[4] For instance, when the analyst convinces the patient that he has an Oedipus complex. In this process, the patient will have to give up autonomous being and reach a state of abject dependence on the analyst. This reduction of the patient to become the analyst's thing is often assumed in popular culture to be the price that has to be paid for the patient's whim to talk endlessly about himself.

The capacity for the psychoanalyst—and, indeed, any therapist—to exert his will over his patient/client is popularly discussed. Elements of this common critique may have a modicum of truth in reality—and certainly some patients may succumb easily to a dependence of this kind. Exploitative therapeutic relationships are undoubtedly found.

However, this picture is a partial one; usually it is a temporary phase during the course of a treatment that will, in the long run,

---

[4] Special considerations obviously apply here in a training analysis, where the analysand is indeed in the process of imbibing psychoanalytic values, partly consciously and partly unconsciously. The suspicion is that he is even less in a position to defend a critical purchase on his thinking about psychoanalytic values.

resolve those dependency wishes. Of course, an analyst such as the author would say this; and an ordinary everyday critic might point to the Wolf Man's interminable dependence on Freud (Freud, 1918b [1914]; Gardiner, 1972). Nevertheless, the intrusive occupation of the patient's mind by the analyst and his views, beliefs, and values is *not* a psychoanalytic intention. The aim—and the ability—is to resolve issues, including those of dependence, that typically arise between patient and analyst. It is to enable the patient's self-expression (not the psychoanalyst's), to learn about him rather than to correct the patient with good ideas implanted by the analyst. In so far as the psychoanalyst does advise and suggest, he is for the moment interrupting his analytic functioning.

Yet, the counter argument might run, whatever the intention of the analyst, the analysand may become quite overpowered, as if transfixed and immobilized by the analyst's presence and power.

This is, at times during an analysis, true, particularly for certain obsessional or passive patients. The analysis, as we have seen, is not a process that follows an ideal route; however, neither is it a condemnatory process—either about the patient's diffidence, or about the analyst's part in it. The psychoanalytic intent is to enquire and, through a raised level of awareness, ultimately to resolve the postures of dominance and submission that are dramatized. The analyst, interestingly, is not there to advise on such postures and to prescribe what to do about them. He does, indeed, put into the patient a series of interpretations; but in the long run he puts into the patient the capacity to make interpretations for himself.

Well—our sceptical interlocutor will return to say—it is not possible to put interpretations into the patient's mind without sliding in, in hidden compartments, a whole slew of beliefs and values. They are, in any case, just part of language—especially of specialist languages.

In fact, it seems to me that this must be so. Any communication an analyst makes must come from a loaded framework of words and concepts derived from his social position on various measures—ethnic, class, gender, age, and so on.

Well—my thoughtful inquirer might add—the position of professional expert has been left off that list. It is most crucial, because it is the most powerful. The professional is infused with a set of socially defined qualities that set him apart, and above, just because of his expertise and the lack of it in the patient.

Whilst acknowledging this—that the expert's expertise does, indeed, risk slithering down into polarized roles of the powerful helper and his helpless client—it is, of course, a risk any person runs in giving any advice or professional suggestion whatever. However, in the case of psychoanalysis the foundation was that "patients knew everything that was of any pathogenic significance and it was only a question of obliging them to communicate it" (Freud, 1895d, p. 110). Thus, fundamentally, we question: who is the one who really knows? This is not expertise as it is with other professional experts. Rather than an expertise in knowing the patient better, it is an expertise in prompting self-knowing (and being known). There is a careful distinction to be made between the analyst knowing about the patient and the analyst enabling both to come to know, with the patient's guidance (from his unconscious). The analyst is in this sense dependent on the patient giving up the knowledge for examination, just as the patient depends on the analyst to spot it.

By this time, my co-debater might have given up in tedium or exasperation at my dogged persistence. But if he were to acknowledge the fine point I have made of the difference between enabling the patient to be known and knowing better about the patient, then I would concede to him something important. The analyst–patient relationship is not quite like an ordinary working partnership, because the knowledge supplied by the patient is unconscious knowledge, supplied through his free associations, his dreams, his roles in the transference. His lack of conscious knowledge of his unconscious does put him at some disadvantage. It makes him *consciously* helpless in the search for his knowledge. Moreover, the patient's unconscious mind is set against the knowledge becoming conscious. But it must be clear that any tussle of wills is just as much between the patient's conscious mind and his unconscious as it is between the patient consciously and the analyst.

It is true, in fact, that the patient is expected to accept some of the analyst's baggage of beliefs—but the core of it is the belief that the patient can know himself best and in a certain sense does already know himself best. The belief is that despite such knowledge being unconscious—or, worse, possibly for the time being located outside the patient altogether and in someone else—the learning that is "found" in the analysis is the patient's own knowledge.

The ethical professional

Psychoanalysis shows that the choices our patients make are suffused with conflicts of an extremely subtle kind. Their consent will have all the variety of distortions that can be manifested by repression, rationalization, and, above all, splitting. Psychoanalysis—like medicine and other humans sciences—is a moral practice that entails choosing what is good for someone (as determined by professional ethics) and working at understanding *their* choices (as in psychoanalysis).

The formulation of an underlying ethical principle—that ethical practices are beneficent if they *aim* to minimize the distortions of identity and unethical if they *aim* to fragment the personality—is one that involves the mental functioning of the professional as well as that of the patient.

We need to give account of this mutuality between the minds of the patient and the professional. Therefore we can add to the principle of integration, as I stated it above. It should then read:

- Professional Ethics:
  Those practices are ethical in which the professional minimizes the distortions of his own identity; and those are unethical in which he colludes with his client to distort both their personalities in an interpersonal spreading.

The professional's integration (or, conversely, his tendency to redistribute his own personality) is a crucial factor in whether his practice is ethical. The principle will clearly include the classical rule of abstinence. However, the principle extends beyond the rule of abstinence, since it must also apply to the unconscious functioning in the professional and cannot be voiced merely as a conscious rule. Consent, therefore, is a negotiated process between intermingled individuals who interact in ways that are benign or malignant. And that negotiation and intermingling is unconscious, though with quite visible results.

Expertise

The professional's own integration affects his capacity to use his knowledge beneficently. One could call it his professional integrity, which depends on his propensity (or not) for interpersonal spreading of himself.[5] If he knows a great deal, but also *knows* that he knows a great deal and *knows* that his client does not know much, then he has already begun to lose his integrity. He has begun a mutual spreading activity in which he acquires the role of knowing and assigns to his client that of ignorance. Whilst there may be some actual truth in the expert having some expertise that his client lacks, the divergence can, through splitting, be carried through to a degree that distorts both their identities. Professional relationships based on this redistribution of knowing will result in the expert enhancing the depletion of the personality of his more vulnerable clients. A collusive situation arises—perhaps even to mutual advantage—but the mutual distortion of each other ensures that it is an unethical mutual advantage. This contributes to establishing the power-relations of professionals that are so potentially threatening.

Returning to the problem posed by Patient C (Chapter 9): should I have influenced my patient to forgo her marriage for the eventual benefit of her psychoanalysis? Had I done so, I could have appealed to rational choice. But it might have opened up a further splendid opportunity, unconsciously, for the patient to install even more firmly in me *her* worry about her future and about her progress in treatment.

Already, such an unwitting (and unwelcome) introjection by myself was occurring and, in effect, breaching my integration, too.

---

[5] For example, we shall shortly note Main's vivid descriptions comparing the personalities of staff and patients of the mental hospital.

However, the compensation for the breach of my own boundaries is an enhancement of my own sense of self. Such an enhancing effect on the professional is not uncommon. It is obtrusively visible within institutions.

The paternalistic institution

Under compulsory detention, the psychiatric patient has his own volition removed from him. He is no longer master of himself, and he loses various citizens' rights. Such a legal order quite clearly removes, in a concrete and legal fashion, much of the patient's own capacities to decide for himself. In more subtle ways, he suffers an ensuing gross and progressive depletion of his personality—"health and stability are too often bought at the excessive price of desocialisation" (Main, 1975, p. 7). This depleting, desocializing effect of orthodox psychiatry is Szasz's (1961) useful contribution to the social phenomenon of madness and psychiatry. However, taken to extremes, it becomes a despair that has allowed professionals to acquiesce in the dismantling of the large mental institutions themselves.

Inevitably, such admission to hospital causes a division in the patient. He no longer has a capacity *within* himself to decide his immediate future in many respects, including his treatment. Is not compulsion of this kind ruled out by the ethical principle I am advocating? Does the principle of integration mean that this psychiatric practice is inevitably unethical? Yet we cannot avoid admitting certain patients, despite their own resistance, to psychiatric wards. On an intuitive basis, it seems clearly to be right practice. The patients are frequently relieved of a considerable portion of their suffering, as are their relatives, who have become ground down. Much modern psychiatric care is effective in emergency situations of this kind. It would seem to be heartless to consign such patients, and their relatives, to further unnecessary suffering if it could be relieved. Ordinary benevolence seems to put out of action the principle of integration. However, we might note that the last argument seems equally to counteract the principle of autonomy, on the basis of benevolence. And it is left to the extreme libertarian arguments of Thomas Szasz to support autonomy (Sedgwick, 1982). In this sense, integration fares no worse than autonomy.

However, there is an important sense in which the principle of integration could contribute to thinking about the way in which the professionals in such a case would go about this compulsory detention. It is a contribution that is not available with the principle of autonomy, which precludes the technical process of compulsory admission. Let us see how, employing the principle of integration, the effects on the mind can be better tracked.

Institutionalization

Certain people who have been admitted to a mental hospital on a compulsory detention order come out after a longer or shorter period of time, and others do not, but remain incarcerated within the hospital for prolonged periods. From that observation, the integration of the patient has two possible fates: either (1) an obliteration of a part—through splitting, projection, depletion, and loss—results, as if displaced to another personality or to the institution itself; or (2) a protection—perhaps, holding in safe-keeping—is afforded, with eventual re-integration, as, say, in the case of a surgical patient with appendicitis. Clearly, there are two diverging processes: (1) an annihilating internal force and (2) a temporary regression, which means giving up more sophisticated functions only for the time being. What makes this difference?

One answer to this is that the nature of the incarcerating institution has something to do with the outcome. Nineteenth-century psychiatrists believed that the disease process was an irreversible physical degeneration of the brain, and patients' depleted states were accepted without question. They stayed incarcerated to the ends of their lives.

During the 1940s, new methods of treatment were tried, notably in the military hospital, Northfield, in Birmingham (Bridger, 1985). These derived in part from social psychology ideas developed in experimental settings (Asch, 1952; Lewin, 1936; Sherif, 1936), blended with the developing practice of psychotherapy. From this social dimension came social psychiatry, group therapy, the therapeutic community, and community psychiatry. There were several important principles that had been learned by this time, arising from the recognition that the individual person, or patient, resides within a context of other people. The social milieu began to be recognized as a cause of the individual patient's condition and therefore perhaps potentially curative. It became important to consider what kind of institution could be curative rather than destructive (Main, 1946). The question that needed to be answered was:

- What ingredients make an institution either therapeutic or damaging?

In fact, it has proved much more difficult to answer this question than to describe what is believed to be wrong with the old asylums. Crucial to this debate in the 1950s were the descriptions of institutionalization (Barton, 1959; Goffman, 1961; Martin, 1955). Though the early writings on the woeful effects of large institutions were often phrased in a campaigning manner, right from early on we can begin to see a much more sophisticated view of the malfunctioning of these institutions. Denis Martin described institutionalization in the large and traditional mental hospital:

> . . . the patient has ceased to rebel against, or to question the fitness of his position in a mental hospital; he has made a more or less total surrender to the institution's life . . . he is co-operative. Here "co-operative" usually implies that the patient does as he is told with a minimum of questioning or opposition. This response on the part of the patient is very different from that true co-operation essential to the success of any treatment, in which the patient strives to understand, and work with, the doctor in his efforts to cure. . . . [The] patient, resigned and co-operative . . . too passive to present any problem of management, has in the process of necessity lost much of his individuality and initiative. [Martin, 1955, pp. 1188–1190]

The distortion of the personality of vulnerable people resulted from the processes inherent in the institution itself. The power relations are clear. But the patient has lost not just power, he has lost significant aspects of himself—individuality, initiative, enquiry, and self-determination. He has lost his active self. There is a kind of deliberateness in the way identity is stripped from these patients, who are already vulnerable to "losing their minds". A rather similar description was given by Main in reviewing his experiences, which started in Northfield Hospital:

> . . . only roles of health or illness are on offer; staff to be only healthy, knowledgeable, kind, powerful and active, and patients to be only ill, suffering, ignorant, passive, obedient and grateful. In most hospitals staff are there because they seek to care for others less able than themselves, while the patients hope to find others *more* able than themselves. The helpful and the helpless meet and put pressures on each other to act not only in realistic, but also fantastic collusion. . . . [The] helpful will unconsciously *require* others to be helpless while the helpless will *require* others to be helpful. Staff and patients are thus inevitably to some extent creatures of each other. [Main, 1975, p. 61]

What patients lose of their healthy side accumulates in the identity of the staff. And what the staff lose in terms of their more negative attributes resurfaces as passivity within patients.

What both these observers pinpoint is how personality characteristics are redistributed in the social field. The redistribution occurs between two groups: that of patients vulnerable to losing their personalities and that of staff who need to build themselves up in successful medical and curative careers. We can see that care is benignly intended, but it can swerve off into malignant effects. And this is to do with the way carers relate to those in their charge. To understand institutions and their capacity to be malign—and therefore perhaps their capacity to be curative—we need to direct our attention to the kind of personality swapping that occurs in the relationships between the two main groups. Moreover, we need to study the aspects of the personalities of one group of individuals that have been transferred, in the course of this odd way of relating, into the other group, and vice versa.

Early work, which I have quoted, targets the characteristic of helpfulness and its matching partner, helplessness. One opinion was that the *whole* of the problem was caused by the malignant institution (Cooper, 1967), but now it is generally accepted that chronic institutionalization is an interaction between (1) particularly vulnerable people, within (2) a particular kind of institution. These institutions—"total institutions", as Goffman (1961) dubbed them—will affect most people, however healthy they are, to some extent. A similar effect of prisons on prisoners may contribute to the phenomenon of recidivism. It would appear that the chronically depleted personalities in the mental hospital could result from progressive splitting and depletion of the individuals, with an institutional response that takes over the functions of those parts of the mind that have been split off—responsibility, caring, thought, awareness, and so on.

In other words the splitting and projection to be found in the category of patients whose illness becomes chronic occurs in some more retrievable way with those patients who recover. For the latter, the process of splitting and projection is not so pernicious, and to protect them, treatment programmes now assume that everyone will recover unless proved otherwise (exactly the reverse of the Victorian attitude). In fact, a great many more people do go out and lead lives that are to a greater or lesser extent "normal", and they will have been protected from being sucked chronically into the institution.

For patients who are seeking to split their minds, mental institutions provide a very useful opportunity. The interactions pithily described by Main (1975), in which the helpful and the helpless inevitably become "creatures of each other", are pernicious in the case of certain individuals willing to cooperate in this splitting. Certain staff members may also need this compliance with the psychological relocation of aspects of their own personalities and those of others.

However, because this division within and between people does not disable everyone, certain kinds of interaction between individual and institution must be less damaging to the person. Main is of the view that institutions have to be carefully reappraised for their therapeutic intentions. In particular, he recommends revising the view that benevolence is solely the relief of suffering.

Thus, the paternalism of the institution has various outcomes, and the test of the institution itself is its capacity to help or hinder recovery. This variance can be gauged according to the principle of integration. The crucial criterion is the possibility of re-integration. Thus we can assert:

- The therapeutic institution:

  A paternalistic institution is more ethical in so far as it allows for the potential re-integration of the patient; and less ethical in so far as it works against the eventual possible re-integration.

The ethical judgement resides in the acts of the institution when faced with a patient who is splitting. Caring institutions, therefore, need to do whatever is possible to minimize the potential of the patient's splitting, but clearly they can only provide a certain amount of protection for the patient against himself. Paternalism is permissible in this sense—with the qualification that the institution should make the sensitive judgement about the eventual re-integration of the personalities of all members. This is the critical issue—not whether large institutions should or should not exist.[6]

Thus paternalistic decisions by individuals or by institutions are informed by the notion of integration, in a way that autonomy cannot.

With this, the treatment of professional ethics is complete. In the final part we return to two issues that have been crucial to the arguments in this book: the nature of personal identity and a view of society and social organizations that is commensurate with the psychoanalytic observations on persons and their integrity.

---

[6] We cannot go into the specific features that make an institution more therapeutic or less depleting, but there is a vast literature on the subject. A useful start can be made with Rapaport (1960), Kennard (1983), Trist and Murray (1990), and Obholzer and Roberts (1994).

PART FOUR

PERSONS AND SOCIETY

CHAPTER SIXTEEN

Identities

Psychoanalytic observations show discontinuities of identity within persons and continuities between them. The idea that personal identity is dependent on the interpersonal world in a way that is to a greater or lesser extent permanent is a familiar one within sociological research, at least since Goffman (1961) and Berger and Luckman (1966). This school, based on the social construction of reality, used the notion of social role and its construction by social institutions; Harré (1983) has attempted to set out the philosophical underpinnings of this approach.

Psychoanalytic work goes beyond merely social roles. It is consistent with Vygotsky (1962, 1978; see also Wertsch, 1985) and also Harré (1983) and establishes that the outer *interpersonal* network of relationships between persons is a constitutive factor in the inward sense of individual personal identity.

The role of psychoanalysis has been important, but ambiguous, in the way that the conception of self and the person has developed over the course of history.[1] Amélie Rorty places the notion

[1] Taylor's (1989) important account of the historical evolution of the notion of the "individual" is authoritative.

of the individual as emerging from historical conditions:

> . . . let us sketch the historical conditions that gave rise to the view of the person as the "I" of reflective consciousness, owner and disowner of experiences, memories, attributes, attitudes. The philosophic conditions: the movement from Descartes' reflective "I" to Locke's substantive center of conscious experience, to Hume's theater of the sequence of impressions and ideas, to Kant's transcendental unity of apperception and the metaphysical postulate of a simple soul, to Sartre's and Heidegger's analysis of consciousness as the quest for its own definition in the face of its non-Being. [Rorty, 1976, p. 11]

The hermeneutic and semiotic influences breaking up the culture of modernism into the culture of post-modernism dissolve the traditional concept of the individual. The kaleidoscope of meanings-within-meanings has an important root in the interpretative method of psychoanalytic thinking. And yet psychoanalysis reinforces the celebration of the individual by virtue of its focus on the single person in treatment. The influence of psychoanalysis in favour of one or other of these trends seems to be multi-valent; it does not take sides.

Psychoanalysis suggests strongly that there are odd occurrences in which identity loses its unity. The person who is not stably self-identified with a single structure of drives and intentions can therefore fail to maintain his own coherence and unity. Identity ceases to be an atomic singularity. Thus, we have addressed this counter-intuitive situation in which personal experience entails feeling less of a person.

The psychoanalytic phenomena described in this book suggest that the basic experience of having a mind and sustaining its constituents is difficult, and the person remains vulnerable throughout life to mental processes such as splitting and projections. As Meltzer (1981) put it:

> These two mechanisms [splitting and projection] imply that the mind is not unified, that it can split itself, and that it can divide itself into component parts which can relate to one another and to the outside world. In that sense it

> appears we can live many separate lives at once. [Meltzer, 1981, p. 179]

These observations summarize the dynamic indicating that the traditional unitary notion of personal identity is too static. Personal identity is deeply moulded and distorted in the interpersonal arena. Wollheim,[2] who has attempted to ground Kleinian thought in philosophic terms and questions, describes this as a "depersonalization". The person loses some or all sense of personhood:

> To grasp the full predicament in which depersonalisation results, it is necessary not only to recognise the two principal thoughts under which the person's phantasies compel him to perceive the world. . . . That others know him better than he knows himself is bad: that others know him in the same way as he knows himself is bad. But combine the two thoughts. . . . Instead of losing parts of his psychology, he has only lost awareness of them: and this awareness he has lost to others, who now possess it, and who thereby gain unlimited power over him. He is Caliban to their Prospero. [Wollheim, 1984, p. 275]

The primitive mechanisms I have described do point to the way constituent parts of the mind, or person, can "go missing": the capacity for feeling (Melanie Klein's patient) or insight (Patient C—Chapter 9), a person's cognition (the shredded mind of Patient J—Chapter 6), a character trait (Patient F—Chapter 6), and the moral conscience (in a crowd). This is not a complete catalogue. Many other parts of the mind can disappear from a person through splitting and can be re-found in another person as a result of the action of projection and introjection. These processes are not confined to seriously ill patients. My psychoanalytic patients were for the most part all quite successfully functioning citizens.

---

[2] Wollheim's *The Thread of Life* (1984) is an attempt to create a correspondence between ontological and epistemological issues of the person on the one hand and the discoveries of psychoanalysis, particularly the Kleinian school, on the other.

Philosophical debates

Earlier we touched on the contemporary philosophical discussion about divided minds. Braude (1996) crystallized a problem for moral philosophy arising from multiple personality. Who takes responsibility for the actions of one of the personalities? Consider, in a court of law:

> What sort of individual is standing trial? An alter or the multiple as a whole? Should courts accept the claim that the subject being questioned on the stand is not the same as the subject who committed the crime? If so, other questions come immediately to mind. For example, would it be appropriate for each alter of a criminal defendant to have separate legal council? [Braude, 1996, p. 37]

Common-sense practice would tend to deal with the problem on the basis that the identity of the person on trial resides in the living body standing in the dock.

Leaving aside the question of how valid the diagnosis of multiple personality disorder may be, these questions might also apply to the phenomena to which we have been attending. If multiple personalities are believed to be several minds residing in one body, then something of the same issue applies to splitting, except that in this case one mind exists in several bodies. The approach that has seemed natural here is to deal with personal identity as residing within mental experience, within the grid of the "self", rather than located in the spatial confines of the bodies.

This touches upon the question of whether identity resides in the mind or in the body (Williams, 1970, 1973). Despite Williams's enthusiasm for such a clear separation, most would agree that the sense of self emerges in interaction at the point of intersection between an immaterial mind and a spatio-temporally located body (Hampshire, 1959).[3]

---

[3] Harré (1983) has added to this grid a "location" in the social world, defined by conversation, to create an extended geometry of personal identity which, he claims, can be treated as Newtonian. His treatment of identity is to bring it close to the natural science method, a project also approached by Searle (1995) in a similar way—through locating culture close to the causality structures of biology.

Bernard Williams (1960) investigated the example of a man—whom we may call Charles—who acquires all the memories of Guy Fawkes in place of his own memories. The question then is: Who is he? Whether he is Guy Fawkes, or Charles is less interesting than the notion of personal identity that is implicit in Williams's arguments. This is the more fundamental, since we do know of situations in which someone, perhaps called Charles, is imbued with *some* thoughts of someone else—that is, the victim of torture and brainwashing. Charles, we would say, is not now his torturer, but he is not himself either. Dr Jekyll had spells when he was not himself, he was Mr Hyde. Where, we might ask, was Mr Hyde when he was Dr Jekyll? The answer, in some sense, is that he was in hiding. But these questions are not very interesting. It is not the content of the person or personality that is crucial. We all have a change of character at times—when on holiday, before an examination, during a period, after a bad dream, with the comfort of a double whiskey, and so on.

These questions arose from the need to explain philosophically the phenomenon of irrationality, but we came upon the issue in a different context, that of professional ethics and informed consenting rather than from the philosophy of mind. However, the philosophical concern is whether these psychoanalytic results cause problems for the validity of psychoanalysis itself—that is, whether these findings could be accepted, despite not conforming to the philosophical understanding of the nature of mind. Are there real metaphysical implications? Is this merely a psychological quirk, so that ethical practices could just make psychological provision to get around the problem?

My claim is that a real division in a mind can be observed in the phenomena of a psychoanalysis, so that it does represent a challenge that philosophy needs to address.

Well-founded common-sense psychology takes the unity of mind and person as an *a priori* assumption. The phenomena cannot be covered by the ordinary concept of repression (or dissociation), which could be compatible with current philosophical views. Thus if these are valid phenomena, then the common-sense metaphysical assumptions and claims about the unity of the mind and of the person have to change. Before a new metaphysics is resorted to, some approaches advanced by Braude (1995b) and Gardner

(1995b) towards dealing with "Kleinian" splitting can be considered.[4] In arguing against splitting being an entity that is distinct from repression, they counter-claim that these psychoanalytic observations fall into the following categories:

1. that the psychoanalytic observations can be explained in terms of more ordinary psychological (psychoanalytical) phenomena—in particular, in terms of self-representations, or of dissociation;
2. that splitting implies parapsychological phenomena that fall outside valid philosophical debate.

Representation

Gardner (1995b), writing from a thorough knowledge of Kleinian psychoanalysis, has argued that the phenomena are reducible to a set of psychological interactions of quite ordinary plausibility:

> X's mental state S is relocated in Y = : (i) Y has entered state S and X has ceased to be in state S; (ii) if Y had not entered state S, X would have remained in state S; (iii) Y is in state S as a result of Y's unconscious sensitivity to X's phantasy of state S being removed from themselves to Y; (iv) X has ceased to be in state S as a result of X's unconscious sensitivity to the fact that Y has entered state S. [Gardner, 1995b, p. 211]

This describes the relocation of parts of the mind as merely *represented* in phantasy by one of the pair, whilst the other is sensitivity to the phantasies of the first. In the paradigm quoted, this occurs on both sides. If, therefore, this is a matter of how people will represent themselves and each other in their own phantasies, then this does not breach common-sense psychology and its metaphysical underpinning.

---

[4] It is of interest that the two philosophers who have examined the Kleinian school of psychoanalysis most closely—Wollheim (1984) and Gardner (1993)—have omitted to give consideration to the radical nature of splitting, which Melanie Klein and her followers have emphasized so strongly. It suggests that Kleinian splitting provokes philosophical unease.

This is an *a priori* argument, which, I have claimed, must be superseded by the empirical findings reported.

Braude (1995b), from the point of view of a different psychological framework, mounted a similar argument, suggesting that parts of the person dissociated from each other (separate "alters") do represent each other: "dissociated systems interfere with each other" (Braude, 1995a, p. 105). Dissociation thus falls within the psychoanalytic phenomenon of repression. In multiple personality disorders, the various "selves" are dissociated from each other. This means that at some level outside the awareness of the person(s)—that is, unconsciously—there is access between the "selves" (Thigpen & Cleckley, 1957). The apparent independence is, in this case, at the conscious level, whilst unconsciously the selves relate, with one (or each) representing others. Braude argues that the primitive phenomena revealed in psychoanalysis are variants of dissociation and therefore cannot qualify as evidence for the divided mind. This is an empirical claim that simply contrasts with mine—and can only be decided by empirical testing of the evidence. I have given my clinical evidence in considerable detail for this purpose. I conclude that Braude incorrectly understands splitting, conflates it wrongly with dissociation, and ignores the loss of self-reflection.

Parapsychology

Gardner has counter-claimed that my claims for splitting imply a claim for parapsychology. His understanding of splitting and projection amounts to "a metaphysical impossibility on a par with telepathy or telekinetic transference of thoughts" (Gardner, 1995b, p. 211); and, in the instance of someone waking up with someone else's memories:

> ... to suppose that projective identification is of the same order as such an exchange of memory is to rank it again alongside parapsychological phenomena, i.e. to place it outside the orbit of commonsense metaphysical possibility. [Gardner, 1995b, p. 211]

He goes back to representation and his limited agreement with

> . . . projection, in the sense that subjects really do *represent* the world as having qualities derived from their own minds—but not in the sense that subjects really do modify the outer world merely through their mental activity. [Gardner, 1995, p. 212]

In this view, the "outer world" is a fixed entity, based, it would seem, on the model of the physical world of inanimate objects—and not, therefore, the external world of other minds. Gardner's assertion does not hold if the "outer world" is composed of animate entities (the minds of other persons).

Metaphysical consistency

The metaphysical status of these psychoanalytic observations is inevitably open to debate, and it is important that such a debate should take place. My assertion is that it cannot be so clearly closed by collapsing splitting back into a form of representation that is repressed. This has been exhaustively discussed in Chapter 8 and will not be rehearsed again here.

If there are unwelcome philosophical consequences to my empirical claims, this may be unfortunate (or exciting), but it cannot be shirked.

If ordinary common-sense psychology is to be claimed as the benchmark of what is allowed philosophically (Gardner, 1995a), it is ironic that Freud's original hypothesis (demonstrations) of the unconscious as an active determining force in personal life created seismic changes in that ordinary psychology (Morton, 1982). Those changes and their inevitable metaphysical consequences have, as it were, now passed as water under the bridge. It is not, therefore, inconceivable that developments in psychoanalysis since Freud's early days might throw up further awkward facts, which, in the course of time, can come to be graced with the ascription "common-sense" psychology.

My claim seems to be warranted that we should at least consider the possibility of what metaphysical adjustments are necessary and what it would mean for the philosophy of mind and for ethics to have to contend with the sort of relocation of identity with which contemporary psychoanalysis presents us.

What is identity?

The identity of a physical object is its continuity in space/time. But there are problems with non-physical objects—notably, cultural objects. Gardner (1995b) cites a novel. It may be the same novel, but you and I may have a copy each. Though the condition for identity is typographical in this case, it cannot apply to all cultural products. Different editions of the same book have a conditional identity. I suppose reproduction of a musical score could be typographical, but concert performances cannot. Repeated theatrical performances are ambiguous—Olivier's Richard III is both separate in terms of the performances and the productions, but also an identifiable entity in its own right. One of the problems about cultural productions is that they *are* reproducible. Typically, this is the distinction between physical objects and information. The latter is reproducible without loss of identity—a photocopy is not the same physical piece of paper, but what is reproduced is exactly the same information.

When it comes to mental entities, are they more in line with physical objects or with information/cultural products? Freud's original project was to explore their physical properties (Freud, 1895d). It was a project that, he felt, had failed. And we on the whole agree that he failed to present psychological "laws" to match physical ones. However, it is not so simple as to say that mental phenomena are, therefore, in line with cultural products and are reproducible outside any "law of conservation".

When we converse with others, we do, indeed, reproduce our thoughts. If I teach my daughter Pythagoras's theorem, she then "knows" it too. There is something about exchanging information that is similar to photocopying. My knowledge has been reproduced as her knowledge, as well. However, it is not quite the same to say that Pythagoras's theorem had become *her* theorem once she had learned it. Her knowledge is of *his* theorem.

There is something we accept about the originator of a thought that, even though it is now our thought, it still has the originator's stamp on it. Some thoughts carry this kind of implicit copyright.

When we come to affects, do we in the same way reproduce our affective states in others? This sounds stranger. In the first place, it is more difficult to imagine a "photocopy" of an emotion. But there is also something that seems more personal about an emotional state. If someone is sympathetic to what I am saying it does not necessarily mean that someone else will feel the emotions in the same way. If I converse about the death of my father and someone else "feels" my pain, it will be on the basis of his imaginative empathy or his own previous loss. Despite this empathic I-know-how-you-feel quality of response, if the conversation is any good, it will involve the other person communicating something of his own experience to compare with mine. There is a reproducibility without an absolute identicality. A separateness creeps in, which does not entirely dismantle similarity but distinguishes who is having the feeling. I reproduce the other's state of mind in my own, but with my own characteristics. This is the difference between the reproduction of a cultural product and the communication of a mental entity. As Gardner states:

> . . . the mental contents of two persons are shared by virtue of a relation of similarity—fundamentally similarity of content—and not by virtue of the interpersonal identity of a mental item. Shared mental phenomena are *qualitatively* identical, but not *numerically* identical. [Gardner, 1995b, p. 210]

Now, the problem, is this: in listening ordinarily to someone else, I am not simply becoming the equivalent of a photocopy of them, but under some circumstances, when primitive processes operate, this does seem to happen. My mental state recreates theirs, without that separation of different personal characteristics. There is a loss of a sense of what belongs to whom. I want to explore this self-ascription that comes to be stamped upon mental contents, and I will do so in terms of ownership and belonging.

CHAPTER SEVENTEEN

Objects and ownership

Montaigne said, "The greatest thing in the world is to know how to belong to ourselves". Mental entities—or "parts of the mind" in psychoanalytic terminology—are not concrete, as are material belongings. However, Parfit (1984) conducted thought experiments as if parts of the mind could be made to behave like material bits and pieces. In imagination he conducted non-surgical excision and exchange of parts of the person. Fantastical though this is, it does bear a resemblance to actual reality encountered between people. When I took over the fears and the awareness of Patient J (Chapter 6), in the clinical illustration of introjection, rendering her bland and indifferent, it was as if mental entities operated in a spatially extended dimension. It was not that she shared her feelings in an ordinary sense, but more as if she had lent me her spectacles or donated her kidney. It was as if we did, in fact, juggle with mental entities as with material ones. And yet it was not quite so, since she no longer had any inkling that the entity was or had been hers.

This was not a matter of an exchange of roles. My subjective experience at the time was of an unsettling sense of uncertainty about who was who. I was not simply changing from one role to another, voluntarily or otherwise. The mental entities—Patient J's hostility, fear, and awareness—were a proper feature of her identity at one moment, and a part of someone else's (mine) at another. Thus, if identity were based simply on the static ownership of mental parts, this becomes very problematic in the light of this fluidity.

Mental belongings

Part of the problem is that our presuppositions restrict the language we use and, in turn, the range of thoughts we can normally have about identity. In ordinary language, I might talk of her anxiety and of *my* feeling it. But is it hers or mine? Psychoanalytic investigation demands a more precise language.

The language that might be developed for this purpose is the language of ownership and belonging. It does two kinds of jobs that we would require of a language of identity. In the first place, possessive pronouns—as in "my" hopes or "my" arm—do this specific work of indicating identity through belonging. There is no ambiguity about where or what that identity is. The language of belonging conveys one important feature of identity. In ordinary experience, identity relates a person to his physical presence, all of it physically bounded, and to his possessions. Identity refers immaterial "parts of the mind" to that space/time location and is thus the one feature of mental life that gives spatial qualities and locations to immaterial entities.

The second job of a language of ownership is to allow belongings to move from one person to another. One person's belongings can become another's, and the primitive psychological mechanisms of exchange we have examined are the mechanics of such a trade.

The language of belonging and ownership allows us to define a locus of identity without implying a consistency of content of that locus. Identity ceases to be a structure, as it is in the "normal" view, and under close scrutiny becomes a process that is in some measure intra-psychic. But it is also in some measure interpersonal—in the sense of being an interaction between intra-psychic worlds. In the latter sense, it is irretrievably linked, therefore, to human relationships, to the process of one identity in the context of another.

We know that a child's identity is forged, from the outset, in a process that involves internalizing (introjecting) aspects of the parents and of significant others, forming the superego and many other aspects of what the child eventually comes to think of as itself. He may grow up to vote Liberal Democrat, play football, fish, and so on and so forth, by derivation from his parents—a "chip off the old block". Such a process involves developing a sense of ownership of those aspects of oneself achieved through an internalizing acquisition.

Eagle (1988) has proposed that the crucial distinction in Freud's later structural view of id, ego, and superego is of me/not-me. Personal identity is, in his terms, a process that organizes the contents of mind and eschews what is alien.

> . . . in examining the implications of psychoanalysis for a theory of mind we would consider not only, or perhaps not even primarily, the question of unconscious mental processes, but the issue of owned versus disowned, the rendering personal or impersonal of mental contents. [Eagle, 1988, p. 94]

Like those of Frankfurt (1976) and Penelhum (1971), this concept of identity arises from a classical Freudian position that places repression at its centre (i.e. ego-psychology). Eagle (1988) is driven to the view that "repression is held to be the motivated disownership of mental contents" (p. 97), and he is confined to considering the displacements within the self of mental contents only; this particular psychoanalytic stance (ego-psychology) does not employ the concepts of splitting or projection in the way that they have been described in this book. Thus, the splitting-off of mental functions (as well as mental contents) and their location in other people does not form part of his psychoanalytic view. Despite these added restrictions imposed by Eagle's view, he nevertheless comes to the conclusion that

> The unity of consciousness and of self is, then, neither a necessary fact nor a given, but a developmental integrative *achievement*". [Eagle, 1988, p. 104]

This conveys an awareness of the dis-integration of personal identity, not just the dispersal of contents, and thus from whatever school of psychoanalysis, there is a need to recognize the potential for division, and incoherence, of identity.

Tulving (1983) made a psychological distinction between "episodic" and "semantic" memories—episodic ones are marked by a belonging to the autobiography of the rememberer, whilst semantic memories are generalized facts, ideas, and so on that have a non-personal existence. For instance, a patient suffering from amnesia will forget all personal details of who he is and what he is doing but retain memories of how to walk, speak his language, use a knife and fork, and so forth. There is thus a stamped-on attribute to certain memories and functions that serves as a label of ownership. Braude (1995a) endorsed a comparable distinction in ownership between autobiographical and indexical senses of "I". A repressed experience, in Braude's terms, is *indexically* one's own, because it is known about as a matter of reflective belief—a belief that one has had that experience: Patient J (Chapter 6) had a quarrel with me, her analyst, the day before, though it could not be recalled to consciousness. It can only be indexed to "J". *Autobiographically* owned experiences are different. They are directly available to thought and consciously owned—for example, Patient J's scene where she wanted to pick up a frightened, crying baby to give it comfort was a heart-felt experience she had and knew was hers. These descriptions—autobiographical and indexical—derive from two different vantage points: autobiographical from the point of view of the subject, his "locus", and indexical from the position of some outside position in which experiences can be assigned without reference to the conscious experience of the subject.

We can extend this to entities that the subject feels are within him, that are within his "locus", but they do not feel as if they belong; they are "unassimilated". When someone comes into my house, I may refer to her as *my* wife, with all those connotations and evaluations that loving and creating as well as grating implies; the "my" indicates a deep sense and complex of belonging and belonging-to. If the person is an intruder, however, I would be less likely to refer to him as, say, *my* burglar. The fear, the violation, and the outrage constitute a very different experience and evaluation, which makes a clear boundary around the sense of ownership.

Similarly, alien objects can seem to be within the person but not to belong, and they remain in an unassimilated existence inside the person. Freud summarized this condition as important in the very founding moments of identity itself: "the judgement is: 'I should like to eat this', or 'I should like to spit it out'" (Freud, 1925h, p. 237). Heimann (1942) described a vivid case of a painter who felt she was inhabited by alien objects, whom she called "devils". The patient felt these devils to be intruders, and they were not experienced as a part of her own identity: "They roamed around inside her, caused her physical pain and illnesses, inhibited her in all her activities, especially painting, and compelled her to do things she did not want to do" (Heimann, 1942, p. 29). These parts of herself were not "assimilated". In this case, the boundary of the patient's identity had reverted to the fragile and uncertain condition characteristic of the originating moment to which Freud referred.

Similar experiences of ownership and of intrusion occur within mental life and between personal boundaries. The distinction of autobiographical from indexical is helpful, Braude claimed, in talking of dissociative states like hypnosis and multiple personality disorder. Could it be applied to the phenomena of psychoanalysis too? In fact, it does not really capture the phenomena described. Patient J (Chapter 6) became bland by losing, both consciously and unconsciously, her fears about becoming hostile. Instead, in her view, that capacity for hostility and fear of it was borne temporarily by the psychoanalyst. In Braude's terms, it was *autobiographically* the analyst's experience: I, the analyst, had the experiences of hostility and responsibility. However, *indexically* it was both Miss J's, in one sense (she could accept the fact of the hostility of the day before, but she could not have the feeling) and not hers in another sense (it was the experience of the analyst, myself).

Ownership of mental entities can carry this ambiguity, in which the psychoanalyst can speak quite naturally of it being his patient's experience, even though he is having it himself. The locations of the origins of the experience and of having-it are different. The "same" experience has quite different loci of belonging for analyst and analysand and creates the boundaries of their identity accordingly. This is not to say that, in practice, the psychoanalyst can easily assess the belongingness of what he experiences—in terms of what has been projected *into him* and what has arisen *as him*. On some occasions it may be straightforward, as he feels invaded by something he feels is quite definitely not he. For instance, a mood of heavy uselessness would often overtake me when listening to Patient F, at times when I knew things were in general going quite well for me personally. Of course, there were times when things were not going so well, and then my own experiences and those with Mr F were more difficult to distinguish. At these latter times, the uselessness with which he could at a moment's notice leave me would then "mate" with something in me (Brenman-Pick, 1985). In the latter case, something with two separate belongings came together *within* the analyst, rather than between analyst and analysand—for instance, when I took over Patient J's awareness of, and interest in, her feelings.

Of course, even the straightforward sense of feeling something alien having invaded oneself is not as straightforward as it looks, as the human mind (according to psychoanalysis) has a capacity to disown its own experiences—as in the case of, for instance, Heimann's (1942) artist patient, who was inhabited by devils. And in principle the analyst, having an ordinary human mind, is, indeed, capable of such disowning as well. We have seen this in the examples discussed. Mace (1997) has complained that these require the analyst to claim a position of total integration—or, at least, superior integration—with respect to his patient, and that this is explicit in the principle of integrity in its supplementary form, as stated in Chapter 15 (p. 167). This is, indeed, a possible claim, as Main's observations of the sharp poles of helpfulness and helplessness illustrate. But it misses my point. I do not claim such a therapeutic arrogance for the psychoanalyst. Lapses actually occur in analytic practice, when they are just that—lapses.

Whilst it is ideal that the analyst is himself in a state of robust integration, this cannot be realized. When it comes to investigating the unconscious there is inevitably a degree of the blind leading the blind! What is special about psychoanalysis is that the setting is constructed such that one partner has *some* greater purchase on what is happening. The feature of the setting is the "rule of abstinence", so that the analyst may know that something odd is happening whenever he manages to recognize that he has stepped out of that rule. Of course, there is the temptation, behind the analyst's couch, to assume the omnipotence of the expert professional, and we have discussed this (p. 164). However, the setting is emphatically not one of an expert who knows and a sufferer who pleads.

Freud's early campaign against suggestive therapies was exactly the argument that psychoanalysis must be an investigation of what neither partner knows—although the patient, in his unconscious, knows very well (Hinshelwood, 1991). Bion's (1970) emphasis on Keats's concept of "Negative Capability" (in contrast to the "irritable reaching after fact and reason") and the picturesque image of shining a beam of darkness are attempts to evoke the state of waiting upon inspiration with which the analyst tries to accompany the patient in his own free association—a state he also called "reverie", as if receptive to the patient's belongings being transplanted into him. There is, as Mace (1997) puts it, a "fixed asymmetry" in the positions of analyst and patient, but the asymmetry is not the one that he describes: it is that one partner is *relatively* protected from too much confusion in his mind, while the other is enabled to descend into his own confusion.

Identity, in this sense, is derived from the negotiations, deeply embedded in human relationships, over the ownership of parts of the mind and the experiences of them. The sense of identity is thus a meeting between a "locus" and a property that we call "belonging". That sense can then be filled out with contents that in one sense belong to that identity but can, in another sense, be swapped with another locus of belonging. In this view, contrary to Braude's descriptions, both indexical and autobiographical identity are transitory; they can come and go and come again.

Thus, we have to extend this classification by describing the belonging of the "contents" of identity from at least three different positions: those of the patient, of the analyst, and of an outside position. And this increases the number of different categories of belonging from two to three: those entities that belong to the subject; those that belong to the subject but once belonged to the object; and those that belong to the object but were once the subject's.

If the crucial element of identity is a sense of belonging, then identity is formed by the process of stamping on that the label of attribution. This central "core" of identity might be seen not so much as substance (content) or as a process, but as an ascription of belongingness—after Hume, in a sense (Strawson, 1959). It gives to the self a contentless quality. It is not a thing or a set of things or a sequence of things (Anscombe, 1975)—it is something like a hallmark on a piece of jewellery.

This might be called self-reflection, were it not that such a term already implies the sense of self upon which the illumination of reflection plays. Harré (1979) attacks this problem—the nature of the "self"—through considering the difference between an actor playing a part in a play—or, for that matter, playing a social role—and the person in that part. He can look upon himself in two senses: as the part he plays and as himself playing that part (and this links with indexical and autobiographical identities promoted by Braude, 1995a). A crucial additional element—the sense of self—adheres in the second of these conditions, looking upon himself playing the part. C. J. F. Williams (1989) explored the conditions for this added component, which distinguishes "himself playing the part". There is an added factor beyond empirical observation (Swinburne, 1973–1974).

In the terms of the present argument the subjective encounter with self is given by self-reflection, and this is the key human property that is generated by the coming together of parts of the person. When they are "owned", the contents of the mind become subjected to self-reflection, which is thereby enlarged in its scope. When disowned, self-reflection shrinks.

CHAPTER EIGHTEEN

Freedom and coherence

Identity might, therefore, be best defined as a "locus of belonging", in that locus within which mental entities—faculties, experiences, awareness, and so on—can be gathered as sets of possessions (or, in some instances, as unassimilated intrusions) and be eliminated through the processes of splitting and projection. I have described clinical material to demonstrate that this definition is one that is actually in general use at a particular level in the human mind, a level at which the sense of identity itself is founded. This level of thinking is largely closed over by more mature development of sophisticated conceptual and symbolic language, but nevertheless it does still push through in the way we might use the possessive pronouns, "my", "his", "yours", and so forth about our own characteristics. It also obtrudes in the experiences of patients in a psychoanalysis and, indeed, significantly in everyday life, where it resides without an adequate language (in our culture) for a proper symbolic representation and expression of it.

Autonomy and identity

With this new grounding of the notion of identity we can pursue the discussion of questions about autonomy and integration.

In earlier chapters the capacity to think clearly and to decide effectively came to be considered to depend on having as much of one's mental possessions available as possible. The primitive processes severely limit this freedom of thought, because they remove from availability certain experiences, memories, and faculties; or at other times intrude extraneous experiences, faculties, and so on, as if the subject owned them.

A number of psychoanalysts have addressed the limits to freedom of thought that arise from problems from within the person (Kennedy, 1993; Segal, 1977) or from cultural influences (Main, 1967). The consensus is that the capacity for freedom of thought and action depends in large measure on reducing the interference to enquiring of oneself—to roam, in effect, among one's mental belongings. Such a freedom entails two preconditions: (1) a fairly open attitude to the ownership of one's own experiences, as unhampered as possible by repression or, particularly, splitting—the "freedom to relate", in Kennedy's terms, to one's own mental belongings; (2) an attitude of enquiring and knowledge-seeking about those entities. This is the capacity for self-reflection and the organ of cohesion—the "K"-link. It is the process of ascribing belonging and sustaining ownership.

These are preconditions for what we would call mental health, or, in this argument, the conditions for integration and the freedom to make choices—in other words, for autonomy.

Pluralism and individuality

Integration implies a plurality of parts available to be known and to be arranged as alternatives to choose between and to be recruited as resources for thought, judgement, and creativity. Integration is a kind of internal pluralism.

The term "pluralism" normally describes a feature of the external social environment. In a successful society, different entities operate flexibly together. It requires their differences to become related and to collaborate. It does not mean the unrelated independence of different things—that would be fragmentation. An unremitting sameness is not a necessary condition for relating and collaboration. Pluralism in society depends on the individuals integrating in a fluid and flexible way, and this can be exactly mirrored in the interior of the person:

> It would seem that optimal integration is as much the goal of world organisation as it is of mental organization. The fundamental principles governing nations and of bringing up children may indeed be identical. [Brierley, 1947, p. 82]

Socially working together is a paradigm for the internal working together of different parts of the mind.[1] Indeed, it is more than an analogy, since the internal and external conditions partly reflect each other. Jaques (1955), in a laconic summary, stated:

> Individuals may put their internal conflicts into persons in the external world, unconsciously follow the course of the conflict by means of projective identification, and re-internalize the course and outcome of the externally perceived conflict. [Jaques, 1955, p. 497]

This to-and-fro process at the social level corresponds to the processes of projection and introjection between patient and analyst in the micro-social setting of the psychoanalytic consulting room. In everyday life, part of the therapeutic knowing is to witness these kinds of conflict being brought together and worked through, without denial of differences; we can say that there is a comparable arrangement in the psychoanalytic setting, where the conflicts between patient and analyst are brought together more flexibly. There the separation of internal from external is deliberately reduced, and working over the splits and differences between analyst and patient is much nearer to the working out of separate and different parts within the patient's own mind.

It is ironic that at the same time that psychoanalysis contributed to the undermining of traditional notions of identity, it also

---

[1] The relation between the plurality of internal parts and external political plurality is discussed extensively from a Jungian point of view by Samuels (1989).

stressed the importance of the discrete individual person. In Wollheim's (1984) account, it is the continuity of the "thread of life" that constitutes being a person. Such an individualized narrative has a long and creative history, and each one of us attempts a continuing act of imagination in sustaining a story of our lives—a storehouse, as it were, of our possessions. We act in accord with the concept of a core self, actualized in a creative history of a self-unfolding life. We demand of ourselves a personal and individual narrative.

The creation anew of a life narrative in each one of us takes on a literary form in the novel, which depends on the unitary concept of the individual. The novel has, in turn, been a powerful pillar of support in sustaining that notion. We accept and aspire to independent, self-creating status as individuals, not only because of the pressures from our cultural, literary, or similar background, but because from inside, too, our psychology may seek such an imagined closure. Unconscious and emotional undercurrents steal our individuality from us, and it just feels better to bolster a contrary sense of oneself as a consistent, discrete, and independent individual. Perhaps we shed, and culturally defend against, feeling divided, spread out on the social domain, a locus with inconstant character.[2] Our perceived discreteness and independence is wishful (Lasch, 1978), and, in the nature of the human world, wishes can easily come to constitute reality.

Psychoanalysis can, therefore, support unwittingly that wishful illusion of an indivisible coherence. It does so by contributing a wide variety of plausible narratives that can be taken down from the shelf for tailoring to individual idiosyncrasies. To this extent, psychoanalysis may work against itself. Enhancing integration is not necessarily achieved through recourse to a coherent narrative, which could, without care, be more a denial of the fluidity of the real experience of the self.

Identity comprises, then, various qualities: (1) a presence in time and space (associated with the physical presence of the

---

[2] The wishful longing for a bounded self is reflected pointedly in certain psychoanalytic ideas—those of self-psychology, or in Bick's idea of the containing skin (Bick, 1968, 1986).

body); (2) variable clusters of contents and personality characteristics; (3) a process of ascribing a locus of belonging; and (4) striving for an elusive and illusory completeness, coherence, and permanence.

If we want to pursue the possibilities that arise from eroding the concept of the discrete person, we are compelled to move on to the world of social relationships. This has a truly reciprocal relation to the individual person. The intra-psychic world of the individual exists within an interpersonal context of other intra-psychic worlds, which dismantle and re-constitute the individual person (Hinshelwood, 1989b). The worlds of social relationships and of the individual are mutually constitutive, and the primitive mechanisms are formative processes through which the different worlds mould each other.

In Chapter 19 we turn to some of the processes on the social side of this equation.

CHAPTER NINETEEN

Coercion: induced splitting

The productive application of psychoanalytic discoveries to society in general has often been attempted. Freud (1921c) adopted the term "contagion", a term derived from LeBon (1895), who had described the interpersonal spreading of something psychological through a crowd. Freud regarded this as based on a form of suggestion, comparable to hypnosis, in which some leading person or idea in the group is identified with. We now know that the process is splitting and projective forms of identification (Jaques, 1955), which correspond to the identity-forming processes that are the essence of transference. Spreading, or contagion, in groups and institutions depends, in part, at least, on the same processes of splitting and projection as occur within the transference.

Not all mental hospitals are good at curbing the patient's self-destructive potential. Instead of exerting a moderating influence on the patient's psychological self-destruction, they may actively induce splitting and projection (see Chapter 15). This is a two-pronged problem: on one side, the individual indulges in psychological self-destruction; on the other, a social process induces his division. Institutions can, in part, induce splitting, and this is evidence in the organized institution of state oppression and torture, which enforces projection and depletion, whatever the victim's contribution to it. In this chapter, I further examine social processes that induce splitting in individuals.

Experimental social coercion[1]

External influences that rob the person of vital mental faculties have been found by experimental social psychologists (Asch, 1952; Mayo, 1933; Milgram, 1964; Sherif, 1936). I shall mention two famous studies that transparently indicate powerful forces acting on individuals and their psychological faculties. These studies were conducted in laboratory conditions. Under social pressure, a group induced an individual to give up his capacity to make ordinary visual judgements. In another experiment, the individual was relieved of his capacity to make a moral judgement about the way to treat other persons.

Some time in the early 1950s, the following laboratory experiment was conducted with some 31 groups. I will quote from the report:

> A group of 7 to 9 individuals are gathered. The experimenter explains that they will be shown lines differing in length and that their task will be to match lines of equal length. The experimenter places on the blackboard in front of the room two white cards on which are pasted vertical black lines. On the card at the left is a single line, the standard. The card at the right has three lines of differing length, one of which is equal to the standard line at the left. The task is to select from among the three lines the one equal in length to the standard line.
>
> . . . In giving his judgement each subject calls out, in accordance with the instructions, the number of the comparison line ("one", "two", "three") that he judges to be equal to the standard. The cards are removed and replaced by a new pair of

[1] Much of this section was previously published in Hinshelwood, 1990.

> cards with new standard and comparison lines. [Asch, 1952, pp. 451–452]

Asch arranged for twelve comparisons in all to be made.

> The experiment proceeds normally during the first two trials for each group. The discriminations are simple; each individual monotonously calls out the same judgement. Suddenly this harmony is disturbed at the third trial. While all other subjects call the middle of the three lines, a single member of the group, seated toward the end, claims the first line to be the correct one. As the experiment progresses, from time to time the same individual continues to disagree with the group.
>
> An outsider, observing the experiment, would, after the first few trials, begin to single out this individual as somehow different from the rest of the group and this impression would grow stronger as the experiment proceeded. After the first one or two disagreements, he would note certain changes in the manner and posture of this person. He would see a perplexity and bewilderment come over this subject's face at the contradicting judgements of the entire group. Often he becomes more active. He fidgets in his seat and changes the position of his head to look at the lines from different angles. He may turn round and whisper to his neighbour seriously or smile sheepishly. He may suddenly stand up to look more closely at the card. At other times he may become especially quiet.
>
> What is the reason for this peculiar behaviour? The answer lies in a crucial feature we have not yet mentioned. The subject whose reactions we have been describing is the only member of the group who is reacting to the situation as it has been described. All the others are, without his knowledge, cooperating with the experimenter by giving at certain times unanimously wrong judgements. . . . Actually the group consists of two parts: the instructed subjects whom we shall call the majority, and one naive person who is in a position of a *minority of one,* and whom we will call the *critical subject.* [Asch, 1952, pp. 453–454]

How did the critical subjects of each group respond to the unanimous opposition of the majority? Did they maintain independence and repudiate the wrong trend of the group? Or did they show a tendency to yield to the majority—and if so, to what extent? (Asch, 1952)

In this experiment by Solomon Asch, he found that the subjects *were* significantly influenced by the group opinion. Nearly 60% gradually moved towards conformity with the others, against the evidence of their own eyes.

But it is not only perceptual judgements that may be affected by social pressure from others. Asch's work inspired a whole branch of psychological experimentation, including one notorious study by Milgram (1964), who showed that behaviour, as well as judgement, could be imposed and distorted by simple social pressure. He could induce behaviour that the subject "knew"[2] to be cruel and dangerous to another human being. This experiment also comprised a "naive subject"—called "critical subjects" by Asch—and three stooges, called "confederates". I will quote from Milgram's account:

> Four adults arrive at a campus laboratory to participate in a study of memory and learning. On arrival each subject is paid $4.50. The experimenter explains that a variety of roles must be performed and subjects are to draw printed slips from a hat. Actually three of the adults are confederates [stooges], and one naive subject. The drawing is rigged so that the naive subject is always assigned the role of "Teacher 3", who whenever the "Learner" [another role] gives an incorrect answer, will administer punishment by activating a shock generator; and confederate B is always the "Learner". The experimenter explains that the purpose of the experiment is to study the effects of punishment on memory in a context of "collective teaching". Confederate B (the "Learner") is taken to an adjoining room and in full view of the others is strapped into an electric chair apparatus. The experimenter explains the nature of the learning task and passing over a remark made by the

[2] The word "knew" has been put in quotation marks because there is a real sense in which his capacity to know may have been taken over by other people present in the experimental setting, and the subject lost the capacity for human judgement.

> [confederate in the electric chair] concerning a mild heart condition, takes [the naive subject and the other two confederates] to the main experiment room. They are seated before an imposing shock generator with 30 lever switches labelled 15–450 volts in 15-volt increments. Verbal designations are spread along the line of switches: Slight Shock, Moderate Shock, Strong Shock, Very Strong Shock, Intense Shock, Extreme Intensity Shock, and Danger: Severe Shock. . . .
>
> They are told that the "Learner" must be shocked each time he errs in the learning task. The amount of punishment is decided by themselves. Each will suggest a shock. And the shock actually administered will be the lowest level suggested; and "Teacher 3" [the naive subject] bids third. Thus the naive subject can effectively control the maximum shock administered. On the other hand he may go along with or move in the direction of the group choice [fixed with the confederates to escalate continuously].
>
> The "Learner" indicates no discomfort until the 75-volt shock at which time there is a slight grunt . . . at 150 volts the "Learner" cries out that he wants to be released complaining of a heart disturbance . . . at 180 volts the "Learner" cries out "I can't stand the pain". . . at 300 volts the victim shouts in desperation he will no longer provide answers to the test, and so forth to 450 volts. [Milgram, 1964, pp. 138–139]

Milgram reported that the presence of the two others—the confederates—substantially influenced the level of shock that the naive subject administered. Shock levels rose regularly from trial to trial; 27 of 40 experimental subjects "went beyond the point of the 'Learner's' first truly vehement protest" (p. 139). In a control experiment, with no social pressure, only 2 subjects out of 40 administered shock beyond this point. This impressive demonstration of social coercion into unethical behaviour provokes alarm and requires a great deal of explanation:

1. How does it happen?
2. In what situations does it occur (including therapeutic ones)?
3. How could it be prevented?

A psychoanalytic view of social psychology

These experimental results clearly point to a real problem in group therapy, where group perceptions and behaviour may be moulded by all sorts of unconscious forces, none of them under the control of the individuals. If something as objective as the length of a line is altered by subjective pressures, how valid, then, are less exact, less objective judgements in a group? Our own or other people's personalities and characteristics are so much less tangible, they must be enormously more vulnerable to distortion by group pressures.

These are forces motivated usually by a disregard of reality and often a motive actually to reconstruct reality. The lone therapist can only be a rather slow and weak influence, and in addition we have to allow for the fact that the therapist will equally feel the coercion of the group.

We might wonder, too, about the individual therapy of psychoanalysis. This kind of experimental result seems to lie alongside the popular fear that psychoanalysis is dangerous (see Chapter 15). We have seen, in fact, that psychoanalysts are not immune from distortions to their perceptions and behaviour. They can, at least temporarily, be dispossessed of their own judgements. And the patient, who is vulnerable in any case, can suffer potentially strong influence by the psychoanalyst. This correspondence emphasizes the psychoanalytic setting as a version of a social one—it is a society of the smallest proportions.

Asch and Milgram were able to fix, as if with a stain under the microscope, the social influences that coerce individuals. They may be explained from the psychoanalytic point of view by referring to the primitive mechanisms of splitting and projection. (1) Asch's critical subjects, whose perceptual judgements were confounded by the group, consisted of a selection of average people whose "normality" was challenged. When 60% accepted the unanimous judgement of the group, their capacity for perceptual judgement was diminished or given up. To put it in the terms we have been using, that part of their mind was obliterated and projected into the rest of the group, who became the perceptual judges. Subjects seemed to buy relief from their disturbance, but at the price of being depleted of an essential psychological function. (2) Milgram's naive subjects similarly gave up an essential part of their personalities, which was split off and projected. In this case, this was not their perceptual judgement, but their capacity for making moral judgements. No experiment whatever could have justified giving a person with a heart condition the strong shocks that were given. This responsibility for moral conduct was passed over by the subjects to the two colleagues who were stooging for the experimenter. Again, one would have to say that the subjects were suffering a crucial depletion of their personalities—an obliteration of moral judgement and responsibility and its projections into others.

These experiments shock us because they show how easily people can give up aspects of themselves. Apparently quite normal people are "splittable" in the psychic sense by group pressures. Clearly this is nonpsychoanalytic evidence of influences that are deeply coercive on the mind. It does show that the personalities of quite ordinary people can be dismantled.

The technical methods used in these experiments can measure group influence on individuals. But their results are ethically unnerving.[3] These results also support the disturbing problems we have discovered in the therapeutic sphere. Especially in group therapy, we can imagine pressures that impinge upon vulnerable people. The clinical illustration in Chapter 7 is an example of group roles being imposed. Identities within that group were pressed into stereotyped modes—those of victim, inquisitor, thoughtful bystander, and so on. Ellen and others could *spread* their separate parts through the group.[4] Such unconscious *role-allotting* is the essence of the group activity, and it concerns more

[3] They are also of interest because of their claim to the ethical neutrality of the experiment and the experimenter. A whole tradition of social psychology experiments have been applied technically to the industrial workplace—the continuing legacy of Taylorism, for instance (Doray, 1988). In advertising, ethical neutrality remains assumed and thereby equally unnerving.

[4] Therapeutic work in groups is largely to bring these role stereotypes and coercions to conscious recognition—a therapeutic knowing, comparable to the "K"-link in a psychoanalysis. See my descriptions of the "reflective space" in groups, which has to be kept open for examining these stereotyping occurrences (Hinshelwood, 1994b).

than just social roles. It is the actual subjectivity of self and identity that is dislocated and reformed as social parts. The social psychology experiments confirm how identity becomes dislocated. We can bear this in mind when concerned with how roles are allotted in the mental hospital. And there are many other social settings where similarly scapegoat roles, stereotyping, and prejudice are underpinned by group pressures.

Torture and brainwashing

These general social processes in ordinary groups coerce individuals into deformed and depleted identities, and it must be true that we all do operate in this way at times. Especially when we consider people in the abstract, say, those from another culture, whom we do not know sufficiently in a direct way, we will risk projecting onto them in all sorts of personal and cultural ways (see Chapter 13).

In some societies, as I mentioned earlier, this kind of influence is raised to a much more conscious and deliberate method of controlling minds, with branches of State administration dedicated to organized violence and political oppression. These, it would seem, have developed out of the "technical neutrality" of social psychology—that is, they work and are methods of operating upon people as the means to other ends. The victim is not an end in himself.

The progressive destruction of a person under brainwashing and torture removes the capacity for thinking, discrimination, and responsibility and creates an enduring loss of reality, so that he is finally reduced only to a relation with his body or his bodily needs (see Chapter 13). Internal resources to survive as a person are notoriously limited, as the experiments of Asch and Milgram convey. We can conclude that the primitive processes are deeply implicated in certain social occurrences, including:

1. *spreading*, or "emotional contagion";
2. the social *moulding of personal identity*;
3. the allotting of one-dimensional roles, or *stereotyping*, which includes scapegoating, racism, sexism, and other prejudices;

4. the demolition of the personality under organized state coercion.

The principle of personal integration that has been derived from psychoanalysis is one that can be employed in social and political contexts. Social influences can induce those primitive mechanisms of splitting, projection, and introjection. Distortions of the person are not, therefore, just the wanton self-destructiveness of disturbed individuals. The engineering of persons by depleting them to one-dimensional identities recognized as social stereotypes is prevalent across human society. It occurs adventitiously on a wide scale in society at large; it can be organized specifically by the State; and it can inadvertently become a feature of group therapy. The pressures in which the analyst gets caught up in the transference/countertransference dynamics of the psychoanalytic setting both exemplify and investigate how the social context can be coercive:

- A general ethic:
  An influence on another person is more ethical the more it promotes an integration of the parts of his personality, and less ethical the more it enhances a split in his personality.

The regulation of individuals' actions with and upon each other creates the interpersonal setting in which the processes operate. That interpersonal medium, in the form of organizations (mental hospital, brainwashing centres, etc.), also impacts itself back upon the individuals. In the final chapter we look at some hypotheses that can be drawn about society in general.

CHAPTER TWENTY

Social health

As soon as we move into the field of changing people—"psychoengineering"—we are involved in an ethical issue (Lakin, 1988). Because of the interactive quality of the ethical criteria (and the primitive mechanisms) I have discussed, this has implications for social science and the "good" society. In this chapter, I want to address, in the widest terms, the nature of political systems (totalitarian and democratic), as well as the nature of moral and ethical activity within a society. Such broad issues can necessarily only be touched on sketchily. The intention is to indicate possible lines of thought.

The coercive moulding of human beings is associated with the social engineering performed by the more odious dictatorships. Margaret Mead, writing during the Second World War, was impressed by the power of scientifically applied coercion. She wrote:

> Before we apply social science to our own national affairs, we must re-examine and change our habits of thought on the subject of means and ends. . . . If we apply the social sciences as crudely instrumental means, using the recipes of science to

manipulate people, we shall arrive at a totalitarian rather than democratic system of life. [quoted in Bateson, 1973, p. 134]

She was assessing the status of the experiments in social engineering at the time, particularly in the Soviet Union and in Nazi Germany. She surveyed a stark choice between a totalitarian system that engineered people through "the recipes of science" and a democratic way. Such technical mastery of social science seems now to be discredited, even in its technical effectiveness, let alone ethically. A method of designating a society for the good of all in it has not been shown to be technically feasible. (I have developed this argument in Chapter 13.)

It might be argued that the development of a democratic State is an exception to this rule, and we could turn to John Stuart Mill's conception of liberty as the founding good of ethical systems and of a beneficent State. The "instrumental means of social science" would not be required. We can put the following question to these liberal systems that rest upon Mill's ideas:

- Is there no coercion of people within a democratic State?

Clearly, there can be. We will use our notion of integration and its social conditions to examine this question.

Political engineering

The move from describing and hypothesizing about social organizations and forces (largely an eighteenth-century invention of the physiocrats) to becoming potent in initiating and controlling them has been a feature of the twentieth century. It has been the century of social psychology—or, perhaps more accurately, of social engineering. Social science has imported from the nineteenth century ideas of harnessing and controlling the forces of nature that have been so fabulously successful within manufacturing industry and technology. In the First World War, the fairly crude attempts to mobilize the country depended on the use of popular songs and poster art. The newness made it effective in this country, and to a lesser extent in the United States in 1917, when it joined the War.

Following that war, the longer-term engineering of a whole society was developed in the Soviet Union through the rather blunt instrument of Stalinism, which, nevertheless, survived for more than 70 years. The German experiment of the 1930s was briefer and, marginally, nastier.

Thereafter, the instruments of the democratic State have become much more subtle: the development of an artistically and psychologically sophisticated advertising industry and of much more penetrating forms of mass communication, and the discovery of a manipulated (as opposed to centrally controlled) economic system, demand-led as opposed to supply-led. These more subtle forms seem (in the present) to be more long-lasting and therefore more technically effective.

However, technical effectiveness has outstripped our capacity for judging ethical validity—biomedical developments in fertility and genetics are two pressing examples of this. It could be that these more subtle forms are better not only technically but also ethically. How can we tell?

The question is difficult—in part because the subtle manipulation is also aimed at getting us to believe the "right" answer. In other words, our society—as all others—cultivates the belief that we live in the best of all possible worlds. As a result, we intuitively believe that a rigid dictatorship just seems more unpleasant than our own liberal consumer economy. To test our intuitive assessments, we need a rigorous criterion for such an ethical judgement, which will, if possible, be immune from any manipulative bias resulting from those forces in society in which that assessment takes place. This is, of course, a tall order.

However, we can see how the principle of integration might perform in this context. We do, in fact, make assessments of how ethically "healthy" dictatorships are and adjudge the milder forms of engineering in the democratic West. Results will come from lining up the societies in the order of their capacity—or otherwise—to promote integration, or at least to limit the disintegration of the individuals within them.

The discussion of torture and state oppression in the preceding chapters has shown that ultimately totalitarian and dictatorial States have no particular *intention* of enhancing integration and will, if the need arises, actively demolish the personalities of certain individuals. Clearly, applying the test of integration, totalitarian States employing coercion, torture, and brainwashing heedlessly expose their peoples to the distorting effects of primitive processes. Thus, ethically they come out very low on the scale. Intuitively, we might then assume that the democracies will approach the opposite end of the scale. In fact, it seems to me that this is not necessarily so. The rhetoric in Western societies on freedom of choice is clamorous and indicates a solid adherence to the principle that their citizens sustain a capacity for autonomous judgement. However, we might also recognize that what is given with one hand may be taken away with the other. The advertising industry and the media are enterprises that—deliberately or otherwise—decide on the choices to be made and also pick the "best buys". The advertising industry's technical effectiveness in manipulating choices is vast and impressive—somewhat similarly to the way in which a professional can assert his knowledge. In the act of giving advice and providing choice, the consumer's own judgement can be taken away. Can we assess the depletion of the ordinary consumer, whose capacity to make judgements is taken over by the swamping impact of advertising, and distinguish it from the depleted subject of the totalitarian regime, who is deliberately deprived of his capacity to judge and choose? In fact, one might even say that possibly the totalitarian regime operates with a greater degree of honesty and straightforwardness; the subject is much more consciously aware of his depletion. Nevertheless, intuitively, there appears to be a significant ethical difference—we could refer back to the discussion comparing torture with therapies that employ manipulation and deceit (Chapter 15). However, I think we can make the distinction between consumerist democracies and dictatorships clearer by addressing briefly some of the specific institutions of consumerism.

Choosing by buying

On the whole, methods of social engineering in the democracies are aimed at influencing what we see, what we do, and especially what we buy. These influences can, by and large, be countered by other institutions—periodicals, consumer associations, certain investigative television programmes, and so on—that are created to analyse advertising claims. A roughly balancing dynamic can be perceived, though fragile and precarious it might sometimes be.

If, therefore, there is pressure on individuals to deplete themselves of the capacities to judge what to do, think, and buy, these elements of mind can be collected into a social institution to restore something of the judging capacity. To some extent, then, the influences on attitudes, actions, and consumption are balanced. The depleted portions of individuals can be refound and identified with. Therefore, an ethical validity is retained within the society *as a whole*. Explicitly, institutional judgements replace individual ones. It remains risky, of course, but this notion of *balancing institutions* seems to be a core feature of "democracies". In this case, special institutions stand as buffers against the individual's loss of his own balancing judgement. This is, of course, only a partial solution; individuals have still lost their individual capacities, however much that external institution can be identified with.

Feeling and being

Coming to other forms of influence, there may not be such a convenient balancing dynamic into which the ethical issues can be submerged. Other influences on "what to feel" and "what to be" can have a deeper impact on the individual (Fromm, 1976). These existential aspects of human life are generally kept separate from the more active thinking, doing, and buying. Contemplative reference to the *internal* states of feeling and being is just not as active in our culture in the same way; it attracts less attention and therefore less balancing critical analysis, though possibly it also receives less manipulative and coercive attention.

This "exclusion" is perhaps a hallmark of Western culture and constitutes the distinction between the technical and the ethical. More outwardly directed mental activity—thinking, acting, consuming—can be measured technically and manipulatively influenced in that way. More inward activity, which has to do with feeling and being, is left as a separate—and perhaps inviolable—

sphere of the person. Moreover, these two spheres of mental activity of the person—the outwardly and the inwardly directed —are radically separated (although this is a false separation and in itself constitutes a social pressure working against integration).

Emotional influencing

The argument that we are not subjected to interpersonal influencing of inner states, "what to feel" and "what to be", might be based on the claim that an "inward" person is a particular individual in himself, separate from society. "Outward"-directed features of the personality—attitudes, doing, and consuming—are, in contrast, socially gained and socially changed. Such a view of "human nature"—being a discrete core formed from the individual alone—feels right. However, we have discovered that, natural though it may seem, this cannot be sustained.

And from childhood, at least, these internal states of feeling and being are highly influenced.

When we come to think about our internal states, we do it within the categories that have been given words by our parental and schooling contexts. How does a child first come to distinguish tears of sadness from those of anger or those of shame? The feeling states to which those tears refer may well have appreciably different emotional tones; however, they can only become part of the social world through being given an indicative definition by parental others. The child is dependent on the accuracy of the parent's empathy to supply him with the correct verbal and social signifiers:

> . . . in infancy the environment largely provides the vocabulary for the infant's experience when the child is learning to speak. [Segal, 1982, p. 16]

A child whose tears of sadness are always identified by the parent as tears of anger will have his internal state profoundly influenced—indeed, limited—when he takes his place in the interpersonal world outside the family and comes into contact there with others' tears, which may be of varying emotional tones. The point is that the relationship with one's internal state (self-reflection) is deeply dependent on social and familial influencing.

However, parental descriptions may carry injunctions—"those are tears of anger" may be an implicit indication that the parent does not want them. Children may often be told not to be angry . . . to cheer up . . . not to make such a fuss . . . dry their tears . . . be grown up . . . and so on. Parental influence is staunchly of the internal as much as the external. Our states of emotion and being are influenced, manipulated, and controlled by parental guidance (Laing, 1959).

This kind of influencing does not stop with childhood. Cultural influences continue, for instance, in art and literature, which elaborate extremely subtle emotional tones of feeling and being and present to us what persons are and what their states are constituted of. Moreover, political influences may also work over emotional themes in highly influential ways. For example, in certain heartrending struggles, sadness may be culturally obliterated. In Nicaragua, after the revolution of 1979, mourning for the dead was almost erased in favour of a cultivated euphoria for the revolution, known as "the triumph". Since almost no family in the country was untouched by violent death, this gave rise on a very wide scale to personal disconfirmation of nearly everyone's internal states. Only those who died incidentally to the revolutionary fighting could be mourned, and anyone who mourned the death of someone who had died for the revolution was put to shame. It came eventually to be known as "frozen grief" (Hollander, 1988). This is an example of a whole national community mobilized towards certain culturally influenced forms of personal feeling. Integration was severely harmed in this respect by social pressure on a national scale.

Culturally, we lack adequate categories and language for identifying states of incoherence, fragmentation, and disintegration; we are, therefore, hampered in our thinking about our internal states, and we may be restricted to non-verbal or even non-symbolic active means (symptoms, for instance) of addressing these personal problems. Awareness of ourselves in these states—"going to pieces"—disqualifies us from the consensus of normality as experienced in our culture.

Influences upon both doing and also on emotional feeling and being are prevalent in Western democracies. In large measure this is a fact of life in social intercourse amongst human beings. The assessment we started to make is the ethical standard of democratic society in promoting or limiting this process. The conclusion seems to be that subtle processes influence what we do and buy, and personal judgement is severely removed from individuals personally. It may be refound in institutions accepted as the repository of a collective judgement. When it comes to more inward states—feeling and being—there is a different situation. In the first place, our culture provides us with a strict but specious separation between doing and being. In the second place, the social, interpersonal, and familial influences over what we are do not receive the same kind of balancing protection. Instead, there is a cultivated belief that personal being is inviolable and is not capable of being split—a rather inadequate and denying response to the reality of interpersonal life.

The verdict, in short, is that consumerist democracies do have an intention to protect the individual's stock of mental belongings, but they do it rather inadequately. With the insights provided by the principle of integration, better social institutions might be developed.

Using the principle of integration can provide some purchase on what is an ethical and healthy (benevolent) society and what is not. Social, cultural, or political forces are capable of deeply influencing the capacity of individuals to experience themselves as whole and can, in addition, exert influences on the normality or otherwise of those experiences. Societies can be ranged, like individuals, on their *intention* to protect their citizens—or the opposite.

Other societies

One could say that in the emotional world and in the world of personalities there is an attempt at least towards a "distributive justice" of personality characteristics. It is an equitable distribution of the person. This contrasts with, and is greatly overshadowed by, a distributive justice in the material world. Other societies—oppressive regimes, dictatorships—do not necessarily intend the kind of "distributive justice" of the person. For instance, the powerful disintegrating forces active in a totalitarian system are clearly unethical in the terms we have developed. They separate out personal authority, which accumulates in "the party" or the President.

However, in Western democracies the deceitful manipulation of outward activities and the obstruction to knowing the full experiences of being in pieces (as well as whole) do not place these democracies particularly high on the ethical scale either.

Other cultures do not necessarily espouse the concept of the discrete and indivisible individual. For instance, Brenan (1993) supports a thesis that historically this is "the age of the ego", the "foundational fantasy", a belief that one finds one's own *self* through the control of the "other". She makes an interesting, though patchy, review of the anthropological literature that demonstrates different and non-individualistic concepts of self. Possibly primitive cultures and their descendants in the third world operate by defining roles and places for persons in a way that constitutes a completely different conception of the relations of the person to society. Having reached this point, we can grasp how culturally relative is the stance of the argument in this book. The ethical principles I have enunciated, those resting on the principle of integration as a beneficence, are deeply embedded in the Western outlook. However, the understanding of the notion of integration does provide a basis for assessment, debate, and argument about the nature of a society, including a Western one. In practice, it could be argued that integration of parts of the personality *within* the person is merely a Western view, and that integration between aspects of the personality via social structures that accumulate and politically represent them is equally valid, or even superior. To argue that integration within the person is a better good than is integration through social structures, which bring together different roles holding different functions, may be *merely* a Western bias. However, the notion of integration at least allows an expansion of thought about this and a more conscious deliberation on the relative merits of different cultures, belief systems, and societies.

An interactive morality

Psychoanalytic views on the structuring and function of institutions (Jaques, 1955; Menzies, 1959; Trist & Murray, 1990) have addressed the *unconscious* components. This provides a radically different perspective on the way people do their work with colleagues in organizations. But analysing organizations in this way also gives a perspective on the interpersonal setting of ethical issues.

Economic factors in the creation and function of institutions, as well as various other cultural and superstructural factors, are important, but the study of unconscious collective psychology of the individuals shows how the identity of the individuals brought into the institution is moulded to employ the primitive mechanisms of splitting, projection, and introjection (see, e.g., de Board, 1978; Hinshelwood, 1987a; Obholzer & Roberts, 1994; Trist & Murray, 1990). For instance, in Isabel Menzies' study (1959), recruits to a nursing service were required to accept certain institutional attitudes that demanded particular kinds of splitting of themselves. This and other studies confirm, for instance, the circulation of personal responsibility, dislocated from the individuals and put into a flow within the institution—generally, responsibility is projected upwards and irresponsibility downwards. Damage is done to the individual, empathy withers, and stereotypes accumulate.

One implication of this is the problem that our ethical actions and intentions are not performed in isolation; our attempts to act ethically will depend for their success partly on others—other individuals, an institution, or a group—towards whom we act. As demonstrated in this work, persons are continually moving across a dimension from integrated to fragmented, and this movement is driven under the internal stresses of the individual but is also induced by the social influence of the interpersonal, institutional, and cultural setting. Thus, movement along this dimension results from two forces: (1) the propensity for the individuals to split and project parts of themselves; and (2) the demands of the "other" (individual or institution) that employs splitting and projective mechanisms.

The oddity in this is that an ethical act of mine depends partly on the other subject being in a state of willingness to accept all the parts of his own personality—or at least to refrain from using my acts as a means of projecting into me. Patient C (Chapter 9) is an example: whenever I opened my mouth to speak, she projected in a doting mother, so that I became, for the patient, the embodiment of her own disowned anxiety and responsibility. My acts left her depleted, despite my intention to make her more aware of, and contain, her own parts. We are even more constrained in this way when the "other" is a group or institution, because of their strong influence towards splitting and the spreading of individuals' minds.

The divided mind and its spreading implies an "interpersonal" identity for the individual. He is invested in others in his world, and the context of others in his world also shapes him deeply. This porosity and malleability of the individual threatens the high evaluation of the independent individual embedded in our contemporary culture. However, it is not quite true to say that the discrete essential identity is a fiction. It has a reality in us as a picture of how we expect ourselves to be. Because of our cultural influences, this is what we actually come to see in others and aspire to in ourselves. Thus, a dynamic exists between, on the one hand, the presented and perceived picture of discrete interacting individuals consciously relating over their tasks and their wants and, on the other hand, the unseen picture of a swirling network of charged emotional interpenetrations between personal nodal points of would-be identity. This contrast in perceptions and apprehensions—both conscious and unconscious—is not easily understood and absorbed, since its full appreciation threatens to revise radically our normal experiences of rational, social, academic, industrial, cultural, and moral life.

If there is a sense in which we have to give up some of our culture's insistence on the discreteness of individual identity and accept that individuals tend to spread interpersonally, then we have to accept that moral acts are very different categories of things, not simply the rational or irrational outcomes of an individual's autonomous thinking. We exist in an uncomfortable tension, carrying full moral responsibility for our actions, whilst constrained to carry them out within the limits imposed by our social and interpersonal context on our scope for moral action. Our culture's capacity to promote or limit splitting and spreading is thus one assessment of its moral worth.

REFERENCES

Abraham, Karl (1919). A particular form of neurotic resistance against the psycho-analytic method. In: Karl Abraham, *Selected Papers on Psycho-Analysis*. London: Hogarth, 1927 [reprinted London: Karnac Books, 1988].

Abraham, Karl (1924). A short study of the development of the libido, viewed in the light of mental disorder. In: Karl Abraham, *Selected Papers on Psycho-Analysis*. London: Hogarth, 1927 [reprinted London: Karnac Books, 1989].

Amati, Sylvia (1987). Some thoughts on torture. *Free Associations, 8*: 94–114.

Anscombe, G. E. M. (1975). The first person. In: S. Guttenplan (Ed.), *Mind and Language*. Oxford: Oxford University Press.

Asch, Solomon (1952). *Social Psychology*. Englewood Cliffs, NJ: Prentice-Hall.

Austin, Kenneth, Moline, Mary, & Williams, George (1990). *Confronting Malpractice: Legal and Ethical Dilemmas in Psychotherapy*. London: Sage.

Barker. P., & Baldwin, S. (1991). Change not adjustment: the ethics of psychotherapy. In: P. Barker & S. Baldwin (Eds.), *Ethical Issues in Mental Health*. London: Chapman & Hall.

Barton, Russell (1959). *Institutional Neurosis*. Bristol: Wright.

Bateson, Gregory (1973). *Steps to an Ecology of Mind*. St Albans: Paladin.

Berger, Peter, & Luckman, Thomas (1966). *The Social Construction of Reality*. London: Allen Lane.

Berlin, Isaiah (1958). Two concepts of liberty. In: *Four Essays on Liberty*. Oxford: Oxford University Press.

Bick, Esther (1968). The experience of the skin in early object relations. *International Journal of Psycho-Analysis, 49*: 484–486. [Also in: M. Harris Williams (Ed.), *Collected Papers of Martha Harris and Esther Bick* (pp. 114–118). Strath Tay, Perthshire: Clunie Press.]

Bick, Esther (1986). Further considerations of the function of the skin in early object relations: findings from infant observation integrated into child and adult analysis. *British Journal of Psychotherapy, 2*: 292–299.

Bion, W. R. (1957). Differentiation of the psychotic from the non-psychotic personalities. *International Journal of Psycho-Analysis, 38*: 266–275. [Also in: W. R. Bion, *Second Thoughts*. London: Heinemann, 1967; reprinted London: Karnac Books, 1988.]

Bion, W. R. (1961). *Experiences in Groups*. London: Tavistock.

Bion, W. R. (1962). *Learning from Experience*. London: Heinemann [reprinted London: Karnac Books, 1989].

Bion, W. R. (1967). *Second Thoughts*. London: Heinemann [reprinted London: Karnac Books, 1988].

Bion, W. R. (1970). *Attention and Interpretation*. London: Tavistock [reprinted London: Karnac Books, 1988].

Bion, W. R. (1974). Seminar 10, Rio de Janeiro. In: W. R. Bion, *Brazilian Lectures*. London: Karnac Books, 1990.

Bion, W. R. (1979). Making the best of a bad job. In: W. R. Bion, *Clinical Seminars and Four Papers*. Abingdon: Fleetwood Press, 1987. [Extended edition: *Clinical Seminars and Other Works*. London: Karnac Books, 1994.]

Bleuler, Eugene (1911). *Dementia Praecox or the Group of Schizophrenias*. New York: International Universities Press, 1950.

Bloch, Sydney (1981). The political misuse of psychiatry in the Soviet Union. In: S. Bloch & P. Chodoff (Eds.), *Psychiatric Ethics*. Oxford: Oxford University Press.

Bloch, Sydney, & Chodoff, Paul (1981). *Psychiatric Ethics*. Oxford: Oxford University Press.

Boorse, C. (1975). On the distinction between disease and illness. *Philosophy and Public Affairs, 5*: 49–68.

Braude, Stephen (1995a). *First Person Plural: Multiple Personality and the Philosophy of Mind*. Lanham: Rowman and Littlefield.

Braude, Stephen (1995b). Comment on "Social relocation of personal identity". *Philosophy, Psychiatry and Psychology, 2*: 209–214.

Braude, Stephen (1996). Multiple personality and moral responsibility. *Philosophy, Psychiatry and Psychology, 3*: 37–54.

Brenman-Pick, Irma (1985). Working through in the counter-transference. *International Journal of Psycho-Analysis, 66*: 157–166. [Also in: Elizabeth Spillius (Ed.), *Melanie Klein Today, Vol. 2: Mainly Practice*. London: Routledge, 1988.]

Brenan, Teresa (1993). *History after Lacan*. London: Routledge.

Bridger, Harold (1985). Northfield revisited. In: Malcolm Pines (Ed.), *Bion and Group Psychotherapy*. London: Routledge.

Brierley, Marjorie (1947). Notes on psycho-analysis and integrative living. *International Journal of Psycho-Analysis, 28*: 58–106.

Buford, Bill (1991). *Among the Thugs*. London: Secker & Warburg.

Cade, B. (1979). The use of paradox in psychotherapy. In: Sue Walrond-Skinner (Ed.), *Family and Marital Therapy: A Critical Approach*. London: Routledge & Kegan Paul.

Cavell, Marcia (1992). Knowing and valuing, some questions of genealogy. In: Jim Hopkins & Anthony Saville (Eds.), *Psychoanalysis, Mind and Art: Perspectives on Richard Wollheim*. Oxford: Blackwells.

Clark, Peter, & Wright, Crispin (Eds.) (1988). *Mind, Psycho-Analysis and Science*. Oxford: Blackwell.

Collier, Andrew (1987). The language of objectivity and the ethics of reframing. In: Sue Walrond-Skinner, *Ethical Issues in Family Therapy* (pp. 118–126). London: Routledge & Kegan Paul.

Conran, Michael (1985). The patient in hospital. *Psychoanalytic Psychotherapy 1*: 31–43.

Cooper, David (1967). *Psychiatry and Anti-Psychiatry*. London: Tavistock.

Culver, Charles, & Gert, Bernard (1982). *Philosophy in Medicine*. Oxford: Oxford University Press.

Davidson, Donald (1982) Paradoxes of irrationality. In: Richard Wollheim & James Hopkins (Eds.), *Philosophical Essays on Freud* (pp. 289–305). Cambridge: Cambridge University Press.

de Board, Robert (1978) *Psychoanalysis of Organisations*. London: Tavistock.

Deutsch, Helene (1942). Some forms of emotional disturbance and their relationship to schizophrenia. *Psychoanalytic Quarterly, 11*: 301– 321.

Dewhurst, K. (1982). *Hughlings Jackson on Psychiatry*. Oxford: Sandford.

Dicks, Henry (1972). *Licensed Mass Murder*. New York: Basic Books.

Dilman, Ilham (1984). *Freud and the Mind*. Oxford: Blackwell.

Dilman, Ilham (1988). Intentions and the unconscious. In: Peter Clark & Crispin Wright (Eds.), *Mind, Psycho-Analysis and Science*. Oxford: Blackwell.

Doray, Bernard (1988). *From Taylorism to Fordism*. London: Free Association Books.

Dyer, Allen (1988). *Ethics and Psychiatry*. Washington, DC: American Psychiatric Press.

Eagle, Moris (1988). Psychoanalysis and the personal. In: Peter Clark & Crispin Wright (Ed.), *Mind, Psycho-Analysis and Science*. Oxford: Blackwell.

Edwards, Ram (1982). Mental health and rational autonomy. In: Ram Edwards (Ed.), *Psychiatry and Ethics*. New York: Prometheus.

Ekstein, Rudolf (1976). Psycho-analysis and education as allies in the acquisition of moral values and virtues in the service of freedom and peace. *International Review of Psycho-Analysis, 3*: 399–408.

Ellenberger, Henri (1970). *The Discovery of the Unconscious*. New York: Basic Books.

Elster, John (Ed.) (1986). *The Multiple Self*. Oxford: Oxford University Press.

Erikson, Erik (1976). Psychoanalysis and ethics—avowed and unavowed. *International Review of Psycho-Analysis, 3*: 409–415.

Erikson, Milton (1939). Experimental demonstrations of the psychopathology of everyday life. *Psychoanalytic Quarterly 8*: 338–353.

Ezriel, Henry (1951). The scientific session as an experimental setting. *British Journal of Medical Psychology, 24*: 30–34.

Fairbairn, W. R. D. (1944). Endopsychic structure considered in terms of object-relationships. *International Journal of Psycho-Analysis, 25*: 70–73. [Also in: W. R. D. Fairbairn, *Psychoanalytic Studies of the Personality* (pp. 82–136). London: Routledge & Kegan Paul, 1952.]

Farrell, B. A. (1981). *The Standing of Psycho-Analysis*. Oxford: Oxford University Press.

Fenichel, Otto (1938). *The Psychoanalytic Theory of Neurosis*. London: Kegan Paul, Trench & Trubner.

Ferenczi, Sandor (1909). Introjection and transference. In: Sandor Ferenczi, *First Contributions to Psycho-Analysis*. London: Hogarth, 1952 [reprinted London: Karnac Books, 1994].

Feuer, Lewis (1955). *Psycho-Analysis and Ethics*. Springfield, IL: Charles Thomas.

Flugel, J. C. (1945). *Men, Morals and Society*. New York: International Universities Press.

Flynn, C. (1993). The patients' pantry: the nature of the nursing task. *Therapeutic Communities, 14*: 227–236.

Fornari, Franco (1966). *Psicanalisi Della Guerra*. Milan: Feltrinelli. English translation: *The Psychoanalysis of War*. Bloomington, IN: Indiana University Press, 1975.

Foster, J. (1971). *Enquiry into the Practice and Effects of Scientology*. London: HMSO.

Frankfurt, Harry (1976). Free will and the concept of a person. In: Amélie Rorty (Ed.), *The Identities of Persons*. Berkeley, CA: University of California Press.

Freud, Anna (1936). *The Ego and Mechanisms of Defence*. London: Hogarth [reprinted London: Karnac Books, 1993].

Freud, Anna (1946). *The Psycho-Analytical Treatment of Children*. London: Imago.

Freud, Sigmund (1895d). With J. Breuer. *Studies in Hysteria*. In: James Strachey (Ed.), *The Standard Edition of the Complete Psychological Works of Sigmund Freud. Vol.* 2: 3–311. London: Hogarth, 1953–1973.

Freud, Sigmund (1900a). *Interpretation of Dreams*. In: *S.E., Vols. 4 & 5*.

Freud, Sigmund (1905e [1901]). Fragment of an analysis of a case of hysteria. In: *S.E., Vol. 7* (pp. 7–122).

Freud, Sigmund (1909d). *Notes upon a Case of Obsessional Neurosis*. In: *S.E., Vol. 10* (pp. 155–318).

Freud, Sigmund (1910a [1909]). Five lectures on psycho-analysis. In: *S.E., Vol. 11* (pp. 9–55).

Freud, Sigmund (1912e). Recommendations to physicians practising psycho-analysis. In: *S.E., Vol. 12* (pp. 109–120).

Freud, Sigmund (1914g). Remembering, repeating and working through. In: *S.E., Vol. 12* (pp. 147–156).

Freud, Sigmund (1915a). Observations on transference-love. In: *S.E., Vol. 12* (pp. 159–171).

Freud, Sigmund (1916d). Some character-types met with in psycho-analytic work. In: *S.E., Vol. 14* (pp. 311–333).

Freud, Sigmund (1916–17). *Introductory Lectures on Psycho-Analysis*. In: *S.E., Vols. 15 & 16*.

Freud, Sigmund (1917e [1915]). Mourning and melancholia. In: *S.E., Vol. 14* (pp. 243–258).

Freud, Sigmund (1918b [1914]). From the history of an infantile neurosis. In: *S.E., Vol. 17* (pp. 7–122).

Freud, Sigmund (1921a). Preface to J. J. Putnam's *Addresses on Psycho-Analysis*. In: *S.E., Vol. 18* (pp. 269–270).

Freud, Sigmund (1921c). *Group Psychology and the Analysis of the Ego*. In: *S.E., Vol. 18* (pp. 69–143).

Freud, Sigmund (1923b). *The Ego and the Id*. In: *S.E., Vol. 19* (pp. 12–66).

Freud, Sigmund (1924c). The economic problem of masochism. In: *S.E., Vol. 19* (pp. 157–170).

Freud, Sigmund (1925h) Negation. In: *S.E., Vol. 19* (pp. 235–239).

Freud, Sigmund (1927e). Fetishism. In: *S.E., Vol. 21* (pp. 152–157).

Freud, Sigmund (1930a). *Civilisation and its Discontents*. In: *S.E., Vol. 21* (pp. 64–145).

Freud, Sigmund (1940e [1938]). Splitting of the ego in the process of defence. In: *S.E., Vol. 23* (pp. 275–278).

Fromm, Erich (1976). *To Have or to Be?* New York: Harper & Row.

Fulford, Bill (1989). *Moral Theory and Medical Practice*. Cambridge: Cambridge University Press.

Gardiner, Muriel (1972). *The Wolfman and Sigmund Freud*. London: Hogarth [reprinted London: Karnac Books, 1989].

Gardner, Sebastian (1993). *Irrationality and the Philosophy of Psycho-Analysis*. Cambridge: Cambridge University Press.

Gardner, Sebastian (1995a). Psychoanalysis, science and common-sense. *Philosophy, Psychiatry and Psychology*, 2: 93–113.

Gardner, Sebastian (1995b). Comment on "Social relocation of personal identity". *Philosophy, Psychiatry and Psychology*, 2: 209–214.

Geleerd, Elizabeth (1963). Evaluation of Melanie Klein's *Narrative of a Child Analysis*. *International Journal of Psycho-Analysis*, *44*: 493–506.

Gillon, Raanan (1986). *Philosophical Medical Ethics*. Chichester: Wiley.

Glover, Edward (1930). Grades of ego-differentiation. In: Edward Glover, *The Birth of the Ego*. London: George Allen & Unwin, 1968.

Glover, Edward (1933). *War, Sadism and Pacifism*. London: George Allen & Unwin.

Glover, Edward (1943). The concept of dissociation. In: Edward Glover, *The Birth of the Ego*. London: George Allen & Unwin, 1968.

Glover, Edward (1955). *The Technique of Psycho-Analysis*. London: Balliere, Tindall & Cox.

Glover, Jonathan (1988). *I: The Philosophy and Psychology of Personal Identity*. London: Allen Lane, The Penguin Press.

Goffman, Erving (1961). *Asylums*. New York: Doubleday.

Greenson, Ralph (1967). *The Technique and Practice of Psychoanalysis*. New York: International Universities Press.

Griffiths, P., & Leach, G. (1997). Establishing a model of psychosocial nursing, through action research. In: E. Barnes et al. (Eds.), *Face to Face with Distress*. London: Butterworth–Heinemann.

Grünbaum, Adolf (1984). *The Foundations of Psycho-Analysis: A Philosophical Critique*. Los Angeles, CA: University of California Press.

Guntrip, Harry (1968). *Personality Structure and Human Interaction*. London: Hogarth [reprinted London: Karnac Books, 1995].

Habermas, Jürgen (1968). *Knowledge and Human Interests*. London: Heinemann, 1971.

Hamilton, Victoria (1996). *The Analyst's Preconscious*. Hillsdale, NJ: Analytic Press.

Hampshire, Stuart (1959). *Thought and Action*. London: Chatto & Windus.

Hampshire, Stuart (1963). Disposition and memory. *International Journal of Psycho-Analysis, 42*: 59–68. [Also in modified form in: Richard Wollheim & James Hopkins (Eds.), *Philosophical Essays on Freud*. Cambridge: Cambridge University Press.]

Hanley, Charles, & Lazerowitz, Morris (Eds.) (1970). *Psycho-Analysis and Philosophy*. New York: International Universities Press.

Harré, Rom (1979). *Social Being*. Oxford: Blackwell.

Harré, Rom (1983). *Personal Being*. Oxford: Blackwell.

Hartmann, Heinz (1960). *Psycho-Analysis and Moral Values*. New York: International Universities Press.

Heimann, Paula (1942). A contribution to the problem of sublimation and its relation to processes of internalization. In: *About Children and Children-No-Longer*. London: Routledge, 1989.

Heimann, Paula (1950). On counter-transference. In: *About Children and Children-No-Longer. Collected Papers, 1942–1980.* London: Routledge, 1989.

Heimann, Paula (1960). Counter-transference. In: *About Children and Children-No-Longer. Collected Papers, 1942–1980.* London: Routledge, 1989.

Hilgard, Ernest (1977). *Divided Consciousness: Multiple Controls in Human Thought and Action.* New York: Wiley (expanded edition, 1986).

Hinshelwood, R. D. (1987a). *What Happens in Groups.* London: Free Association Books.

Hinshelwood, R. D. (1987b). Social dynamics and individual symptoms. *International Journal of Therapeutic Communities, 8*: 265–272.

Hinshelwood, R. D. (1989a). *A Dictionary of Kleinian Thought.* London: Free Association Books.

Hinshelwood R. D. (1989b). Social possession of identity. In: Barry Richards (Ed.), *Crises of the Self.* London: Free Association Books.

Hinshelwood, R. D. (1990). Therapy or coercion: a clinical note on personal change in a therapeutic community. *International Journal of Therapeutic Communities, 11*: 53–59.

Hinshelwood, R. D. (1991). Psychodynamic psychiatry before the First World War. In: German Berrios & Hugh Freeman, *One Hundred and Fifty Years of British Psychiatry*. London: Royal College of Psychiatrists.

Hinshelwood, R. D. (1994a). *Clinical Klein.* London: Free Association Books.

Hinshelwood, R. D. (1994b). Attacks on the reflective space. In: Malcolm Pines & Vic Shermer, *Ring of Fire.* London: Routledge.

Hinshelwood, R. D. (1995). Social relocation of personal identity through splitting, projection and introjection. *Philosophy, Psychiatry, Psychology* 2: 185–204.

Hinshelwood, R. D. (1997). Primitive mental processes: psychoanalysis and the ethics of integration. *Philosophy, Psychiatry, Psychology.*

Hollander, Nancy (1988). Introduction. In: Marie Langer, *From Vienna to Managua.* London: Free Association Books.

Holmes, J., & Lindley, R. (1989). *The Values of Psychotherapy.* Oxford: Oxford University Press.

Home, H. J. (1966). The concept of mind. *International Journal of Psycho-Analysis, 47*: 42–49.

Hook, Sidney (Ed.), (1959). *Psycho-Analysis, Scientific Method and Philosophy*. New York: New York University Press.

Hopkins, James (1982). Introduction. In: Richard Wollheim & James Hopkins (Eds.), *Philosophical Essays on Freud*. Cambridge: Cambridge University Press.

Hospers, John (1959). Philosophy and psycho-analysis. In: Sidney Hook (Ed.), *Psycho-Analysis, Scientific Method and Philosophy*. New York: New York University Press.

Irwin, Fritha (1995). The therapeutic ingredients of baking a cake. *Therapeutic Communities, 16*: 263–268.

Jackson, J. Hughlings (1931). *Selected Writings from John Hughlings Jackson*. London: Hodder & Stoughton.

Janet, Pierre (1892). *États mental des hysteriques*. Paris: J. Rueff.

Jaques, Elliott (1955). Social systems as a defence against persecutory and depressive anxiety. In: Melanie Klein, Paula Heimann, & Roger Money-Kyrle (Eds.), *New Directions in Psycho-Analysis*. London: Tavistock.

Jehu, Derek (1994). *Patients as Victims*. Chichester: Wiley.

Johnston, Paul (1989). *Wittgenstein and Moral Philosophy*. London: Routledge.

Jones, Ernest (1908). Rationalization in everyday life. *Journal of Abnormal Psychology, 3*: 161.

Jones, Ernest (1953–1957). *The Life and Work of Sigmund Freud*. London: Hogarth.

Joseph, Betty (1985). Transference: the total situation. *International Journal of Psycho-Analysis, 66*: 447–454. [Reprinted in: Elizabeth Bott Spillius (Ed.), *Melanie Klein Today: Developments in Theory and Practice, Vol. 2: Mainly Practice* (pp. 61–72). London: Routledge, 1988; and in: Betty Joseph, *Psychic Change and Psychic Equilibrium* (pp. 156–167). London: Routledge, 1989.]

Joseph, Betty (1989). *Psychic Change and Psychic Equilibrium*. London: Routledge.

Kaplan, Abraham (1958). Freud and modern philosophy. In: Benjamin Nelson (Ed.), *Freud and the 20th Century*. London: George Allen & Unwin.

Karle, Helmut, & Boys, Jennifer (1987). *Hypnotherapy: A Practical Handbook*. London: Free Association Books.

Kendall, R. E. (1975). The concept of disease and its implications for psychiatry. *British Journal of Psychiatry, 127*: 305–315.

Kennard, David (1983). *An Introduction to Therapeutic Communities.* London: Routledge & Kegan Paul.

Kennedy, R. (1993). *Freedom to Relate.* London: Free Association Books.

Kestenberg, Judith (1991). Children under the Nazi yoke. *British Journal of Psychotherapy, 8*: 374–390.

Klein, Melanie (1932). *The Psycho-Analysis of Children.* In: Roger Money-Kyrle (Ed.), *The Writings of Melanie Klein, Vol. 3: Envy and Gratitude and Other Works.* London: Hogarth [reprinted London: Karnac Books, 1993].

Klein, Melanie (1933). The early development of conscience in the child. In: Roger Money-Kyrle (Ed.), *The Writings of Melanie Klein, Vol. 1: Love, Guilt and Reparation* (pp. 248–257). London: Hogarth [reprinted London: Karnac Books, 1992.]

Klein, Melanie (1934). On criminality. In: Roger Money-Kyrle (Ed.), *The Writings of Melanie Klein, Vol. 1: Love, Guilt and Reparation* (pp. 258—261). London: Hogarth [reprinted London: Karnac Books, 1992].

Klein, Melanie (1946). Notes on some schizoid mechanisms. In: Roger Money-Kyrle (Ed.), *The Writings of Melanie Klein, Vol. 3: Envy and Gratitude and Other Works* (pp. 1–24). London: Hogarth [reprinted London: Karnac Books, 1993].

Klein, Melanie (1952). The origins of transference. In: Roger Money-Kyrle (Ed.), *The Writings of Melanie Klein, Vol. 3: Envy and Gratitude and Other Works* (pp. 48–56). London: Hogarth [reprinted London: Karnac Books, 1993].

Kohut, Heinz (1971). *The Analysis of the Self.* New York: International Universities Press.

Kuleshnyk, Irka (1984). The Stockholm syndrome: towards an understanding. *Social Action and the Law, 10*: 37–42.

Lacan, Jaques (1986). *Le Seminaire, Livre VII: L'ethique de la psychanalyse 1959–1960.* Paris: Seuil. [English translation: *The Ethics of Psychoanalysis.* London: Routledge, 1992.]

Laing, R. D. (1959). *The Divided Self.* London: Tavistock.

Lakin, Martin (1988). *Ethical Issues in the Psychotherapies.* Oxford: Oxford University Press.

Lakoff, Robin, & Coyne, James (1993). *Father Knows Best: The Use and Abuse of Power in Freud's Case of "Dora".* New York: Teacher's College Press.

Lasch, Christopher (1978). *The Culture of Narcissism.* New York: Norton.

Lear, Jonathan (1990). *Love and Its Place in Nature*. New York: Farrar, Strauss & Giroux.

Lear, Jonathan (1995). The heterogeneity of the mental. *Mind, 104*: 416–431.

Lear, Jonathan (1996). Irrationality and the concept of mind. Paper give at a conference on Morality and Ideology, Oxford (June).

LeBon, Gustav (1895). *Psychologie des Foules*. Paris Alcan. [English edition: *The Crowd*. New Brunswick: Transaction, 1995]

Levine, Howard (1992). Freudian and Kleinian theory: a dialogue of comparative perspectives. *Journal of the American Psychoanalytic Association, 40*: 801–826.

Lewin, Kurt (1936). *Principles of Topological Psychology*. New York: McGraw-Hill.

Lifton, Robert Jay (1961). *Thought Reform and the Psychology of Totalism*. London: Gollancz.

Lifton, Robert Jay (1976). Advocacy and corruption in the healing professions. *International Review of Psycho-Analysis, 3*: 385–398.

Lifton, Robert Jay (1982). Medicalized killing in Auschwitz. *Psychiatry, 45*: 283–297.

Lindley, Richard (1986). *Autonomy*. London: Macmillan.

Lindley, Richard (1987). Family therapy and respect for people. In: Sue Walrond-Skinner, *Ethical Issues in Family Therapy* (pp. 104–117). London: Routledge & Kegan Paul.

London, P. (1964). *The Modes and Morals of Psychotherapy*. New York: Holt, Rinehart & Winston (2nd edition, Washington, DC: Hemisphere, 1986).

Mace, Chris (1997). Comment on "Primitive mental processes". *Philosophy, Psychiatry and Psychology*.

Mackie, John (1985). *Persons and Values*. Oxford: Oxford University Press.

Main, T. F. (1946). The hospital as a therapeutic institution. *Bulletin of the Menninger Clinic, 10*: 66–70. [Also in: T. F. Main, *The Ailment and Other Psycho-Analytic Essays*. London: Free Association Books, 1990.]

Main, T. F. (1967). Knowledge, learning and freedom from thought. *The Australian and New Zealand Journal of Psychiatry, 1*: 64–71. [Also in: *Psychoanalytic Psychotherapy, 5*: 59–74.]

Main, T. F. (1975). Some psychodynamics of large groups. In: Kreeger, Lionel (Ed.), *The Large Group*. London: Constable. [Also in: T. F.

Main, *The Ailment and Other Psycho-Analytic Essays*. London: Free Association Books, 1989.]

Martin, Denis (1955). Institutionalisation. *Lancet*, *2*: 1188–1190.

Matte-Blanco, Ignacio (1975). *The Unconscious as Infinite Sets*. London: Duckworth.

Mayo, Elton (1933). *The Human Problems of an Industrial Civilisation*. Boston, MA: Harvard University Press.

Meltzer, Donald (1981). The Kleinian expansion of Freudian metapsychology. *International Journal of Psycho-Analysis*, *62*: 177–85.

Menzies, Isabel (1959). A case study in the functioning of social systems as a defence against anxiety. *Human Relations* *13*: 95–121. [Also in: *Containing Anxiety in Institutions*. London: Free Association Books, 1988.]

Michels, Robert (1976). Professional ethics and social values. *International Review of Psycho-Analysis*, *3*: 377–384.

Milgram, Stanley (1964). Group pressure and action against a person. *Journal of Abnormal and Social Psychology*, *69*: 137–143.

Mill, John Stuart (1859). *On Liberty*. London: J. M. Dent, 1972.

Money-Kyrle, Roger (1944). Towards a common aim: a psycho-analytic contribution to ethics. *British Journal of Medical Psychology*, *20*: 105–117. [Also in: *The Collected Papers of Roger Money-Kyrle*. Strath Tay, Perthshire: Clunie Press, 1978.]

Money-Kyrle, Roger (1952). Psycho-analysis and ethics. *International Journal of Psycho-Analysis*, *33*: 225–234. [Also in: M. Klein, P. Heimann, & R. Money-Kyrle (Eds.), *New Directions in Psycho-Analysis*. London: Tavistock, 1955; and in: *The Collected Papers of Roger Money-Kyrle*. Strath Tay, Perthshire: Clunie Press, 1978.]

Money-Kyrle, Roger (1956). Normal counter-transference and some of its variations. *International Journal of Psycho-Analysis*, *37*: 360–366. [Also in: *The Collected Papers of Roger Money-Kyrle*. Strath Tay, Perthshire: Clunie Press, 1978; and in: Elizabeth Spillius (Ed.), *Melanie Klein Today, Vol. 2: Mainly Practice*. London: Routledge, 1988.]

Money-Kyrle, Roger (1958). Psycho-analysis and philosophy. In: John Sutherland (Ed.), *Psycho-Analysis and Contemporary Thought*. London: Karnac.

Morton, Adam (1982). Freudian commonsense. In: Jim Hopkins & Richard Wollheim (Eds.), *Philosophical Essays on Freud*. Cambridge: Cambridge University Press.

Moscovici, Serge (1981). *L'âge des foules*. Paris: Fayard. [English translation: *The Age of the Crowd*. Cambridge: Cambridge University Press.]

Myers, Frederic (1903). *Human Personality and Its Survival of the Body*. London: Longmans Green.

Nagel, Thomas (1971). Brain bisection and the unity of consciousness. *Synthese, 2*: 396–413. [Also in: Thomas Nagel, *Mortal Questions*. Cambridge: Cambridge University Press, 1979.]

Nye, Robert (1975). *The Origins of Crowd Psychology*. London: Sage.

Obholzer, Anton, & Roberts, Vega (1994). *The Unconscious at Work*. London: Routledge.

Oppenheim, Janet (1985). *The Other World: Spiritualism and Psychical Research in England, 1850–1914*. Cambridge: Cambridge University Press.

O'Shaughnessy, Edna (1994). What is a clinical fact? *International Journal of Psycho-Analysis, 75*: 939–947.

Parfit, Derek (1984). *Reasons and Persons*. Oxford: Oxford University Press.

Pears, David (1982). Motivated irrationality, Freudian theory and cognitive dissonance. In: Richard Wollheim & James Hopkins (Eds.), *Philosophical Essays on Freud*. Cambridge: Cambridge University Press.

Penelhum, T. (1971). The importance of self-identity. *Journal of Philosophy, 68*: 667–678.

Pierce, A. H. (1895). Subliminal self or unconscious cerebration? *Proceedings of the Society for Psychical Research, 11*: 317–325.

Podmore, Frank (1895). Subliminal self or unconscious cerebration? *Proceedings of the Society for Psychical Research, 11*: 325–332.

Prince, Morton (1906). *The Dissociation of a Personality*. New York: Longmans Green.

Puccetti, Roland (1973). Brain bisection and personal identity. *British Journal for the Philosophy of Science, 24*: 339–355.

Puget, Janine (1988a). Social violence and psycho-analysis in the Argentinian context. *British Journal of Psychotherapy, 5*: 363–369.

Puget, Janine (1988b). Social violence and psycho-analysis in Argentina: the unthinkable and the unthought. *Free Associations, 13*: 84–140.

Rapaport, Robert (1960). *The Community as Doctor*. London: Tavistock.

Raphael, D. D. (1981). *Moral Philosophy*. Oxford: Oxford University Press.

Reich, Wilhelm (1933). *Character Analysis*. New York: Farrar, Strauss & Giroux, 1949.

Reid, J. R. (1955). The problem of value in psycho-analysis. *American Journal of Psychoanalysis, 15*: 115–122.

Reyes, Alejandro (1989). The destruction of the soul. *British Journal of Psychotherapy, 6*: 185–202.

Ricoeur, Paul (1970). *Freud and Philosophy: An Essay in Interpretation*. New Haven, CT: Yale University Press.

Rivers, W. H. R. (1920). *Dreams and the Unconscious*. Cambridge: Cambridge University Press.

Rorty, Amélie (Ed.) (1976). *The Identities of Persons*. Berkeley, CA: California University Press.

Rosenfeld, Herbert (1947). Analysis of a schizophrenic state with depersonalisation. *International Journal of Psycho-Analysis, 28*: 130–139. [Also in: *Psychotic States: A Psychoanalytical Approach*. London: Hogarth, 1965; reprinted London: Karnac Books, 1990.]

Russell, Bertrand (1921). *The Analysis of Mind*. London: George Allen.

Russell, Bertrand (1956). On denoting. In: R. C. Marsh (Ed.), *Logic and Knowledge*. London: George Allen & Unwin.

Rustin, Michael (1991). *The Good Society and the Inner World*. London: Verso.

Samuels, Andrew (1985). *Jung and the Post-Jungians*. London: Routledge.

Samuels, Andrew (1989). *The Plural Psyche*. London: Routledge.

Sandler, Joseph (1976). Counter-transference and role-responsiveness. *International Review of Psycho-Analysis, 3*: 43–47.

Sandler, Joseph (1987). *From Safety to Super-Ego. Selected Papers of Joseph Sandler*. London: Karnac Books.

Sartre, Jean-Paul (1943). *L'Etre et le Neant*. Paris: Gallimard.

Scheffler, Samuel (Ed.) (1988). *Consequentialism and Its Critics*. Oxford: Oxford University Press.

Seaborn-Jones, Gareth (1968). *Treatment or Torture*. London: Tavistock.

Searle, John R. (1995). *The Construction of Social Reality*. London: Allen Lane.

Sedgwick, Peter (1982). *Psychopolitics*. London: Pluto.

Segal, Hanna (1950). Some aspects of the analysis of a schizophrenic. *International Journal of Psycho-Analysis, 31*: 268–278. [Also in: *The*

Work of Hanna Segal. New York: Jason Aronson, 1981; and in: Elizabeth Spillius (Ed.), *Melanie Klein Today, Vol. 2: Mainly Practice*. London: Routledge, 1988.]

Segal, Hanna (1975). A psycho-analytic approach to the treatment of schizophrenia. In: Malcolm Lader (Ed.), *Studies of Schizophrenia*. Ashford: Headley Brothers. [Also in: *The Work of Hanna Segal*. New York: Jason Aronson, 1981.]

Segal, Hanna (1977). *Psycho-Analysis and Freedom of Thought*. London: H. K. Lewis. [Also in: *The Work of Hanna Segal*. New York: Jason Aronson, 1981.]

Segal, Hanna (1982). Early infantile development as reflected in the psycho-analytic process: steps in integration. *International Journal of Psycho-Analysis, 63*: 15–22.

Segal, Hanna (1992). Acting on phantasy and acting on desire. In: Jim Hopkins & Anthony Saville (Eds.), *Psychoanalysis, Mind and Art: Perspectives on Richard Wollheim*. Oxford: Blackwells.

Serota, H. M. (1976). Ethics, moral values and psychological interventions: opening remarks. *International Review of Psycho-Analysis, 3*: 373–375.

Sherif, Muzafer (1936). *The Psychology of Social Norms*. New York: Harper.

Shoemaker, Sydney (1963). *Self-Knowledge and Self-Identity*. Ithaca, NY: Cornell University Press.

Sinason, Valerie (1997). *Memory in Dispute*. London: Karnac Books.

Spillius, Elizabeth (Ed.) (1988). *Melanie Klein Today, Vols. 1 & 2*. London: Routledge.

Strachey, Alix (1957). *The Unconscious Motives of War*. London: George Allen & Unwin.

Strachey, James (1934). The nature of the therapeutic action of psychoanalysis. *International Journal of Psycho-Analysis, 15*: 127–159.

Steiner, John (1982). Perverse relations between parts of the self: a clinical illustration. *International Journal of Psycho-Analysis, 63*: 241–252.

Strawson, P. F. (1959). *Individuals*. London: Methuen.

Storr, Anthony (1960). *Integrity of the Personality*. London: Penguin.

Sturdee, Paul (1995). Irrationality and the dynamic unconscious. *Philosophy, Psychiatry and Psychology, 2*: 163–174.

Swinburne, Richard (1973–1974). Personal identity. *Proceedings of the Aristotelian Society, 74*: 231–248.

Szasz, Thomas (1961). *The Myth of Mental Illness*. New York: Hoeber-Harper.

Szasz, Thomas (1965). *The Ethics of Psychoanalysis*. New York: Macmillan.

Taylor, Charles (1989). *The Sources of the Self*. Cambridge: Cambridge University Press.

Thigpen, Corbett, & Cleckley, Hervey (1957). *The Three Faces of Eve*. London: Secker & Warburg.

Treacher, Andy (1987). "Family therapists are potentially damaging to families and their wider networks." Discuss. In: Sue Walrond-Skinner (Ed.), *Ethical Issues in Family Therapy* (pp 87–103). London: Routledge & Kegan Paul.

Trist, Eric, & Murray, Hugh (Eds.) (1990). *The Social Engagement of Social Science*. London: Free Associations.

Tulving, E. (1983). *Elements of Episodic Memory*. Oxford: Oxford University Press.

Vinar, Michel (1989). Pedro or the demolition: a psycho-analytic look at torture. *British Journal of Psychotherapy, 5*: 353–362.

Vygotsky, Lev Semonovitch (1962). *Thought and Language*. Cambridge, MA: MIT Press.

Vygotsky, Lev Semonovitch (1978). *Mind in Society*. Cambridge, MA: Harvard University Press.

Wallerstein, Robert (1976). Introduction to symposium on "Ethics, moral values and psychological interventions". *International Review of Psycho-Analysis, 3*: 369–372.

Walrond-Skinner, Sue (1987). *Ethical Issues in Family Therapy*. London: Routledge & Kegan Paul.

Watzlawick, P., Weakland, J., & Fisch, R. (1974). *Changes: Principles of Problem Formation and Problem Resolution*. New York: Norton.

Wertsch, James (1985). *Vygotsky and the Social Formation of Mind*. Cambridge, MA: Harvard University Press.

Wilkes, Kathleen (1988). *Real People: Personal Identity Without Thought Experiments*. Oxford: Clarendon Press.

Williams, Bernard (1960). Personal identity and individuation. In: Bernard Williams, *Problems of the Self*. Cambridge: Cambridge University Press, 1973.

Williams, Bernard (1970). The self and the future. In: *Problems of the Self*. Cambridge: Cambridge University Press, 1973.

Williams, Bernard (1973). *Problems of the Self.* Cambridge: Cambridge University Press.

Williams, C. J. F. (1989). *What Is Identity?* Oxford: Oxford University Press.

Winnicott, Donald (1945). Primitive emotional experience. *International Journal of Psycho-Analysis, 26*: 137–143. [Also in: *Collected Papers: Through Paediatrics to Psycho-Analysis.* London: Tavistock, 1958; reprinted as: *Through Paediatrics to Psycho-Analysis.* London: Hogarth Press & the Institute of Psychoanalysis, 1975 (reprinted London: Karnac Books, 1992).]

Winnicott, Donald (1960). The theory of the parent–infant relationship. *International Journal of Psycho-Analysis, 41*: 585–595. [Also in: *The Maturational Processes and the Facilitating Environment.* London: Hogarth Press & The Institute of Psychoanalysis (reprinted London: Karnac Books, 1995).]

Wisdom, John (1953). *Philosophy and Psycho-Analysis.* Oxford: Blackwell.

Wittgenstein, Ludwig (1942). Conversations on Freud. In: *Lectures and Conversations on Aesthetics, Psychology and Religious Belief.* Oxford: Blackwell, 1966.

Wittgenstein, Ludwig (1979). Remarks on Frazer's *Golden Bough.* In: G. Luckhardt (Ed.), *Wittgenstein: Sources and Perspectives.* Ithaca, NY: Cornell University Press.

Wolf, Ernest (1988). *Treating the Self.* Hillsdale, NJ: Analytic Press.

Wollheim, Richard (Ed.) (1974). *Freud: A Collection of Critical Essays.* New York: Doubleday.

Wollheim, Richard (1984). *The Thread of Life.* Cambridge: Cambridge University Press.

Wollheim, Richard, & Hopkins, James (Eds.) (1982). *Philosophical Essays on Freud.* Cambridge: Cambridge University Press.

Wortis, Joseph (1954). *Fragments of an Analysis with Freud.* New York: McGraw-Hill.

Zetzel, Elizabeth (1956). Current concepts of transference. *International Journal of Psycho-Analysis, 37*: 369–376.

INDEX